RAISING EDUCATIONAL STANDARDS IN THE INNER CITIES

Practical Initiatives in Action

Edited by
Michael Barber
and
Ruth Dann

CASSELL

Cassell
Wellington House
125 Strand
London WC2R 0BB

215 Park Avenue South
New York
NY 10003

First published 1996

British Library Cataloguing-in-Publication Data
A catalogue record for this book is available from the British Library.

ISBN 0–304–33136–8 (hardback)
     0–304–33138–4 (paperback)

Typeset by Mayhew Typesetting, Rhayader, Powys
Printed and bound in Great Britain by Redwood Books Ltd, Trowbridge, Wiltshire

Contents

Notes on Contributors   vii

Series Editors' Foreword   ix

Preface   x

Introduction   1
Ruth Dann

1   Creating a Framework for Success in Urban Areas   6
    Michael Barber

Part One: Urban Education – The National Context

2   Urban Education: Current Position and Future Possibilities   27
    George Smith

3   Urban Education Initiatives: The National Pattern   56
    Michael Barber, Tim Denning, Gerry Gough and Michael Johnson

4   Urban Education Initiatives: Future Progress   76
    Michael Barber, Tim Denning, Gerry Gough and Michael Johnson

5   Urban Education Initiatives: Three Case Studies   85
    Michael Barber, Tim Denning, Gerry Gough and Michael Johnson

Part Two: Policy into Practice   99

6   The Role of Partnerships and Networking in School Improvement   101
    Louise Stoll

7   Urban Deserts or Fine Cities?   118
    Tim Brighouse

8   Collaboration for School Improvement: The Power of Partnership   129
    Michael Barber and Michael Johnson

Part Three: Policy and Practice in American City Schooling

9   Implications of Restructuring and Site-level Decentralization upon
    District-level Leadership   145
    Robert L. Crowson and William Lowe Boyd

Contents

10 Education for Urban America   169
     Paul Hill

Appendices   187

Name Index   212

Subject Index   214

Notes on Contributors

Michael Barber is Professor of Education and Director of the Centre for Successful Schools at Keele University.

Ruth Dann is a Lecturer in Education at Keele University.

Tim Brighouse is Chief Education Officer for Birmingham.

Robert Crowson is Professor of Education at Vanderbilt University, USA.

Tim Denning is Lecturer in Education at Keele University.

Gerry Gough is a Senior Research Fellow in the Centre for Successful Schools at Keele University.

Paul Hill is a Research Professor at the University of Washington's Institute for Public Policy Management.

Michael Johnson is a Senior Research Fellow in the Centre for Successful Schools at Keele University.

William Lowe Boyd if Professor of Education at Penn State University, Pennsylvania, USA.

George Smith is a Research Consultant at the Office for Standards in Education.

Louise Stoll is Co-ordinator of the International School Effectiveness and Improvement Centre at the Institute of Education, London.

Foreword

The problems and challenges of education in inner city schools are familiar to us all. Politicians and the press, almost daily it seems, talk about or report on disruption, crises of confidence and poor teaching. Similarly, many commentators on national surveys and examination results point to falling standards. Whilst some of this may be posturing for a particular audience, there is no gainsaying the very real difficulties of being a student and a teacher in an inner city school.

That much of the debate has been conducted at the level of rhetoric is understandable, given the lack of research in the area. In this book Michael Barber, Ruth Dann and their colleagues provide some of Britain's first evidence to inform serious discussion. Drawing on their own experience at the University of Keele's Centre for Successful Schools, the report 'Success and Achievement in Urban Education' they produced for OFSTED, and on reviews of the literature and other urban education initiatives in the United Kingdom and the United States, they begin to map the territory of urban education. Although incomplete, the picture that Barber, Dann and their contributors present is not one of unmitigated gloom. Despite the very real problems that they identify, graphically in some cases, an air of optimism pervades these pages. A key message is that we can raise standards and, more importantly perhaps, enhance the feelings of self-worth of young people in inner city schools, if we really want to.

What is so exciting about many of the proposals or 'aspects of success' contained in this book is that they are not necessarily dependent upon external factors, but reflect concerted action within the school. The focus on the classroom and, in particular, the ways in which teachers and students interact, is to be welcomed. What is needed is more research to tease out the in-school variables that contribute to success. We need to focus research work on the in-school factors leading to success and the external supports required to support schools in a decentralised system. We read much in this book about networking and the spread of best practice – but do we yet know how to facilitate this in all situations?

The case studies contained here begin to give us some clues. We are also particularly pleased that the work of Robin Slavin and his colleagues features prominently. The 'Success for All' project demonstrates unequivocally that high standards can be achieved in high poverty inner city environments. A major contribution of this book is that it demonstrates that, against the odds, standards can rise given the right conditions and high expectations.

We trust that this book will not only contribute to and inform the debate on raising educational standards in the inner city, but also convince the wider public to raise their expectations of what is possible for all students.

David Hopkins
David Reynolds

Preface

There is a paradox at the heart of the contributions to this book. Those responsible for urban education – teachers, parents, administrators, academics and others – face a daunting, almost overwhelming challenge; and yet, simultaneously, there are increasingly grounds for optimism.

It is hoped that this book will provide a combination of inspiration, explanation and practical ideas relevant to those working to improve schools in urban areas. For this reason it is dedicated to urban educators everywhere.

A number of acknowledgements are due. The Office for Standards in Education helped to raise the profile of urban education in the UK with its sombre but important report 'Access and Achievement in Urban Education' published in 1993. It also funded the research which is reported in Chapter 2, 3, 4 and 5.

We are grateful to the many people responsible for urban education who took the trouble to respond to the inquiries of the research team and to the teachers and LEA officers in the three case-study areas (see Chapter 5) who were unfailingly welcoming, open and frank about their experiences.

Finally, a tribute ought to be paid here to the work on urban education of Tim Brighouse. He has provided a chapter here – based on his 1994 TES/ Greenwich lecture – but his contribution to this volume goes far beyond that. He was one of the originators of the Two Towns Project described in Chapter 8. He also founded – and provided a vision for – the Centre for Successful Schools at Keele University which undertook the research reported here. Finally, through his commitment, energy, vision and imagination he has helped Birmingham's educators to provide a lead which others in this country, and perhaps elsewhere, will surely follow. The problems of urban education are not insurmountable.

Introduction

Ruth Dann

When the Stranger says: 'What is the meaning of this city?
Do you huddle close together because you love each other?'
What will you answer? 'We all dwell together
To make money from each other'? or 'This is a community'?
And the Stranger will depart and return to the desert.
O my soul, be prepared for the coming of the Stranger,
Be prepared for him who knows how to ask questions.
      (T.S. Eliot, Choruses from 'The Rock', 1934, p. 111)

These questions concerning the city in Eliot's critical chorus call for profound comment. With Eliot's Stranger, those who know how to ask questions have returned, posing disturbing questions about our inner cities. All the contributions in this volume raise questions concerning education in city schools. The questions posed refuse easy answers. However, stemming as it does from such questions, this volume adds to recent educational research into inner-city conditions and the effects of a variety of policies and services which offers evidence markedly more compelling than that previously gained.

The identification of concentrations of educational under-achievement in inner cities was followed nearly thirty years ago by the introduction of specific measures to help urban regeneration. Since then considerable disquiet at the growing evidence of continued failure to give effective education and training to young people so that they can meet the needs of the modern world has inspired many initiatives aimed at raising educational standards. A growing number of such initiatives, concerned with the inner cities in particular, and with urban issues in general, have been prompted by and have prompted a wide range of research projects specifically designed to explore the complex interactive factors involved in education.

Indeed the rapid growth of evidence relating to urban education initiatives, the large number of bold conjectures – many of which still await structured refutation or confirmation – and the exciting, yet sometimes bewildering, proposals for further initiatives all combine to provide a lively context for further explanation.

However, this evidence, with its associated conjectures and proposals, has not overcome the ambivalence about urban education so clearly portrayed in the literature. For some, the problems of inner cities seem insurmountable. Poorly-motivated pupils from whom little is expected, and for whom little is provided, may loom so large in the collective consciousness that despair is virtually inevitable. A more positive picture, however, emphasizes the existence in urban areas of effective schools, innovative programmes and sometimes monumental accomplishment against the odds.

Whatever the case, it may well be that this very ambivalence offers a life-line to all of us who are concerned to raise educational standards in our inner cities. It may prompt us to seek a deeper understanding of the complexities surrounding such a task. It may discourage us from over-simplification. It may protect us from offering premature and potentially destructive resolutions. The conviction underlying this book, however, is that it is entirely feasible to provide a high-quality education for all in the inner city.

The contributors to this volume share the conviction that, in the task of raising educational standards in the inner cities, we are not at the mercy of uncontrollable forces. There is a choice of responses, and it is here contended that a healthy optimism is in fact an appropriate ingredient in rational decision-making. Our optimism, however, is tempered by proper caution as we invite the reader to take due account of the incomplete evidence advanced. Contextual issues are also highlighted, for the structural and human factors contributing to patterns and possibilities for inner-city education call for insightful exploration in the light of such issues.

Focusing on the UK, Chapter 1 maps the quest for educational renewal in our inner cities. It traces the route, and inspects the landmarks. The overriding concern is to understand the factors facilitating schools' improvement in urban areas – the features creating a 'learning school'. In this endeavour, a vision for educational development is highlighted. It is this vision which gives unity and direction to the mission. The chapter 'looks forward, with hindsight', to the time when high-quality education will contribute to the self-discovery, high standards and heightened self-esteem of all young people in the inner city.

Whilst Smith's chapter (Chapter 2) also beckons us to future possibilities, its main emphasis is on current issues in urban education. It outlines the context for the first part of the book. A critical review of selected research in the UK, with some reference to recent developments in the USA, leads us to an optimistic and constructive outlook. Drawing on Slavin's research on effective schooling for disadvantaged pupils, Smith examines a wide range of programmes aimed at raising the educational performance of these pupils. The long-term effects of high-quality pre-school provision and parental involvement emerge as the key elements in ensuring the long-term impact of such programmes. Of particular significance in Smith's offering is the evidence that the impact of specific developments tends to fade away once they have finished. A careful reading of the text may well deter the critic from seeking a well-developed theory of 'what works'. Perhaps further evaluation will ultimately produce a 'theory'. Perhaps not. Meanwhile we do well to heed Smith's concluding caveat. His optimism 'should not be taken to mean that anything will work'.

Such concerns are expressed again in Chapters 3 and 4, which are adapted from a report for OFSTED by the Keele University Centre for Successful Schools. The research highlights the fact that in some projects there is a lack of clarity about the criteria of success. Furthermore, it is noted that a tendency to rely on subjective judgement and anecdotal evidence hardly makes for accuracy or offers reliable guidance for future planning. Chapter 3 identifies the scope and extent of urban initiatives in England while Chapter 4 probes issues relating to the continuation of these initiatives. Despite disappointment at the absence of success criteria in some cases, six aspects of success are identified: increased awareness of the characteristics of school improvement in urban areas, particularly among teachers, headteachers, parents and governors; raised morale; improved teaching skills; better management; enhanced communication with parents; and improved pupil performance. Implying a theory of evidence which combines concepts of probability and explanation, this contribution advances evidence which is sufficiently convincing to be acceptable to even the most sceptical reader. Such a reader may well seek the defining characteristic of any empirical statement in the possibility of its being tested by some kind of confrontation with experimental findings. Many of the propositions advanced in Chapter 4 serve as useful starting points for focused observation designed to test them.

The three case studies presented in Chapter 5 provide carefully chosen examples of such focused observation. After the identification of serious under-achievement and low expectations in some schools in the town, the Tilbury initiative was launched. Even in the early stages, it promises significant improve-ment in levels of educational achievement. Again, however, the importance of clearly specified success criteria was highlighted. The second case study, 'The Schools-Make-a-Difference Project', in the London Borough of Hammersmith and Fulham, clearly identified an important determinant of the success of the project: 'the development of young people as autonomous and independent learners, with all that implies for flexible learning, and the emphasis on curriculum enrichment and extension.' Significantly the main 'guiding principle' of the SMAD initiative is the importance of high expectations for children and young people in inner cities.

This principle features prominently in the third case study, which involves nine inner-city primary schools in Nottingham. Distinctive educational challenges resulting from typical inner-city social problems are here grouped under three headings: recovering achievement; behaviour-management; and home/school partnership. Perhaps the most poignant pedagogical experiment in this project is the movement from the traditional Plowdenesque primary philosophy to a new mix of informal and more directive approaches. Target-grouping, directive teaching and performance-monitoring constitute the main ingredients in this major advance in primary practice. The evidence from Nottingham may not yet be conclusive but it certainly demands further and deeper consideration.

The second part of this volume concerns the translation of policy into practice so that the persistent marginalization and disempowerment of young people in the inner city can be alleviated – even eradicated. An understanding of the relevant educational changes required necessarily embodies a vision of 'what might be'. Stoll (Chapter 6) highlights the idea that during a time of uncertainty and rapid socio-cultural change, allegiance shifts from membership of organiz-ations to membership of networks. This shift sets the framework for considering a link between policy and practice. It focuses on the development and function of perhaps the most important national network for school improvement, based at the London Institute of Education's International School Effectiveness and Improvement Centre.

Stoll points to the tension between the decentralization represented by Local Management of Schools (LMS) and an increase in central control and account-ability in terms of a National Curriculum and its associated assessments; and she reminds us that schools are discovering an agenda which can properly be called their own. Most significant is the tendency for schools to favour networking and clustering opportunities as distinct from any crude competition which could well be the effect, if not the intention, of the publication of league tables of raw academic results. This chapter plots the movement towards partnerships and networks in one higher-education institution working with schools. Critical ques-tions are confronted, enabling the reader to glimpse something of their signifi-cance. In this particular project the process of implementation was facilitated when the focus for improvement was a specific target of the school's development plan set out in its management documents. Additional facilitation derived from the empathy and commitment of headteachers, coupled with an emphasis on leadership through a small group, and the involvement of staff beyond this group. Finally and unapologetically an emphasis on classrooms is presented as a vital factor in the facilitating process.

Not surprisingly Brighouse (Chapter 7) too proclaims the primacy of the classroom in securing hope for our cities. For him neither policy nor practice can prevail if they are restricted to the macro level. Inescapably they require sharpening in particular schools and in particular classrooms. More than that, though, there is no pre-formed pattern of performance apart from the problems and provisions of the classroom. Certainly many of his considered proposals are, at the same time, contentious. Who can fail to respond, even react, to his contention that a para-professional workforce in schools will offer no mean contribution to the task of raising educational standards? Who can resist the temptation to pull his 'golden cracker of teaching'? Who can deny the wit and wisdom in this attempt to discover the alchemists' stone?

Clearly such a challenge calls for the sustained collaboration of all those actively concerned to create the climate in which commitment and achievement are celebrated. In Chapter 8 Johnson and Barber explore the collaborative initiative called the 'Two Towns Project'. Prominent in this project is the partner-ship between pupils, parents and the staff of the three high schools involved. Additionally, this partnership involves the Careers Service, the post-16 institutions, the post-18 institutions, the local primary schools and the business and industrial community. The value of a loose network in this partnership is clearly recognized. Moreover, management structures reflect the loose nature of this collaboration. Two generalizable lessons emerge from this project: firstly, that participation in an initiative is not an alternative to getting the in-school factors right; secondly, that cooperating agencies as well as schools can benefit from school-improvement initiatives.

The issues raised in translating policy into practice in this initiative suggest the importance of developing closer links with parents, post-16 institutions and other supporting services. Additionally, lessons learned from initiatives in the USA, such as the 'Headstart' programme, should be built upon and extended. Advances in the USA offer valuable insights into the problems and possibilities for education in the inner city. Attempts to raise standards in American urban education, through structural reform and initiative implementation, form the focus of Part Three of this volume.

In Chapter 9, Crowson and Boyd consider the impact of decentralizing urban schooling, in relation to reconceptualizing hierarchical roles. Any attempt to distinguish centralized from decentralized structures, in terms of a simple dichotomy, is forcefully dismissed. Rather, their concern is to consider the changing nature of school-based organization in relation to a changing and restructured central framework. For Crowson and Boyd, neither centralization nor decentralization will work. They call for strength both at school and central-office levels. The complexities involved are immense, yet, with vision and leadership from central office and with coordination and redevelopment at school level, there is every indication that the difficulties encountered with large-scale restructuring can be reconceptualized in order to 'make good things happen for children'. Even in the vast areas of urban deprivation, on a scale as yet unknown in Britain, optimism about raising educational standards is emerging.

Hill, in Chapter 10, in outlining the nature and cause of poverty in parts of large American cities, offers suggestions for improving educational standards that are based on examples of success. As part of the centralized and bureaucratized educational system many teachers, he claims, have little sense of responsibility for their work. Pupils' expectations are often low and the relevance of school to society is often minimal. In addition to the lower funding revenues in some inner-city areas, and to the lower qualifications of teachers, the education on offer is poor. For Hill the answer lies not in increased funding or policies to alleviate other social and economic problems, but in the capacity of teachers to transform their teaching so that outcomes are clear, expectations are high and content is challenging. This draws on the reconceptualization of school-based practices previously considered by Crowson and Boyd. Hill calls for schools to take a lead, to consider for themselves the curriculum on offer, to draw on the interests of parents and the expertise of other public services. Local networking and collaboration provide an important dimension to the success of schools. Hill illustrates the successes, and he appeals for a shift away from the prevalent notion that city schools will fail children. However, any such shift, he claims, must start in the community.

Each contributor in this book offers insights, problems and possibilities concerning the raising of educational standards in inner cities. They add to a developing literature concerned with exploring, analysing, evaluating and implementing urban education. While the various chapters here fall far short of providing all the answers, it is hoped they will contribute to preparing for the coming of T.S. Eliot's Stranger.

Chapter 1

Creating a Framework for Success in Urban Areas

Michael Barber

INTRODUCTION

There has been a huge amount of structural change in education over the last seven years. This chapter attempts to answer two questions. Firstly, to what extent have the changes that have been made assisted in creating a framework for school improvement in urban areas? And secondly, what more might need to be done to ensure that every school has the possibility of success, whatever its circumstances? However, before examining these two questions in the third section of this chapter, it is important to set the context. The first part of the chapter looks at the question of standards and whether they are rising or falling. The second section discusses what we know about school effectiveness and school improvement. The third section then deals with the two questions which form the heart of this opening chapter. Finally, the fourth section analyses the implications for national government, local government and schools of the principles set out in the third section.

As a prelude to that discussion it is worth highlighting one point. Educators, a group of people whose professional skills and expertise depend on language, often underestimate its power and importance in bringing about change. John Oakland, in his book *Total Quality Management*, says:

> Quality, the way we have defined it as meeting the customer
> requirements, gives people in different functions of an organisation a
> common language for improvement. It enables all the people, with
> different abilities and priorities, to communicate readily with one
> another, in pursuit of a common goal.

> (Oakland, 1989, p. 13)

Underpinning the argument of this chapter is a similar point. In schools and LEAs where school improvement is taking place, one feature tends to be the existence of a common language of school improvement. The language in which we discussed education prior to the 1990s, in terms of equal opportunities, equality, and the comprehensive principle, has been extended to include words such as standards, ambition, diversity, openness, accountability and fairness. These words are all part of the vocabulary of improvement. Through the use of terms such as these, the expectations of both pupils and teachers are being raised and their vision of what is possible is being extended. Efforts to improve schools which do not include these changes in the language are unlikely to be wholly effective.

STANDARDS

The first and perhaps most important point to make about standards is that, in absolute terms, they are currently inadequate. The revised National Education and Training Targets (NETTs) will include one suggesting that 85 per cent of young people should achieve five grades A–C at GCSE (or the equivalent) by the year 2000. The young people who will take GCSE in that year start secondary school in September 1995. The challenge of meeting this target is therefore immediate. To many in the education service the target seems ludicrously unrealistic, yet it is pitched at the kind of level needed if this country is to keep up with the international competition, as the tables below make clear.

Raising standards, however, is not just a matter of international competition. It is also necessary to take account of the rapidly-changing job market.

> By the year 2000 70 per cent of all jobs in Europe will require cerebral rather than manual skills. Some experts suggest that as many as 50 per cent of these jobs will require the equivalent of higher education or a professional qualification.
>
> (*Eurotechnet Report*, 1994, p. 15)

Furthermore, the case for higher standards is not purely a matter of economics. It is also an issue fundamentally related to the success of a democratic society in the twenty-first century. The social consequences of extensive under-achievement will become increasingly dire. Already we have evidence of a clear link between educational failure and crime. We also know that a high degree of education and

Table 1.1. *Sixteen-year-olds in certain countries reaching equivalent of GCSE grades A–C in mathematics, the national language and one science, 1990–91*

Country	Percentages
Germany	62
France	66
Japan	50
England	27

Table 1.2. *Young people in certain countries obtaining a comparable upper-secondary school qualification at 18+, 1990.*

Country	Percentages
Germany	68
France	48
Japan	80
England	27

(*National Commission on Education Report*, 1993, p. 3)

self-confidence are requirements for full participation in democratic society. The fruits of a successful education system are, therefore, much more than purely economic.

Even this is not the full extent of the case for higher standards. The fact is that the range of threats to the future existence of the planet, from global warming to the pressure of population growth, will all increasingly focus minds. We will require more ingenuity, knowledge, and understanding than ever before to solve these immense challenges early in the next century.

Although standards, measured in these terms, are clearly too low, it is important to recognize that for many young people they are rising and have been rising for a number of years. Indeed if the available indicators are to be believed there has never been a time when standards have risen as fast as they have in the last decade. In 1994 over 53 per cent of those entered achieved five grades A–C at GCSE compared to fewer than 30 per cent in 1987. The average improvement at GCSE is, therefore, around 3 per cent per annum since 1988. There has been a similarly steady improvement at A Level over the same period. Meanwhile staying-on rates at both 16+ and 18+ have soared. By 1994 over 70 per cent of the age group remained in education after the age of 16 compared to only 35 per cent 15 years earlier. Participation in higher education has more than doubled since the mid-1980s. Thus, for a significant proportion of young people, indeed perhaps for the majority, standards appear to have risen.

However, there is simultaneous and disturbing evidence that for other young people standards are at best static, and perhaps falling. The evidence from both OFSTED and the NFER suggests that reading standards in primary schools may have fallen in the early 1990s. As many as 30 per cent of lessons in junior schools were considered inadequate in the 1995 report of Her Majesty's Chief Inspector. It is not uncommon, these days, for secondary heads, normally in private, to explain that they are admitting ever more pupils at age eleven with reading ages of nine of less. Indeed a significant number of secondary schools are now employing reading tests at the beginning of year seven in order to set a base-line for examining their own value added. In one of the more successful inner London boroughs, the average reading age of pupils in the first year of secondary schools is nine years and nine months. This kind of disadvantage at the start of secondary school is all too likely to prevent pupils from making the most of the crucial years between eleven and sixteen. It may be for this reason that the Adult Literacy and Basic Skills Unit (ALBSU) has discovered that as many as 15 per cent of 21-year-olds have limited literacy competence and 20 per cent have limited competence in mathematics.

It is interesting to set this evidence on standards against the Keele University database of 'Pupil Attitudes to Secondary Schools'. This shows that somewhere between 20 and 30 per cent of secondary-school pupils are disappointed or lacking in motivation. Another 10–15 per cent are disaffected and likely to disrupt the education of others. As many as another 5–10 per cent truant regularly or in some urban areas have unofficially left school altogether and become the 'disappeared'. In short, it would seem that the attitudinal data confirms the data on standards. While half or slightly over half are doing reasonably well, concern over the rest remains justifiable. It is a sobering reality that reaching the 85-per-cent target envisaged in the NETTs will involve switching-on all of 'the disappointed' and some of 'the disaffected' too.

If this is the overall national picture than it should be borne in mind that the gloomy parts of it are likely to be accentuated in Britain's urban areas. The group who are under-achieving and who are disappointed or disaffected include a disproportionately high number of boys, working-class students and students in deprived urban areas. The fact that a disproportionate number of those who underachieve are in urban areas does not, in any sense, justify having lower expectations or setting lower standards for pupils there. It does mean acknowledging, given the social circumstances in many of Britain's urban areas, that it takes more time, energy, commitment, skill and resources to enable pupils to reach those high standards. The distinctive feature of urban education is the concentration of social challenges, whether in terms of poverty, poor housing, poor health or other aspects of social deprivation. Many schools in urban areas work against the odds to provide an excellent education in spite of this concentration of challenges that pass daily through the door.

Perhaps not surprisingly not all schools manage. Some become ground down by the weight of social pressures and the demands of a never-ending series of educational policy changes. The central issue for policy-makers is to create a framework which increases the chances of success and reduces the chances of failure for urban schools. The starting point for such a policy must surely be the extensive knowledge we now have of what characterizes effective schools and what can be done to help schools that are not yet effective to improve. This is the theme of the next section of this chapter.

IMPROVING PERFORMANCE

There is now an overwhelming consensus about the characteristics of effective schools. The last year or two has seen the publication of a series of reviews of the literature in this field and the conclusions of all of them are very similar. A typical list of characteristics would include:

1 Strong, positive leadership by the head and senior staff.
2 A good atmosphere or spirit, generated both by shared aims and values and by a physical environment that is as attractive and stimulating as possible.
3 High and consistent expectations of all pupils.
4 A clear and continuing focus on teaching and learning.
5 Well-developed procedures for assessing how pupils are progressing.
6 Responsibility for learning shared by the pupils themselves.
7 Participation by pupils in the life of the school.
8 Rewards and incentives to encourage pupils to succeed.
9 Parental involvement in children's education and in supporting the aims of the school.

9

10 Extra-curricular activities which broaden pupils' interests and experiences, expand their opportunities to succeed, and help to build good relationships within the school.

(National Commission on Education Report, 1993, pp. 142–3)

Ongoing research is demonstrating that even within an effective school there are significant variations in the effectiveness of different departments or aspects and indeed that within a particular school the extent of effectiveness for different ability-groups varies too. These findings can help school managers to analyse and understand what is required to help their own schools improve. They are unlikely, however, to change significantly our understanding of what characterizes effectiveness. Indeed it is worth noting how similar the list of effectiveness characteristics is to the lists of effectiveness for all organizations that appear in management textbooks such as the Peters and Waterman classic *In Search of Excellence*.

Helpful though it is to be able to describe an effective school, doing so does not solve some important problems. Firstly the evidence from major studies in school effectiveness in this country has limitations. There has, for example, been little work on the study of historically ineffective schools and the evidence suggests that one cannot easily take the characteristics of effectiveness determined through studies of effective schools and apply them, unthinking, to schools that are less than effective. Secondly, the studies of school effectiveness have tended to focus on school- and departmental-level factors rather than on aspects of classroom practice. Surely one of the next frontiers for research in this country, and indeed elsewhere, is to examine what it is that characterizes effective teaching since we know already that the quality of the teacher is one of the key determinants of the quality of learning for pupils. Thirdly, there has until recently been insufficient overlap between the study of school effectiveness and the study and application of the processes of school improvement. Increasingly in this third area there is progress both in terms of research and practice. For example, the work of the London Institute of Education's School Improvement Network and the Keele Centre for Successful Schools is consciously designed to bridge the school effectiveness/school improvement divide.

The most significant problem, unaddressed in the school-effectiveness research findings, is that being able to describe an effective school does not necessarily indicate what is needed to help an unsuccessful school to become successful. The steps required to help a school turn itself round are, from a policy point of view, more important to know yet significantly less researched. However, there is a growing body of evidence about what works and it is important to summarize this as a prelude to determining a policy framework.

Some or all of the following strategies used in combination can contribute to school improvement:

(i) *Changing the Head*
Where the leadership has been poor this helps, but it is not necessarily the solution nor, on its own, is it likely to be sufficient.

(ii) *Providing External Consultancy*
A school that is failing may well be incapable of designing its own improvement strategy. An external consultant, from an LEA or elsewhere, can make an important contribution. The 'critical friend' beloved in education jargon does appear to be effective. The focus, however, should be on creating the capacity for sustainable improvement rather than on creating dependency.

(iii) *Changes in the Staff*
These are sometimes necessary but often prove very difficult to achieve through normal procedures. Some heads who have successfully turned round schools talk of the 'unofficial' means they used to drive out inadequate teachers.

(iv) *Changing the Culture*
More important than changing staff, which at most affects a tiny minority, is the changing culture. This involves:

● a sense of purpose and direction;

● high expectations of staff and pupils;

● a focus on teaching and learning;

● a belief in the possibility of success, This is easier to say than do, but undoubtedly involves attention to small but symbolic details as well as larger structural issues.

(v)   *Learning Networks*
Some schools have found that their improvement is enhanced if they link up with other schools either via an LEA or via a university. Being part of a network encourages risk-taking and enables schools to share ideas and expertise. It also enables the development of a shared language of school improvement. Later chapters provide many examples of effective networks currently in operation.

(vi) *Greater Openness about Performance Information*
It is important that schools monitor performance both in academic terms and others (e.g. attendance and behaviour). It is vital that data is shared across the school and that, however, uncomfortable it may be for some or all of the staff, it is never hidden.

(vii) *An Agreed Constructive Approach to Discipline*
A consistently applied behaviour policy which provides for both rewards and punishments is a precondition of success.

(viii) *An Effective Staff Development Policy Related to the School's Overall Development Strategy*
A school's policy for professional development needs to make effective use of limited resources, and to be seen to be fair. Above all, it needs to contribute to the notion of a learning staff among whom professional development and reflection are a constant feature of practice.

11

(ix)   *Actions*
There is then a menu of possible actions that might be necessary and from which a school might be encouraged to select. These include:

- more effective use of teaching support;
- additional voluntary classes/extra-curricular activities at the end of the day or in lunch hours;
- the provision of mentors from within the school or outside for some pupils, particularly those without stable family support;
- improved liaison with primary schools (in the case of secondary schools);
- a whole-school approach to literacy.

This list is not exhaustive.

(x)   *A School Development Plan*
The school needs a development plan which pulls together its strategy and relates it to available resources. It should include targets for improved achievement as well as specified changes. Each aspect of it needs success criteria, time-scales and an identification of staff responsibility and appropriate resources.

These are school-focused factors. There are other related factors which concern wider networks or initiatives. In 1994 Keele University was commissioned to study the characteristics of successful urban-education initiatives involving more than one school and the results of that study, which have a direct bearing on the argument here, are reported in the next few chapters in this book.

THE POLICY FRAMEWORK

Education Acts have followed each other with such bewildering rapidity over the years since 1988 that it is sometimes difficult to pick out the underlying principles from the mass of detail. Though there are many ways in which, in my view, the present policy-framework is in need of amendment, the reforms of the last few years have pointed the way to some important principles. In the following paragraphs I have attempted to identify and refine these emerging principles and show how their application would need to be altered for them to have their full potential impact. I am conscious, at this point in the argument, of moving from summarizing what is essentially a set of research findings to making proposals for the future which are inevitably controversial. Though I intend to write these principles in robust and confident style (partly in order to provoke controversy), I recognize that they are open to question and indeed will admit to sensing more doubt myself than might be apparent from the written style. This approach may seem, in some ways, unscholarly but the rapid pace of social, technological and economic change demands a change from traditional approaches in any case. Take for example the contrast between the following two approaches to the study of science:

It is not in the nature of things for any one man (*sic*) to make a
sudden, violent, discovery: science goes step by step.

(Rutherford, 1937)

A lucky guess based on shaky arguments and absurd *ad hoc*
assumptions gives a formula that turns out to be right, though at first
no one can see why on earth it should be.

(Robert March, 1978)

The contrast is startling and instructive for education researchers Peter
Mortimore, in his magisterial inaugural lecture (Mortimore, 1995, p. 30) arrived at
a similar point in a rather different language:

> . . . the historians will write their accounts in due course but I suspect
> that some of the factors which have led policy-makers to see the work
> of university departments of education as generally irrelevant have
> been the failure of academics to engage sufficiently with the real-life
> problems of schooling, their inability to work to timescales which
> correspond more closely with policy needs and the tendency to engage
> in what seem to the outside world to be rather esoteric debates.

There does, therefore, seem to be a growing body of opinion which supports the
idea of drawing tentative conclusions from what we do know and putting them
forward as proposals at the very least to provoke debate, even if they have not yet
been subjected to the traditional (and time-consuming) process of academic
critique or, for that matter, demonstrated beyond reasonable doubt.

The first principle I want to put forward is that *school improvement is a
task for the schools*. This apparently simple statement is far from being universally
accepted. However, the argument for placing responsibility for school improvement with the schools seems to me to be powerful. Most of the evidence on LMS
suggests that on the whole headteachers are very positive about taking control of
their budgets. Teachers so far are, understandably, less enthusiastic, but they too
are far from negative. Had LMS been introduced at a time of less-rigid budget
stringency, my guess is that it would have been even more enthusiastically
embraced. What is more, the general management literature argues powerfully for
placing responsibility at the level where it can be most effectively exercised.
Delegation to teams operating at the front line while cutting out tiers of bureaucracy has been one of the central features of changing organizational structures in
the late 1980s and early 1990s.

So far, again not surprisingly, there has been less enthusiasm for schools
becoming the point of accountability as well as the holders of budgets. The league
tables have been the subject of continuing controversy and OFSTED inspection
has hardly been welcomed. Nevertheless, above all in a public service in a
democracy, it seems difficult to construct an argument against those with
responsibility being held to account for their use of public money and their
contribution to the public good. It seems improbable that any imaginable
government in the rest of this decade, and probably beyond, would undo this shift
towards both greater autonomy and accountability at school level.

Thus, in a fundamental way, the government has been right about this issue. The problem is that in crucial details of its approach to both autonomy and accountability, the government's policy has been flawed. The result has been, at times, to discredit an otherwise unimpeachable principle. For example, in respect of its view of autonomy, the flaws include unnecessary restrictions on LMS formulae which prevent them being sufficiently sensitive to need, unnecessary uncertainty about funding prospects from one year to the next, a blatant bias in funding towards the GM sector and a flawed policy on admissions. With respect to policy on accountability the flaws have included basing performance tables solely on raw results, a heavy-handed and inflexible model of inspection and an over-dependence on the belief that the market will identify successful and unsuccessful schools. Proposals later in this chapter will suggest how each of these flaws might be corrected.

The second principle, that follows from the first, is that *the task of those outside schools is to create a framework which increases the chances of success in schools and the chances of failure*. Michael Fullan (1991) has argued that successful implementation of any given policy requires those implementing it to be simultaneously provided with support and put under pressure. This pressure–support paradox seems to me a profound insight into successful public policy. Since the war this country has rarely achieved the right balance of pressure and support in its education policy. One might generalize ruthlessly and argue that we had thirty years of support without pressure and then (since the mid-1980s) ten years of pressure without support. The job for government in the late 1990s and beyond is to provide both.

There are various ways in which effective pressure might be applied. In addition to the National Education and Training Targets that have already been established, it is essential that all schools should have targets for improvement against their previous performance. This was one powerful message of the Keele research on 'Urban Education Initiatives' which is examined later in the book. It has also been a vital feature of Tim Brighouse's strategy for raising standards in Birmingham (see Chapter 7).

The second means of applying pressure is to establish the case for the publication of performance data. The debate has so far been an unsatisfactory one, with the government arguing in favour of publishing solely raw results and the profession arguing against publication of anything at all. It ought to be possible to move towards the model outlined in the School Curriculum and Assessment Authorities Value-Added Working Group report or something similar to it. The first point to make about published performance data is that no single number, whether a raw one or a value-added one, can effectively summarize something as compli-cated as the academic performance of a school. Any single indicator will always be open to criticism and comment. Instead, we need to move towards the notion of three or four indicators which, taken together, summarize the performance of the school. The SCAA report suggests that in addition to raw results a value-added indicator and a school-improvement index should be published. These three statistics taken together would in fact give a broadly accurate picture of whether or not a school was performing successfully. A shift away from dependence on raw results is essential for urban schools since they will, on that indicator, always appear to be relatively unsuccessful. However, if data about improvement and value added are published too, then justice will be done. That combination of indicators would also ensure that any school which is failing, or relatively speaking underperforming, would be unable to hide behind the misleading statistics that are currently published.

The third element of pressure on schools should be through the cycle of inspections. The inspection system needs to be refined to give greater emphasis to school self-evaluation and to provide greater opportunity for improvement in the post-inspection period. In particular the inspection system ought to be more subtle in its distribution of time and resources and to concentrate any post-inspection improvement resources on the schools which have been found, either through the published performance indicators or through inspection, to be relatively under-performing. Finally, in terms of pressure, there needs to be a much clearer national policy for ensuring effective intervention in schools which are found to be failing. This aspect of pressure is examined in greater detail later in the chapter.

The support, which is an essential corollary of the pressure, should come from a range of factors too. Firstly, there should be a commitment to resourcing education consistently over a long period and a consideration of introducing three-year funding horizons to replace the completely inadequate system of staggering from one year to the next. This was a point made vigorously by OFSTED in its report on 'Access and Achievement in Urban Education' where it was argued that 'Resources need to be allocated on a more consistent and long term basis and bear a closer relationship to educational need'.

Secondly, there needs to be much greater investment in teachers' pro-fessional development, particularly in urban areas. The evidence suggests that in many cases teachers simply become ground down by the multiple pressures of working in such areas. For this reason investment in their continuing development ought to be a priority. The idea of vouchers for professional development, specifi-cally for teachers in urban areas, ought to be considered as one means of attracting the best teachers into some of the country's more difficult schools. Thirdly, there ought to be much greater investment in local and school-level innovation through a reform of the current Grants for Education Support and Training (GEST), which currently are excessively focused on the implementation of national priorities. Consideration might also be given to the use of the funds, which have been allocated to the technology schools initiative and its successors, being opened up for schools that want to develop an innovative approach to their choice rather than the government's.

It is also essential for government to invest in the provision of a range of extra-curricular activities, homework clubs, and other after-school options which would provide attractive alternatives to the dubious attractions of the street. Where schools have provided such an array of after-school activities, as in parts of Stoke-on-Trent and in Hammersmith and Fulham for example, they have been successful both in attracting significant numbers of pupils and in raising standards of achievement. Indeed there is some evidence to suggest that by encouraging significant numbers of young people to choose to achieve more, such activities have a positive effect on the formal curriculum through contributing to changing the peer-group culture.

Tim Brighouse has begun to explore, in Birmingham, how a wide range of activities after school and in school holidays might be given priority, coherence and structure through coming under what he has described as a University of the First Age. This would be a means of both enabling enthusiastic teachers to provide activities in their chosen areas of expertise – from chess to soccer, from design to Latin – for pupils interested in pursuing them, and a system of accrediting that range of activities so that it could be recognized by employers and higher-education institutions.

Finally – and it is a tragedy that it still needs to be said – schools in urban areas would be greatly assisted if there were a coherent policy for the education of children between birth and age five. While universally available nursery education would provide part of this, it also requires making use of the health-visitor system to begin to provide educational advice and support for parents from the moment their child is born, if not before.

Given this range of pressure and support, it is possible to imagine that many more schools than at present would succeed in urban areas. In general the aim clearly is to encourage schools to achieve conditions for sustainable improvement. From this, one can deduce a third policy-principle. Namely *that external intervention should be in inverse proportion to success*. This of course requires that there are nationally accepted performance indicators and a credible inspection system so that the extent of each school's success is publicly known. Once this was the case intervention would come when there was clear evidence of school failure or at those moments when the risk of failure is known to be higher, such as at the moment when the headship passes from one head to another or when, for whatever reason, there is excessively high staff turnover.

THE IMPLICATIONS FOR POLICY

If these are the policy principles, what do they mean for national government, local government and schools? The final section of this chapter looks at each of these levels of the education service in turn. The role of national government is relatively straightforward to establish, given the discussion above. First, of course, it has responsibility for establishing the policy framework. This does not mean only the laws and regulations governing education but also the climate in which policy development takes place and the establishment of effective working relationships with the teaching profession, governors, local-education authorities and other participants in the provision of education-policy debate. Secondly, national government clearly has the prime responsibility for setting out the resource framework. This is not simply a matter for the Department for Education incidentally; it also requires the Department of the Environment and, ultimately, the Treasury to think carefully about the impact of their decisions on education, as the governors' revolt over education spending in 1995 demonstrates.

National government also has responsibility for the National Curriculum and the national framework for assessment and examinations. Now that the government has finally established a workable National Curriculum, the main task for it and its successors over the next five years is to keep it under review and prepare for a thorough overhaul of it in the year 2000. There is no doubt that as and when various crises arise in the next few years, there will be repeated demand for the revision of one or other part of the National Curriculum. National government must resist the temptation to tamper with the curriculum until the five years of promised stability are over.

More challenging still will be establishing and improving the national assessment system. This is critical for standards in urban areas since only through national assessment can schools across the country gain the common language of standards and achievement that is so essential. However, for the national assessment system to succeed it will need a judicious combination of externally-marked tests and teacher assessment. At present the balance seems to be tipped too heavily in favour of the former at the expense of the latter. Another challenge for national government between now and the end of the century in relation to assessment is to establish a common framework for qualifications for the 14–19 age range. Some trends are working in favour of this: for example, the modularization of some A-Level courses and the increased uptake of GNVQ. Nevertheless there is a still a welter of confusion and many young people at the age of 16 have to face the dilemma of deciding whether or not to take A-Levels with the risk that if they do they could end up with nothing to show for two years' hard work and otherwise productive learning.

With the National Curriculum, and potentially national assessment, in place, it becomes another crucial function of government to establish a national set of performance-indicators. So far the government has insisted on the publication only of raw examination data but its welcome for the recent Value Added Working Group report of the School Curriculum and Assessment Authority suggests that there is room for movement even before an election. Since the Labour Party has also advocated the publication of raw results, improvement indices and value-added data there is a welcome outbreak of consensus in this area. In order to build sufficient credibility into the system and to develop support for it, the government will have to enter into dialogue with governors and teachers as well as the wider public. Performance-indicators can only play a significant role in the national policy framework if they have widespread credibility.

The national inspection system ought then to be related integrally to the performance-indicators. Applying the policy principle outlined above (that external intervention should be in inverse proportion to success) it would make sense for OFSTED inspection to vary in its intensity according to how well a school appeared to be performing according to the national performance-indicators. Where there were significant concerns a more thorough inspection would be required with the possibility of clear follow-up action. In any case, as a prelude to external inspection, each school ought to undertake a self-review which ought to be validated by an external consultant, perhaps provided by the local education authority.

With these elements in place the next crucial task for central government is to provide genuine and consistent leadership. That requires leading politicians, especially the Prime Minister, to urge consistently higher standards and to draw the public's attention both to the pressure the government is applying and the support it is providing. It is interesting to note that it is not uncommon for political leaders in the western world (including George Bush, John Major and Bill Clinton) to begin their terms of office by emphasising the importance of education and then to lose interest in it rapidly when they discovered how difficult it can be to bring about change in the sector. That kind of fleeting leadership will be inadequate in the decade ahead.

As part of its leadership role government should set demanding targets for the education service. It can be expected that the national education and training targets which are currently being revised will be in place for the rest of this decade. However, in addition to these absolute national targets there ought to be targets relating to the rate of improvement as well. This has worked very effectively in some local education authorities such as Birmingham and a number of urban-education initiatives.

The government also has an obligation (which over recent years it has failed to carry out) to promote research and development in education. The Department for Education has a budget for research which is barely over £1,000,000. This compares very unfavourably with those of the Departments of Health and Employment and is a totally inadequate sum in the context of the many challenges facing the education service. In particular, for example, there has been far too little national investment in the relationship between communications technology, pedagogy and educational achievement. This area is rich in possibilities but remains, sadly, for the moment undiscovered territory.

Finally, national government needs to build a creative functioning partnership with local government. There is some evidence that in 1994 and 1995 the government began to recognize the need to rebuild its relations with local government. This followed the early 1990s in which the relationship reached a low ebb, at a great cost to young people and teachers across the country. Now that central government has become increasingly pragmatic, local government has been slow to respond, not least because the bruises of the previous decade are still very much in evidence. The progress that was made in 1994 and early 1995 has also been set back by the conflict over the under-funding of the education system and the teachers' salary increase in early 1995. It seems improbable that the huge leap in standards we require can be brought about while different tiers of government are at war or at even merely working towards an armed and uneasy truce. This is a major concern and depends on both national and local government focusing not on short-term self-interest but on long-term educational standards.

The Role of Local Government

There have been times in the early 1990s when it appeared that local education authorities were about to become irrelevant. Partly this was a result of central government's hostility, partly it was a result of legislative change and partly it was a result of some local education authorities becoming so demoralized that they began to write themselves out of the script. However, during 1994, when it became apparent that the GM movement was dying on its feet, there was a positive revival of morale and activity at local education authority level. Local authorities such as Birmingham, Nottinghamshire, Lewisham and Essex have begun to create a new role for themselves in spite of the deprivations of the early part of the decade. What is more, this role is turning out in many ways to be more creative and constructive than the old management and administration functions that LEAs have been forced to surrender.

Central to the role of a successful local education authority in the late 1990s will be the offer of community leadership and the provision of a sense of direction for a three- to five-year period. It is interesting that recently a spate of LEAs have taken to writing strategic plans which cover the period through to the end of the century. This suggests a growth in confidence and a renewed determination to provide the local leadership that is so essential to successful education, particularly in urban areas. The evidence presented later in the book shows that in the vast majority of urban-education initiatives, it is the LEA which has played the leading role in bringing together training and enterprise councils (TECs), community organizations, local higher-education institutions, FE colleges and other organizations in support of school improvement. Though it is possible to imagine urban-education initiatives without LEAs, it seems from the evidence that there would be far fewer of them and that they would be significantly less likely to succeed. Even the successful higher-education urban-education networks such as the one at the Institute of Education in London depend on working through local education authorities in many cases. The same is true of the work of the Centre for Successful Schools at Keele. It is worth pointing out that this function of LEAs is of immense significance although it is not written down in statute.

The same applies to the next important function. LEAs are well placed to provide schools with extensive performance data relating, for example, to examination results, test results and financial and management information. Comparative data which enables schools to examine their own success and approaches in comparison with those of other schools in the same geographical area or of similar intakes cannot, by definition, be provided by a school alone. It is almost unthinkable that any school on its own could find the time to gather sufficient data from other schools in order to provide itself with comparative data even if it had the expertise. For an LEA, on the other hand, this is a relatively straightforward matter. Many LEAs are already performing this role excellently. Nottinghamshire, Surrey and Shropshire, for example, provide excellent data to all their schools. In urban areas LEAs such as Islington are doing a similarly effective job.

Information is only one aspect of the support that LEAs can provide. Many LEAs now offer schools a range of training, consultancy and advice which schools are able to buy into as and when they believe they need it. This too can be helpful, and the delegation of the funding of it to schools has, as many people in LEAs will admit, often improved the quality and responsiveness of the services that LEAs provide. In addition some LEAs have been able, even in times of financial stringency, to find small but significant sums of money at the margin of the projects in order to fund local-level innovation. Lewisham, for example, has funded a highly successful school-improvement initiative for its secondary schools, as has Hammersmith and Fulham. Essex has provided £300,000 to assist the deprived urban area of Tilbury in recovering from devastating OFSTED reports in 1992 and 1993. Since any successful organization depends, as the management textbooks constantly remind us, on innovation coming from all levels, it is essential that

LEAs' innovation is promoted at school and local as well as national level. While it is also constructive if schools take the initiative in innovation, it is a substantial risk for any single school to invest a substantial amount in any given innovation. For one thing such innovation can draw away precious resources from core activity, and for another, innovation is often treated with caution and suspicion by parents. Keele's data on parents' attitudes to schools suggests that while about 60 per cent of parents would like, in general, to see some changes in the school that their child attends, it is virtually impossible to put together a majority of parents in favour of any specific change. In our national database the highest percentage of parents in favour of any given change is about 47 per cent who would like to see improved discipline. No other suggestions however have the support of more than a third of the parents and most have significantly less. LEAs on the other hand – even small ones – can sometimes find money, and a group of schools can have the confidence to take risks (Barber, 1994).

Another critical role for local education authorities, particularly relevant in urban areas, is to intervene in cases where there is a risk of failure. Central government has, with some justification, often pointed out that LEAs are hardly in a position to claim the role of intervening in failing schools since there are too many cases in which failing schools have been consistently neglected by LEAs over a long period. However, in the new climate that I have tried to outline here, and in which LEAs are not responsible for the day-to-day management of schools, it seems sensible that this responsibility be placed, at least in the first instance, with LEAs. They ought to have the power to intervene specifically in schools described as failing by OFSTED but also in schools described by OFSTED as being in serious difficulties. Under the present arrangements LEAs have no more power over a school in serious difficulties than they do over any other school. The result is that LEAs find themselves waiting for such a school to drift into more serious failure before they can take the kind of action that may be necessary. While this should be a primary responsibility for LEAs it is surely right for government to retain the right to intervene ultimately, if an LEA has not succeeded in tackling a failing school. It is interesting that during 1995 one or two LEAs have been pressed into taking firmer action with failing schools because central government has been able to threaten the establishment of an Education Association. Without that power some LEAs might continue to abdicate their responsibilities in the way that some did in the past.

Another area awaiting solution is that of school admission policies. In rural areas this is rarely a problem since parents tend to choose the nearest school. In urban areas it is becoming a major problem. The arrangements at present do not seem to be working and the evidence collected by the Association of Metropolitan Authorities (AMA) suggests that fewer first preferences are being satisfied than some years ago. It seems both unwise and improbable for some national agency, whether the Funding Agency for Schools or the Department for Education, to take responsibility for admission policies in any given area. One important aspect of establishing successful admissions policies is detailed knowledge of the locality. LEAs, therefore, are surely best placed to establish an admissions policy for an area. It would therefore make sense for LEAs to have the first-line responsibility for drawing up admissions policies, with schools having the right of appeal to the Department of Education in cases where they believed they had been harshly treated.

LEAs have many other statutory responsibilities, for example in relation to special education, which need not be tackled here. What I have tried to identify in this section is the potentially highly-productive role that local government can play in a new education order where schools are simultaneously autonomous and accountable. LEAs that choose to take on the role described in this section can become the driving force of this country's efforts to raise standards, just as after the war they drove the expansion of the secondary sector.

A Learning School in a Learning City

A great deal has been written about effective schools and the process of school improvement. Some of it has already been referred to earlier in the chapter. In this final section I want to pick out six features of improving schools in urban areas that seem to me are emerging as the new agenda of school improvement. The first of these six features is that urban schools, like all schools, need a clear sense of direction. This is harder to establish in urban schools because of the many pressures upon them but it is also more crucial, since the *status quo* is rarely acceptable to the staff, the pupils or the local community. There is thus a premium in such schools on effective leadership and on a management approach that can generate both a vision of the future and a shared culture and commitment to the schools' direction. In order to achieve this the school-development plan ought to be formulated on the basis of widespread consultation and ought to become the central text for individual teachers, departments (in secondary schools) and others involved in planning aspects of a school's provision. In short everyone must believe in it.

Once this is established, it is also important that urban schools, to use Michael Fullan's phrase, 'practise fearlessness'. This means that once the school has established its own destiny and its plans for how to move towards it, then school leaders need to recognize that they cannot do all the things that external organizations, such as the DFE, LEAs, OFSTED and others will ask them to do. There is simply not enough time for them to be able to do so and implement their own plan. Thus the choice is stark: either things fail to happen by default, or, surely more sensibly, schools decide that they will not do some of the things that they have been asked to do. A good example of schools practising fearlessness, which is particularly a feature of urban areas, is schools refusing to carry out the daily act of collective worship. The evidence suggests that 80 per cent of schools have decided not to do this although it is a statutory requirement, not least because it often proves unmanageable in an ethnically diverse school.

Thirdly, once the school knows what it is going to do and what it is not going to do, it ought to set clear targets. These ought to identify timescales, success criteria, necessary resources and the staff responsible. It then becomes a vital part of management to monitor the implementation of agreed targets and to build on them. Where targets are not met the school is then in a position to ask itself the question why, and engage in a process of review and development. Where targets are met they can contribute to building confidence among the staff.

Fourthly, there seems to be growing evidence to suggest that openness about performance data within a school is a vital ingredient of improvement. This is part of the process of developing a common language about performance. It is also critical to ensuring that no part of a school or individual teacher is able to hide relatively poor performance. Where there is under-performance it ought to be out in the open, debated and, if necessary, tackled properly. However, openness does not apply solely to performance data. It also applies to discussions about teaching approaches and philosophies and about the budget. Roland Barth, for example, in *Improving Schools from Within*, suggests that encouraging discussion in staff rooms about approaches to teaching is an important feature of a successful school and of a learning staff. The same applies in general to the whole process of evaluating a school's performance: essentially the staff should both formally and informally be constantly engaged in researching and reflecting upon their own practice across all aspects of the school. This is more a matter of culture among the staff than of time or resources.

Fifthly, and following directly from the previous point, a successful urban school requires a learning staff. This is partly a matter of having a carefully planned professional development strategy which is related both to the school-development plan and to the school's teacher-appraisal scheme. It is partly too a matter of ensuring that staff have opportunities to take part in INSET events away from the school, and in some cases, in higher-degree courses. However, it is also very much a matter of encouraging staff to learn from everyday events and from management processes. For example, a debate about budget priorities, either at school- or departmental level, can be an important learning experience if it is handled in the right way. It is also essential that the school culture encourages classroom observation. One of the great benefits of the national scheme of teacher appraisal has been to encourage much more widespread classroom observation. Again and again in a recent evaluation of teacher appraisal (DFE, 1995) teachers refer to the value they gained from being appraisers, which provided them with the opportunity to watch other colleagues teach. Often the learning experience of being the appraiser has been as valuable as being appraised.

Finally, it is demonstrably good practice for a school to consider all its staff, not just its teachers, as members of the learning community. For many years teaching-support staff were neglected in professional-development terms as indeed in many other ways. There is now a growing body of evidence of good practice in the involvement of teaching-support staff in all aspects of the management of a school, including planning processes, professional development and decision-making. The best example we identified in our study of urban-education initiatives was in Nottingham city, where the nine primary schools were making highly-effective use of teaching-support staff, not only in administrative and support functions but also in the teaching and learning process. The teachers in these schools did not feel threatened by support staff in a classroom. On the contrary they recognized that having additional support in the classroom enabled them to play their role as teacher and professional leader much more effectively. This is not a minor issue. The number of teaching-support staff in schools in this country is growing rapidly. According to the 1995 *School Teachers' Review Body Report* 'there was an increase of nearly 40,000 in the number of non-teaching staff employed in schools between 1991 and 1994' (STRB, p. 9).

These six roles are picked from among many aspects of improving schools that might have been examined. They seem to me to be those that need most explanation at this stage in the development of urban-education policy. In the chapters that follow many of the points discussed in this section and indeed in the sections before are explored in greater depth. Many other points that it has not been possible to raise in this chapter are raised too. The overall picture, in England and Wales at any rate, is in my view not as depressing as it sometimes appears.

There have been times too in the last decade when a sense of gloom seemed to pervade the consideration of urban education. The growing social problems in urban areas seemed overwhelming. The pace of educational change and its poor implementation at times looked as though they might bring complete demoralization in many urban schools. Funding, never abundant, has been tightly constrained throughout the first half of the 1990s. In spite of all these difficulties there are grounds for optimism. Many of the policies that have been implemented could have benefit so long as this government and its successors are prepared to refine and extend them in accordance with the emerging evidence of progress in cities such as Birmingham and Nottingham.

REFERENCES

Barber, M. (1994) *Parents and their Attitudes to School*. Keele: Keele University.

Barber, M. *et al.* (1995) *An Evaluation of the National Scheme of Teacher Appraisal for the DFE*. London: DFE.

Barth, R. (1990) *Improving Schools from Within*. San Francisco: Jossey-Bass.

Evans, A. (1994) *Industrial Change in Europe*: Eurotecnet Synthesis Report. London: HMSO.

Fullan, M. (1991) *The New Meaning of Educational Change*. London: Cassell.

Mortimore, P. (1995) *Effective Schools: Current Impact and Future Potential*. London: Institute of Education.

National Commission on Education (1993) *Learning to Succeed*. London: Heinemann.

Oakland, J.S. (1989) *Total Quality Management*. Oxford: Butterworth-Heinemann.

OFSTED (1993) *Access and Achievement in Urban Education*. London: HMSO.

School Teachers' Review Body (1995) *Fourth Report*. London: HMSO.

Part One

Urban Education – The National Context

Chapter 2

Urban Education: Current Position and Future Possibilities[1]

George Smith

INTRODUCTION

This paper is intended as a broad-ranging review of research on some aspects of urban education. It is by no means an exhaustive survey of available research or indeed of all the issues that might be raised under the general heading of 'urban education'. It draws on research from this country, but also includes some reference to recent developments in the United States, where issues such as educational disadvantage have in recent years again returned to the centre of the policy agenda. Thus the federal legislation for the 'Goals 2000: Educate America' Act and the re-authorization of 'Title 1' (Chapter 1) (a major source of federal funding for American schools), both passed in 1994, focus strongly on educational disadvantage. The paper also makes some limited use of unpublished data from OFSTED's own EIS database, including limited data from the first year of secondary school inspections carried out under the new inspection system.

The first section describes the sources of information and coverage. Section 2 looks at the changing urban context in this country and Section 3 presents some recent data on urban education and urban disadvantage. These sections provide the backdrop to looking in more detail at the evidence about 'what works' in Section 4.

URBAN EDUCATION: DEFINITIONS AND ISSUES

Scope, Definitions and Data

'Urban education' is a term used loosely to cover a range of educational issues particularly educational disadvantage, not merely to distinguish 'urban' from 'rural' concerns (not surprisingly when 70 per cent or more of the population in England could now be classified as living in 'urban' areas on some definitions). In the original OFSTED *Access and Achievement in Urban Education* (OFSTED, 1993) report (henceforth AAUE) the areas selected for study included a number of peripheral estates (Orchard Park in Kingston-upon-Hull, Hartcliffe in South Bristol) rather than some of the better-known and much-studied 'inner city' areas. As is now well demonstrated, many of the social and economic problems that were particularly concentrated in the central parts of cities and large towns in the 1960s were increasingly evident in outlying estates during the 1970s and 1980s, though there is a strong argument to be made that the term 'inner city', an idea drawn from the American model of 'concentric rings' of urban development, has never fitted at all well with most patterns of urban development in this country. Urban disadvantage now applies to many central urban areas, including the so-called 'inner cities', and to outlying estates and smaller towns as well, particularly those with declining or defunct industries, such as mining, steel-making, shipbuilding and docking.

This description could be sufficient to delimit urban disadvantage – except that we need a way of drawing a precise boundary for data purposes. For this paper I have therefore defined 'urban' as those areas that fall within metropolitan districts, and also those areas in shire counties with population densities greater than ten persons per hectare. This has been done at the level of local electoral wards (of which there were more than 8,000 in England in 1991 with an average population of about 5,500). This definition inevitably has an element of 'rough justice'; there are some wards at the edge of metropolitan areas that have rural-level densities, that will be classified *urban* under this procedure. And there may be clusters of 'villages' that produce wards with densities greater than ten persons per hectare that will be classified 'urban'. However, 'fine-tuning' to remove these anomalies would be laborious and would not be likely to alter the overall picture very substantially.

Second, we need a working definition of 'disadvantage'. Here I have drawn on the recently published Department of the Environment's 'Index of Local Conditions' survey (DoE, 1994). This provides an overall index score for every area in the country, based primarily on 1991 census data. This 'local conditions index' is the successor to the 1981 DoE 'z score' index which was widely used to classify areas on the basis of their *overall* disadvantage. The 1991 index is similarly a nationally 'standardized' measure with a score of 0.00 representing a notional 'national' average; positive values represent increasing disadvantage; negative values advantage. The index at ward level is based on aggregating seven separate measures from the 1991 census (see Appendix 1 for further details of the DoE index).

To link this data to individual schools the school postcode, which can be related to the local census ward, is used. OFSTED data on the school's social setting currently includes the ward where the school is physically located and the three adjoining wards. In some cases the ward selected will not represent the area from which the school draws its pupils, particularly for selective or denominational schools. For an individual school this needs to be checked carefully. However, the overall effect in a large data-set may be relatively small.

'Disadvantage' has been defined in terms of those areas with the 10 per cent highest scores on the DoE 'index of local conditions'. This measure, it should be underlined, is based on the *area* rather than the school. We could of course have used a school-based measure (such as the proportion of pupils eligible for free school meals) or indeed a composite measure of school- and locality-based

Table 2.1. *Primary schools by urban disadvantage and LEA type: all primaries*

Urban area	10% highest disadvantage	Middle 80%	Lowest 10%	No. of schools
Metropolitan districts	1,523	3,606	712	5,841
Urban parts of shire counties	212	4,606	662	5,480
Rural parts of shire counties	10	5,742	380	6,132
Total number of schools	1,745	13,954	1,754	17,453

Table 2.2. *Secondary schools by urban disadvantage: LEA-maintained comprehensives only, 1993*

Urban	10% highest disadvantage	Middle 80%	Lowest 10%	No. of schools
Metropolitan districts	243	675	112	1,030
Urban parts of shire counties	23	894	104	1,021
Rural parts of shire counties	8	607	62	677
Total number of schools	274	2,176	278	2,728

measures as in the recently published OFSTED study on assessing secondary-school performance (Sammons *et al.*, 1994). However as a first stage it seemed preferable to use an area-based measure which is independent of any school-based information. This avoids one problem of measures such as 'eligibility for free school meals', as these figures may be affected by LEA- or school-based registration procedures and variations in take-up at the local level.

At this stage, analysis at secondary level has been restricted to LEA-maintained comprehensive schools only. Selective schools and GM schools have been excluded. For comparative or 'benchmark' purposes we have used the overall group of urban comprehensive schools, showing the middle 80 per cent and the bottom or 'most advantaged' 10 per cent of schools.

These definitions result in the distribution of primary and secondary schools in terms of disadvantage and urban location shown in Tables 2.1 and 2.2. Note that restricting the focus to urban disadvantage does not mean that a large number of highly disadvantaged areas are excluded. Only eight secondary schools and ten primary schools in 'rural' areas fall into the highest 10 per cent of ward in terms of disadvantage, although altering the 'cut-points' up or down from 10 per cent will change the number in the different categories. Also note that the metropolitan districts have most of the schools in the most disadvantaged areas (more than 85 per cent), but they also have slightly more schools in the most advantaged areas. In other words large towns and cities contain proportionately more of the most disadvantaged areas but also a few more of the most advantaged. Appendix 1 provides more details of the technical methods.

Current Issues in Urban Education

Educational Performance Much of the discussion on educational disadvantage has concentrated on performance data, such as examination results, and, where

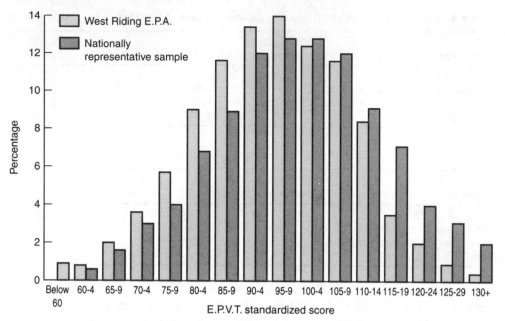

Figure 2.1. *Distribution of performance of primary-age children on a standardized vocabulary test. An educational priority area and national distribution*

available, pupil performance at other key stages. A broader approach would include a range of other measures such as staying-on rates, as well as measures of other educational achievements.

Much of the data on educational performance tends to be presented at an aggregate or average level, for example for schools, for districts or for particular groups. We should not forget that underlying such aggregates are a wide range of individual scores. Thus even in the most disadvantaged school or area, there is likely to be a wide range of individual pupils' scores. Figure 2.1 illustrates this point for the complete primary-age group tested in an (all-white) mining community. The overall range of performance in standardized terms (national average = 100) on a simple picture vocabulary test, shows the slightly skewed distribution in comparison to the theoretical national pattern. What is important to underline is that the data for this socially disadvantaged area shows pupils in *all* performance categories, but there are fewer above-average and more below-average pupils than the national distribution. The overall effect is to depress the average to about 95 points in standardized terms. Presented in this way the problem may look less daunting. Clearly not all children are 'failing' in terms of national norms.

It is important to stress that underlying any aggregate performance data are overall distributions of this type. These will vary from area to area, school to school, and may not look like Figure 2.1, which was drawn from a socially homogeneous and settled community. They may also vary with age. Thus secondary-school data for the same area showed an increasing divergence from the national distribution as the effect of disadvantage accumulated over time. These distributions also raise questions about improvement objectives. Clearly there are many ways that the average could be raised to 100 (assuming that this was the objective); thus every pupil could improve a little, or particular groups could be targeted. This distribution may also say something about the issue of teacher and parental expectations, which is sometimes held to be a factor in explaining under-performance in disadvantaged areas.

Access Questions of access apply most strongly to provision outside the statutory age range. Thus while many forms of preschool have in the past been set up explicitly to meet social needs, the present picture is one of very considerable variation from area to area in terms of both levels and types of provision. This also applies to full day-care provision for young children. Greater diversity of provision at the compulsory stages of education, one of the objectives of current policies, also raises the question of differential access to the full range of opportunities. Questions of access also apply to informal education in youth work, adult and further education. Some forms of provision, for example nursery classes, may be more extensively provided in inner-city areas, but we know much less about provision for disadvantaged groups and areas within traditionally more prosperous authorities. It is reasonable to ask 'who gets what?'

Resourcing The introduction of formula funding has made it much easier to examine levels of resourcing for schools in different types of area. In the 1960s and 1970s there was a move to provide some compensatory funding to schools in defined educational-priority areas (EPAs) or later 'social priority schools'. Some of these patterns continue into the LMS system. At national level, central government allocations to local authorities have been influenced by the Additional Educational Needs (AEN) formula that determines part of each local authority's education Standard Spending Assessment (SSA). This is currently based on three LEA-wide measures (the proportion of children from families receiving income support, the proportion from lone parents and the proportion whose parents were born outside the UK). Together (in the ratio 2.4, 2.4 and 1.0 respectively) these form the AEN index score which is currently (1994/5) used to weight 17 per cent (down from 21 per cent in 1993/4) of the total primary- and secondary-school spending block. AEN index scores run from 2.786 in Hackney to 0.6148 in Surrey. These significantly determine levels of resourcing for LEAs. But we can also ask how well schools in disadvantaged areas do in comparison to others within the same LEAs, since the AEN formula applies only to the national distribution.

Local support for schools Recent government policies have meant a substantial increase in the powers and responsibilities of individual schools and their governing bodies and a related reduction in those of the LEA. In the case of 'failing schools' the remedy is again focused on the individual school, though with the addition of external assistance. There is now clear evidence that individual schools may be able to 'bootstrap' themselves up in this way. However in the United States the emphasis has distinctly shifted from individual school improvement to

31

'systemic reform' – attempts to improve education across the board. While there is some rhetoric associated with the 'buzz word', the starting point is clear. In the words of the 'Goals 2000: Educate America' Act 1994: 'the reforms in education since 1977 have achieved some good results, but such reform efforts have been limited to a few schools or a single part of the educational system . . .' (Section 301, Title III: State and Local Systemic Improvement). There is also some indication from the USA that gains for some schools may have been partially at the expense of others, for example by attracting away better pupils or funding. The extent to which educational improvement in urban disadvantaged areas can depend wholly on individual school effort and how far it requires external support is clearly a key issue of debate.

THE CHANGING URBAN CONTEXT

The National Pattern

There is growing evidence of some fairly fundamental changes occurring during the 1980s and early 1990s that have had a very sharp effect on many urban areas. We have already referred to the shift during the 1970s to include many of the poorer peripheral estates as well as the older inner cities among the most highly disadvantaged urban areas.

At national level, surveys such as that by the IFS (Institute for Fiscal Studies: Goodman and Webb, 1994), which has analyzed the government's annual Family Expenditure Survey (FES) since 1961, show a widening gap between the top-income decile (10 per cent) and the bottom decile over the last decade. After housing costs (AHC) had been taken into account income levels in the bottom 5 per cent were only marginally higher in real terms in 1991 than they had been in 1961.

Data from the IFS survey and the government's *Households Below Average Income* (HBAI) (DSS, 1994a) series show that in addition to the relative shifts in the income distribution, a further important change was in the composition of low-income families over this same period. It is particularly families with children who have increased as a proportion of those in the lowest-income decile or quintile (20 per cent). Pensioners, a group traditionally concentrated in the lower-income bands, have moved up as more of them receive occupational pensions lifting them out of the lowest income deciles. Figure 2.2, from Goodman and Webb, shows the changing proportions of the bottom 10 per cent of households by family type over this 30-year period.

These trends are supported by the latest DSS figures on income support (DSS, 1994b) which show roughly one in four of all children under sixteen years living in households on income support (figures for 1993). These have risen from just over one in five children in 1991. These children are concentrated among the younger-ages groups – 38 per cent (972,600) being under five years, and about the same proportion (979,180) aged 5 to 10. The number of children on free school meals – since 1988 effectively a proxy for income support – has risen from 821,400 in 1991 to 1,141,300 in 1993, a rise of nearly 40 per cent to make up more than 15 per cent of all pupils (figures for England only).

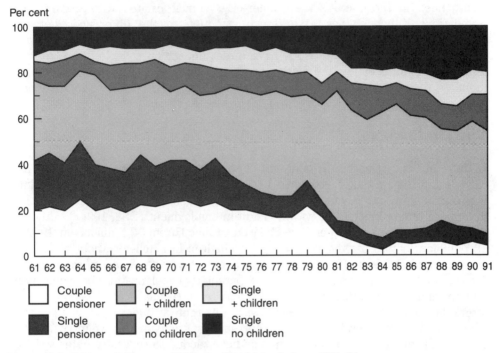

Per cent

Figure 2.2. *Bottom decile group (AHC) classified by family type, 1961–91*

Local Studies

These data chart the changing national pattern of social and economic disadvantage. Several studies have indicated the way that low-income families are distributed geographically. Basing his work on comparison between the 1981 and 1991 censuses, Green (1994) demonstrates how the degree, extent and intensity of disadvantage increased in inner London and the other large metropolitan areas over the decade; particularly in inner and east London she draws attention to the concentration of poor families and their isolation 'from the social and economic mainstream'. Other areas doing badly included those heavily dependent on single industries now in decline – coal mining, heavy manufacturing and port-related industries. More detailed local studies (Noble *et al.*, 1994) have shown the way that low-income families are increasingly concentrated in particular neighbourhoods, especially some of the more disadvantaged council estates, even in more prosperous cities. Both studies show that while there has been some change regionally there is also a considerable stability in the geographical distributions of low-income and disadvantaged families over time (data from 1981 to 1993).

However, we should be careful to avoid a stereotype of such areas. Thus it is important to distinguish areas in rapid transition from those with stable populations. These may present very different types of problem for schools. In analyses for Liverpool, Webber (1975) demonstrated some years ago that the types of social problems linked to his transitional 'rooming house areas' were rather different from those in the more settled inner-city council estates with quite stable populations. Other studies have drawn attention to the differences between 'transitional' and 'residual' areas, for example areas where traditional industries have closed. These characteristics have direct impact on schools: there may be less teacher turnover in more settled areas and certainly fewer problems of pupil mobility, though there may be other issues such as fixed and low expectations.

The Underclass

Is there an 'underclass' in Britain, and, if so, is it growing? The term 'underclass' carries unfortunate moral overtones, and may also suggest a continuity over time. It is certainly the case that a growing percentage of children and young people live in families on low incomes or with no adult in employment (DSS, 1994a): although the actual *numbers* of dependent children dropped from 13.8 million in 1979 to 12.7 million in 1991/92, the *percentage* of children in families without a full-time worker increased from 18 per cent to 30 per cent over the same period (figures for the UK). In some areas, it is also apparent that 'polarization' between more affluent and poor neighbourhoods is on the increase (Noble *et al.*, 1994). However attempts to identify an 'underclass' with different attitudes and values from mainstream society have not picked out such a group in this country (Heath, 1992), and the use of 'snapshot' data may have tended to suggest greater stability than is in fact the case. Longitudinal studies show that families do move in and out of disadvantage over time.

While it would be naive to expect that these social and economic changes would have a direct linear effect on schools and education, it would be equally surprising if they had made no impact. Evidence of the way low-income families are increasingly concentrated in particular neighbourhoods also has implications for schools which serve these areas. Schools only a few streets away may be catering for a very different type of population. This will clearly be more likely in areas outside London. In inner London some LEAs cater for a highly disadvantaged population across their area. Metropolitan districts outside London often include a much wider cross-section.

SOME RECENT DATA ON URBAN EDUCATION

Resourcing

Questions of resources raise a number of difficult issues. However, they cannot be ignored on the grounds that they do not matter. While adequate resourcing is by itself no guarantee of success, this may not mean that it makes no difference. Indeed there is now some more concrete evidence from American research on the effects of enhanced funding where this is targeted at specific developments. The results of underfunding are also clear, for example in the US system where disadvantaged areas may have per-pupil funding less than half that of the more prosperous districts, with dramatic consequences for the overall quality of education (see Kozol, 1993, for a searing account). Such gross inequalities do not exist in this country – the weighting of central government grant by the AEN factor ensures that poorer LEAs generally receive more grant – but this is no reason not to look at this topic.

Under LMS, LEAs are required to allocate 80 per cent of the 'potential schools budget' (PSB) to schools on a 'pupil-led' basis. The remaining 20 per cent can be allocated for special needs, for small schools and for difficult buildings such as split sites, etc. A very wide variety of measures is used by LEAs to allocate the special needs/social needs amounts. The majority take account of the proportion of free school meals; some use educational-test scores or measures of English as a second language; others use general population data or professional assessment (Lee, 1992/3). However CIPFA estimates for 1993/4 indicate a total of £298m allocated to schools under the category 'special needs'. While £298m is a lot of money, it is in fact just 2.6 per cent of the total Aggregate Schools Budget (ASB) for England and Wales. Some of the 'social needs' allocation may be recorded under the 'other expenditure' category, a further 5.4 per cent of the ASB. However it is still less than the total allocated to 'premises-related' (e.g. schools with split sites). And this total is, of course, the sum differentially allocated to schools, not the total available to schools with high social needs. Of course there are some significant variations between LEAs. Some allocate more than 10 per cent of the total ASB on this basis, but others probably less than 1 per cent.

If we now turn to school-budget data based on section 42 returns, we find that overall there appears to be only a modest premium effect for schools in the 10 per cent most disadvantaged areas. Tables 2.4 and 2.5 show the data for all primary schools and all LEA-maintained comprehensive schools (see Appendix 1 for technical details). In each LEA type, primary schools in the most disadvantaged 10 per cent of areas receive on average somewhere between £50 and £100 per pupil more than the bulk of schools in the same LEA type. The differences between LEA types are more marked than between schools within the same LEA type.

The pattern for secondary schools is similar. Here the premium varies on average between £30 and £150 per pupil extra, being most marked between schools in the outer London boroughs. However some part of this could be the result of differences in expenditure at the LEA level. The number of shire-county urban secondary schools in the most highly-disadvantaged urban areas is probably too small to pick up the full impact of expenditure on disadvantage. At both primary and secondary level these figures require further analysis to unravel the LEA differences from any premium for disadvantage. However at this stage it is clear that any premiums for schools in disadvantaged areas are not very large.

Tables 2.5 and 2.6 demonstrate the ways higher per-pupil resources feed through into primary- and secondary-school pupil-teacher ratios (PTRs). Again, while the patterns are consistently in favour of the more disadvantaged areas, the differences are again quite small, more marked at primary than secondary level.

These are of course aggregate figures, and in both cases individual LEAs may have different patterns. Support for schools in disadvantaged areas may come in forms other than through the ASB allocations or in the shape of increased teacher numbers. However the scope for LEAs to provide such other forms of support are sharply reduced by LMS requirements.

Table 2.3. *Overall per-pupil expenditure (3 p.a.): all primary schools 1992/3 by disadvantage and LEA type: urban schools only*

LEA type	10% highest disadvantage	Middle 80%	Lowest 10%	All schools
Inner London	£1,828	£1,737	no cases	£1,809
	(525)	(142)		(667)
Outer London	£1,581	£1,522	£1,460	£1,531
	(281)	(770)	(105)	(1,156)
Metropolitan districts	£1,399	£1,336	£1,349	£1,350
	(631)	(2,511)	(601)	(3,743)
Shire counties	£1,415	£1,311	£1,264	£1,309
	(203)	(3,803)	(520)	(4,526)
All schools	£1,568	£1,353	£1,322	£1,387
	(1,640)	(7,226)	(1,226)	(10,092)

Table 2.4. *Overall per-pupil expenditure (£ p.a.): secondary schools 1992/3 by level of disadvantage and LEA type: urban maintained comprehensive schools only*

LEA type	10% highest disadvantage	Middle 80%	Lowest 10%	All schools
Inner London	£2,455	£2,384	no cases	£2,437
	(97)	(29)		(126)
Outer London	£2,277	£2,122	£2,082	£2,144
	(42)	(163)	(27)	(232)
Metropolitan districts	£2,069	£1,978	£1,939	£1,985
	(104)	(483)	(85)	(672)
Shire counties	£1,990	£1,958	£1,937	£1,956
	(23)	(894)	(104)	(1,021)
All schools	£2,237	£1,990	£1,956	£2,015
	(266)	(1,569)	(216)	(2,051)

There is however considerable difference between LEAs in both funding levels and average PTRs. This is partly a function of central-government allocations. The Education Committee of the House of Commons, purely for illustrative purposes, has demonstrated what would happen if the allocation criteria currently used in the national SSA and AEN allocations were carried down to the school level into per-pupil funding. Table 2.7 shows the result for an 11–15 year old.

As the Committee notes, a pupil who falls into the first three categories would bring in £4,479 to the school. If this became the basis of allocation the effects on school budgets would be dramatic. Schools serving disadvantaged populations would receive an enormous boost to their funding. The present disparities of funding between LEAs would be transferred to schools within the same LEAs, where these differed sharply in terms of social and educational disadvantage.

Nobody is seriously proposing so radical a change in funding allocation. However the two sets of figures for the present allocation, and a theoretical allocation based on the AEN criteria, raise in sharp form the question of how much additional funding support should be linked to disadvantage.

Table 2.5. *Overall PTRs: primary schools 1993: by level of disadvantage and area type: urban schools only*

LEA type	10% highest disadvantage	Middle 80%	Lowest 10%	All schools
Inner London	19.5	20.7	no cases	19.7
	(525)	(142)		(667)
Outer London	21.8	21.8	23.1	21.9
	(281)	(770)	(105)	(1,156)
Metropolitan districts	21.9	22.6	23.0	22.5
	(631)	(2,511)	(601)	(3,743)
Shire counties	20.7	23.0	24.1	23.0
	(203)	(3,803)	(520)	(4,526)
All schools	21.0	22.7	23.5	22.4
	(1,640)	(7,226)	(1,226)	(10,092)

Table 2.6. *Overall PTRs: secondary schools 1993: by level of disadvantage and area type: urban maintained comprehensive schools only*

LEA type	10% highest disadvantage	Middle 80%	Lowest 10%	All schools
Inner London	15.4	15.5	(no cases)	15.4
	(97)	(29)		(126)
Outer London	15.5	16.1	17.0	16.1
	(42)	(163)	(27)	(232)
Metropolitan districts	15.5	15.8	16.3	15.8
	(104)	(483)	(85)	(672)
Shire counties	15.7	16.1	16.5	16.1
	(23)	(894)	(104)	(1,021)
All schools	15.5	15.9	16.6	16.0
	(266)	(1,569)	(216)	(2,051)

Table 2.7. *Funding per pupil if SSA allocations to LEAs were devolved to schools*

Basic amount for pupil aged 11–15	£2,096 p.a.
Additional if from lone-parent family	£958
Additional if parent(s) on income support	£960
Additional if parent(s) from New Commonwealth	£465
Additional for each child receiving a free school meal	£50
Additional if school in sparsely populated area	(£43 average)
Additional if school in London/South East	(£109 average)

Educational Performance

While funding levels may vary by less than 10 per cent, performance levels are rather more varied. Table 8 shows the performance by pupils in secondary schools at GCSE level for 1992 and 1993, using the standard criteria of the proportion of the year group obtaining 5+ grades A–C, again with the same breakdown by urban disadvantage and LEA type.

Table 2.8. *Percentage of year group getting 5+GCSE A–C, 1992 and 1993, by level of disadvantage and type of area: all urban comprehensive secondary schools*

LEA type	10% highest disadvantage 1992	10% highest disadvantage 1993	Middle 80% 1992	Middle 80% 1993	Lowest 10% 1992	Lowest 10% 1993	No. of schools 1992/1993
Inner London	22.9	25.6	25.1	26.9	no cases	no cases	126/125
Outer London	22.7	24.3	33.7	35.6	50.9	52.2	232/230
Metropolitan districts	20.2	21.1	27.4	30.5	46.8	48.8	672/667
Shire counties	22.2	26.8	33.9	36.3	46.9	48.7	1,021/1,006
All schools	21.8	23.7	31.7	24.3	47.3	49.2	2,051
	(266)	(264)	(1,569)	(1,549)	(216)	(215)	2,028

It is important to underline that there is very considerable variation within each of these categories, but overall the difference in proportions gaining 5+ A–C between the highest and lowest disadvantaged areas is approximately twofold. The gap has closed marginally between 1992 and 1993, but we would need more years to be sure of any trends. Difference between the middle 80 per cent by type of area will, to an extent, reflect the different way that these are bunched within the middle band. Thus in inner London there are no areas that fall into the lowest 10 per cent band of disadvantage and the schools in the middle 80 per cent band are bunched towards the disadvantaged end.

A Brief Note on Inspection Evidence

The first year of secondary-school inspection (1993–4) is beginning to yield more information on secondary schools in disadvantaged areas. The advantage of a data-set of this type is that it includes large numbers of schools in different types of areas. Currently the system includes data on nearly 700 secondary schools, including data on the social setting of the school. When some of the inspection judgements are analysed against this criterion, it is clear that there are, *prima facie*, some very sharp differences of judgement on secondary schools at different points on the social spectrum, as the following figures demonstrate (Figures 2.3–2.7 below). There are considerable variations in the way these judgements are distributed according to the different items covered, suggesting that inspectors do indeed discriminate between different facets of a school's overall performance. However, this data requires further analysis to yield a clearer picture of the pattern of strengths and weaknesses and its relationship with other features of the schools.

What is presented here (with very strong health warnings about the need for further analysis) is simply the inspectors' overall ratings of performance at KS3 on five different features (Figures 2.3–2.7). These are split into judgements at the top end ('favourably judged') and judgements in the lower half ('unfavourably judged') in terms of the overall percentage of schools. These are broken down into five social categories, with social context 1–2 representing the most advantaged areas and social context 6–7 the most disadvantaged. The number of schools in each

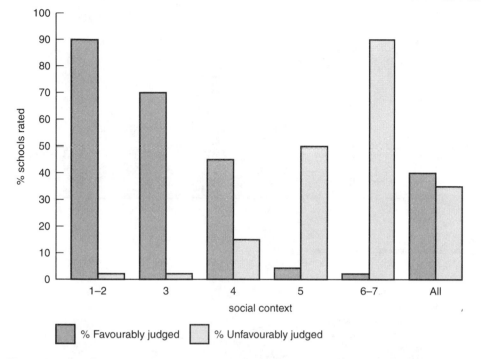

Figure 2.3. *Inspector rating of schools by social setting, standards of achievement in relation to national norms: KS3*

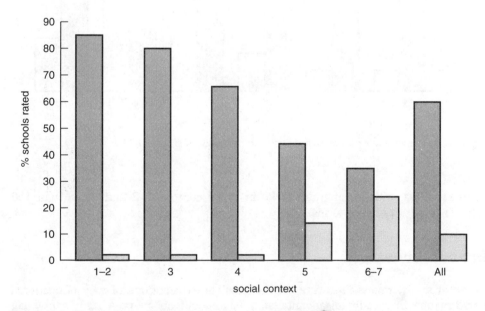

Figure 2.4. *Standards of achievement in relation to pupils' capabilities: KS3*

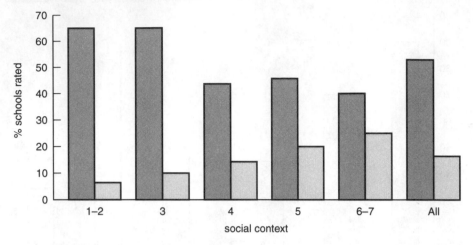

Figure 2.5. *Quality of learning resources: KS3*

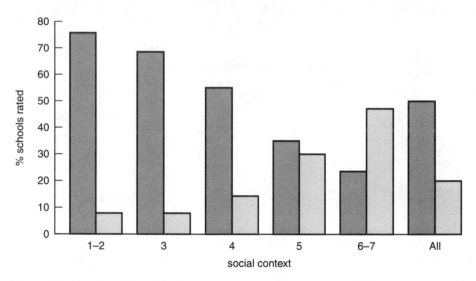

Figure 2.6. *Inspector rating of challenge pace and motivation in lessons: KS3*

context varies, with a minimum of 90 in social context 1–2 and more than 100 schools in all other categories.

Explanations

There is an enormous literature on the possible explanations of why educational performance in socially disadvantaged areas should on average significantly lag behind that of the nation as a whole and even more so that of advantaged areas. This is not only a British phenomenon it is found in most Western industrialized

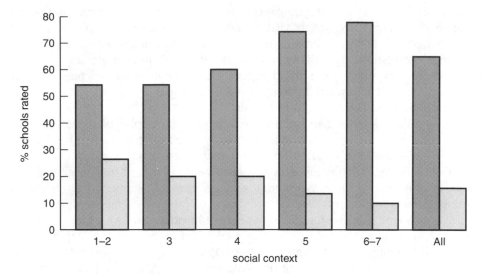

Figure 2.7. *Availability of accommodation: KS3*

countries in varying degrees, and in the United States is particularly marked. Nor is it a recent phenomenon, since it dates back almost to the point where formal assessment began.

At different times different factors have been held to be the main cause of this shortfall. For much of the post-war period the emphasis has been on social and educational and therefore potentially open to remediation factors. For a time it was broadly attributed to social conditions and the environment. In the 1960s and 1970s there was considerable emphasis on family conditions and family support as well as on child-rearing practices. Schools and education were also implicated. The Plowden Report in 1967 called for additional resources for educational priority areas (EPAs). A major issue in the United States at present is that of providing adequate funding for the most-disadvantaged areas to recruit better-qualified staff and meet essential repairs to buildings; there have been a growing number of successful legal challenges to American states on the basis of equity in funding. In this country the question of expectations, not just by schools and teachers, but by pupils and parents themselves are held to be important contributors to under-achievement, for example in many HMI publications and AAUE itself. Beyond school the opportunity structure of wider society is also held to be a factor: for example, the demoralizing effects of poor job opportunities and high youth unemployment on those approaching school-leaving age.

This is not the time and place to examine these different claims in any detail. It seems very unlikely that any one set of explanations could fully explain what is a complex series of events and processes. Thus school-based explanations are not in themselves sufficient, as average performance differences emerge almost as soon as assessment can be conducted and before school entry. One of the arguments for early intervention at preschool was to get in before any circle of failure had built up. But neither are conditions in the home and early socialization sufficient

41

explanation. There is a wide range of performance in most areas, and some evidence of a 'cumulative deficit' that on aggregate, children from disadvantaged circumstances fall further behind as they get older. Studies also demonstrate that children of equal measured ability tend to do less well on average later in their schooling, if they come from disadvantaged circumstances. They may not for example persist in education as long beyond the minimum leaving age as their more fortunate counterparts in other areas.

Longitudinal studies give some indication of the interplay of these different factors. Studies of the long-term impact of early-years programmes in the United States (e.g. Schweinhart *et al.*, 1993) show that there is no simple linear effect, but an initial boost to attainment at preschool was translated into greater confidence in the early school years and greater parental support for children's learning. Equally important was the avoidance of problems (for example, in the American system, grade retention or special education tracks) which held the child back. It was as much avoiding the 'snakes' as getting on the 'ladders' that determined the long-term outcomes, that is staying on at school and getting a job, rather than dropping out and being unemployed. It may simply be that the risk of meeting one or more such 'handicapping' factors throughout childhood (at home, at school or in the local environment) are statistically much higher in disadvantaged areas than in 'better-off' districts.

The current American jargon is to refer broadly to 'barriers to learning' that inhibit children's progress. These would include personal ill-health or accident, family breakdown or other problems, but also school-based factors. In sum these may constitute the basis of educational disadvantage, and over time have a cumulative effect, which produces the type of performance distribution seen in Figure 2.1 above.

This very simple sketch perhaps removes the need to identify a primary or critical reason for underachievement. It stresses the dynamic and continuing nature of the pressures and pitfalls that may hold up progress or perhaps even more important, divert family energy to meet other more immediate or pressing needs than long-term educational goals. It also suggests the possibility of improvement, though it also reminds us that successful education is a long-term activity. Short but temporary boosts to performance may be encouraging but they are not the solution.

IMPROVING URBAN EDUCATION: WHAT WORKS?

This section covers a limited number of developments that have been shown to 'work', in the sense that research has with some consistency found evidence of programme effectiveness. This section inevitably has to be selective: it is not an exhaustive list. Also the criteria of selection, as has often been pointed out, tend to favour the discrete and specific intervention that can be evaluated, rather than more 'organic' developmental activities which are intrinsically more difficult to assess. At this stage some of the sub-sections are more developed than others, but this should not be taken to imply differences in their importance. I have also drawn quite heavily on the work of Bob Slavin from the Johns Hopkins' Center for

Research on Effective Schooling and Disadvantaged Students at Baltimore, who has carried out a number of wide-ranging quantitative reviews of 'what works', particularly for young children.

Preschool

There is now little doubt that high-quality preschool programmes can have lasting impact on children's later development, in social and economic as well as educational terms, and may help reduce the gap between disadvantaged and advantaged pupils. One of the most fully-evaluated programmes established in the 1960s – the Perry Preschool Project (now known as High/Scope) has now followed its 'graduates' up to age 27.

Studies in the 1960s in the United States of early-learning programmes established in the heady days of the War on Poverty suggested that although there might be startling improvements by school entry these 'washed out' after a few years in school. Thus early optimism, in both the States and Britain, that it would be possible to break the 'cycle of poverty' and prevent school failure through intervention at the preschool stage gave way to a more pessimistic view. Both positions have now in turn been replaced by a more realistic assessment of the outcomes from 'high quality' preschool provision.

Early studies, for example of Head Start, typically compared children's scores on IQ or attainment tests (Zigler and Valentine, 1979). These evaluations seriously underestimated the value of programmes by concentrating solely on measures of 'intelligence'. Later studies – for example, Lazar and Darlington's analysis (1982) of eleven high-quality programmes – looked at measures of school competence (need for remedial work or 'special education'), children's attitudes and self-esteem, and the impact on the family, as well as achievement and intelligence. This study suggested that high-quality early intervention could establish a 'positive cycle' of 'mutual reinforcement' between child and parents, and change children from 'passive to active learners who begin to take the initiative in seeking information, help and interaction with others' (Lazar and Darlington, 1982, p. 63). Young people who had participated in preschool programmes were more likely to succeed in school, showed better self-esteem, were prouder of their achievements, and more realistic about their expectations.

In the follow-up study of the American High/Scope programme (Schweinhart et al., 1993), at age 27 the preschool 'graduates' were more likely than the 'home' control group to have stayed on at school (71 per cent as against 54 per cent completing 12th grade or higher), to be home owners and high earners, and to have less need of social-services support (59 per cent as against 80 per cent in the last ten years) and less contact with crime (7 per cent as against 35 per cent with five or more arrests, and 7 per cent as against 25 per cent with drug offences). These findings of social and economic competence add to those at age 19, when 16 per cent of the programme 'graduates' had needed special-education support (as against 28 per cent of the control group), 59 per cent were employed (versus 32 per cent), and 38 per cent had college or vocational training (versus 21 per cent), though it should be underlined that the group still remained quite socially disadvantaged.

Longitudinal work on this scale and detail has not been conducted in Britain. Here the principal longitudinal study with such data is the Child Health and Education Study (CHES), which followed a cohort of children born in 1970 and assessed their behavioural problems and school performance on reading and mathematics at age ten (Osborn and Milbank, 1987). This study showed that children who had attended small, home-based playgroups in their preschool years did best at primary school. But its findings have been challenged on the grounds that cohort studies of this type are 'weaker' than experimental programmes such as High/Scope, and that social-class differences are more difficult to control for: children attending playgroups tended to come from higher-status and better-educated backgrounds so would be expected to do well. Other studies comparing children in reception class with nursery-class or playgroup experience suggest that the former are more likely to be 'learning-oriented' in their activities and contacts with the teacher, to play in a purposeful and creative way, to engage in connected conversation, to show greater motivation for school, and to persevere when they encounter difficulties in their school work (Jowett and Sylva, 1986).

Studies of day care also show that high-quality day care can have positive outcomes for children in terms of secure attachments, social competence, social-emotional development, autonomy and exploration of their environment, as well as school performance (Sylva, 1994; Andersson, 1992; Howes, 1991). Key features include favourable adult-child ratios, small group size, developmentally appropriate activities, training of the caregiver, and adult-child interactions that are 'sensitive, responsive and contingent' (Howes, p. 187)

Children using day care in Britain tend to show poorer results, however, in terms of both behaviour and educational performance, than those shown by children in nursery education (see, for example, Osborn and Milbank, 1982). The explanation may be that day-nursery places in Britain tend to be highly selective, restricted to children with health or behavioural problems or from families under stress (McGuire and Richman, 1986). Staff in social-services-run day nurseries tend to be less familiar with an educational curriculum to meet the demands of the National Curriculum than their teacher colleagues in nursery classes or schools (Sylva, 1992).

Provision of preschool places shows very wide variation between regions and local authorities, and by type of neighbourhood, ethnic and social group. For example, in January 1993, 'under-fives' in one shire county had no opportunity to attend nursery schools or classes although 32 per cent of the age group entered school before the statutory age, while in another, 57 per cent of the age group was in nursery schools or classes in primary schools, with an additional 35 per cent already in school. In metropolitan districts, 60 per cent of under-fives in one authority were in nursery schools or classes, and a further 34 per cent in school; while in another only 2 per cent had the chance of a nursery school or class and only 18 per cent got into school early (DFE, 1994). Recent expansion over the last decade has been primarily by four-year-old entry and 'rising fives' in reception classes (DFE, 1994). There is clear evidence that more disadvantaged areas tend to have better levels of nursery provision, in part through the impact of the Urban Programme. However it is still important to ask which groups have gained access to this provision.

Parental Involvement

Almost everybody favours more 'parental involvement' in schooling, but the meaning given to this term has gradually shifted. At the time of the Plowden Report, the emphasis was on the importance of 'good practice' in home–school links as a two-way communication and information between parents and teachers (Young and McGeeney, 1968).

But by the 1980s attention had shifted to 'parents as educators' and children as 'active learners' (Bruner, 1980). A more careful definition of 'involvement' ranged from parents simply 'being there' at one end of the continuum, to a home–school 'partnership' based on notions of 'reciprocity' at the other (Pugh and De'Ath, 1987; Pugh et al., 1987; Wolfendale, 1983).

In the 1990s interest is focused much more sharply than before on programmes where parental 'involvement' is a crucial element in a specific piece of children's learning for example, children's literacy. Hannon (1994) argues that the concept of family literacy has been helpful in understanding how children develop literacy at home, and how literacy patterns of the whole family affect, and are affected by, individual children's levels of development.

Parental involvement has also been seen as a key element in ensuring the long-term impact of educational programmes. This is probably a combination of the child practising a skill, and positive reinforcement on the part of the parents. Hewison (1985) writes of a form of skill-acquisition plus motivation, where the key is 'extra practice in a motivating context' provided by the parents: 'when parents hear their children read, they are providing them with a very special and potent combination of benefits'. As Lazar and Darlington described their findings (p. 63–4),

> . . . it seems possible that mutual reinforcement processes occurred between the early education participants and their parents. Perhaps the children's participation in a program raised the mothers' hopes and expectations for their children . . . Perhaps children interpreted these parental attitudes as a belief in and support of their efforts, and it served to spur them on . . .

Special Programmes

It has been clear for some years that it is possible to raise pupil achievement by the introduction of special programmes. The key requirements include well-designed and targeted programmes that concentrate on particular skills, often using intensive methods to achieve progress. The problem in the past has been, as with preschooling, that gains made have not always lasted. Also there has been a problem of where to concentrate effort.

The increasing use of standardized measures of effectiveness, such as the so-called 'effect size' (technically the difference in gain scores between the groups being compared, divided by the standard deviation of the control group), allows some broad benchmark comparisons between otherwise very different programmes, using different measures. Thus Wasik and Slavin (1994) used this method to review the results from five different early-reading programmes that used one-to-one tutoring to prevent reading failure. These included Reading Recovery. These programmes all showed significant impact at first grade. Reading Recovery programmes continued to show lasting but reduced effects up to two years later. Research in this country has shown a similar advantage to pupils following Reading Recovery programmes, with some evidence that gains may continue once the programme is complete.

Slavin and Madden (1989) use the same techniques to review a wide range of other developments that have had a measured impact on children's progress in the early years. See also Slavin *et al.* (1992) for an overview of these developments. They conclude that a combination of these different programmes could be sufficient to 'prevent school failure for nearly all students' at this level. They argue the importance of successful beginning reading as a key to later development. They also underline the value of brief structured one-to-one tutoring using qualified teachers for 'at risk' pupils.

Class Size

Reducing school-class size is frequently presented as one of the most effective ways — and certainly one of the most popular among parents and teachers — of raising achievement in schools. It seems self-evident that increasing the amount of contact between pupil and teacher *must* result in improvement. Unfortunately the research on the impact of class size is far from giving a clear-cut answer, though recent experiments in the United States such as the STAR project in Tennessee have produced some more encouraging results.

The first point to establish is the type of improvement that changes in class size might be likely to affect. Researchers have generally focused on changes in *pupil performance*, but there are also objectives such as pupil behaviour and attitudes, teacher attitudes and morale as well as teacher work-load that might all be affected by changes in classroom numbers.

Unfortunately results from large-scale surveys that have included information on class size and pupil performance have tended to show that even where other factors are taken into account there is a *positive* relationship between class size and pupil performance, that is larger classes are associated with better results. However this counter-intuitive finding has been challenged on a number of grounds, particularly that the analysis might not have taken into account all the reasons for smaller classes (for example, small remedial classes or economically growing areas with expanding populations and large classes, and the reverse in declining areas). Crucially, such studies typically lacked any information about performance at entry to school and therefore had no information about the educational progress children made under different class sizes. Where research studies have been able to include prior attainment, there is some evidence for better rates of progress, but it is not very marked. Thus Mortimore *et al.* (1988) found greater progress in maths at age eight and some other positive results for pupils in smaller classes in their study of London junior schools, but this did not extend to other subjects or age groups. One conclusion from this type of research was that *naturally-occurring* variations in class size might not result in any great impact, since these might not be very large and would often take some time to develop, as pupil numbers rose or fell over time. There was also some suggestion from school-based studies that *larger* classes might be associated with *more effective* teaching methods (Galton and Simon, 1980; Mortimore *et al.*, 1988).

Reviews of research studies into the effects of substantially altering class size experimentally, for example that by Gene Glass and colleagues (Glass *et al.*, 1982), suggested that lowering class size dramatically, for example *below* 20 or 15 pupils, could make a significant impact on pupil achievement. Changes, however, at the upper range, say from 30 to 25 pupils, made very little difference. However, pupil and teacher attitudes and instructional processes seemed to respond to class-size changes quite evenly across the size ranges. Critics of the Glass review, such as Slavin (1984, 1986) cast some doubt on the studies that Glass used in his data. Some, it seemed, were about introducing individual tutorial teaching in place of classes or seminars, and others were concerned with non-cognitive skills such as tennis coaching, not normally – Slavin pointed out – what one would have in mind when thinking about school class size. These criticisms threw some doubt on the effects of class-size change on pupil achievement but rather less on the effects on pupil and teacher attitudes.

There have been a limited number of large-scale experiments in the United States. Here class size has been radically altered and the results assessed. One of the earliest of these studies, the More Effective Schools project in New York City, where class size was effectively halved, proved not to be very effective, despite strong support from teachers, parents and administrators. It was concluded that teaching methods and styles had not altered and thus the impact on pupils was limited (Fox, 1967).

The most recent studies include the STAR (Student Teacher Achievement Ratio) experiment in Tennessee and PRIME TIME in Indiana. The STAR project is probably the largest experiment ever conducted on this topic. Some 6,000 pupils in 75 elementary schools were randomly allocated to three class sizes at grades K-3 (Small, 13 to 17; Regular, 22 to 26; and Regular with full-time teacher aide), and their progress studied over three to four years. Using reading achievement as the criterion of success, children in the small classes did better than the other two groups. 'Effect sizes', a standardized way of comparing gains from different programmes, were larger for younger children and for the more disadvantaged. Follow-up to the end of fourth grade when children had been in smaller classes for grades K-3 showed continuing but much-reduced 'effect sizes'.

In a review of eleven recent studies of reducing class size Slavin (1994) concludes that it does have a positive effect at first grade, but this can be 'small and short-lived'. Only the STAR project had evidence of continuing effects, though even this was not large. He underlines the very significant reductions in class size in this study, down to 15 pupils. It was also a 'one-off' experiment, which would be difficult to replicate under normal conditions. However these studies would appear to have demonstrated that very substantial class reductions can benefit younger age-groups particularly. They require a correspondingly large increase in funding, and raise the question whether similar improvements in performance could be achieved by other less costly approaches. Many conclude that there are more cost-effective ways of raising performance. Certainly there are many programmes with larger 'effect-sizes' on the reading criterion, sustained over the same length of time, for example Reading Recovery.

The STAR project made no other changes to the classes. Some years ago Rutter concluded that it was not sensible to focus simply on the effects of class size irrespective of other features in the classroom, such as teaching methods or classroom organization. Despite the STAR results, this would still seem to be very wise advice.

School Effectiveness and School Improvement

Since the pioneering work of Rutter and colleagues (Rutter et al., 1979) a series of studies in this country have demonstrated that there are measurable differences in effectiveness between schools, and that it is possible to identify some of the characteristics associated with more effective schools. This development occurred when researchers began to measure 'progress' made by pupils over time, rather than simply study performance at a single time-point. Initially there was a tendency to see school effectiveness in global terms as truly a 'school' effect and search for a general factor such as 'school ethos' as the cause. However more recent work has tended to break down this overall view. Work on progress up to A-level suggests that it makes more sense to think in terms of departments within schools. Similar results may emerge at earlier stages as overall performance measures are broken down, for example, by subject. Peter Mortimore's work (Mortimore et al., 1988) on junior schools contained both cognitive measures. This study indicated that while many schools were effective in both areas and a few ineffective in both, there was also a scatter of schools with a more mixed pattern of results.

Many school-effectiveness studies have found fairly uniform effects for different groups of pupils within the school: that is, these schools are equally effective or ineffective with all groups. However there is some evidence from London secondary-school data that there may be differential effects for different groups. As a handle on the importance of the school effect, the junior-school study (Mortimore et al., 1988) showed that in both reading and maths pupils from manual backgrounds in the most effective junior schools scored better on average than pupils from non-manual backgrounds in the least effective schools.

The next stage of such research is to use the findings on the characteristics of effective schools to focus school-improvement work. But school-improvement research has come from a very different starting point, rooted strongly in the culture of the school and in 'action-research'-style development work. Programmes now under way in this country and in Scotland will throw light on how far it is possible to draw on the school-effectiveness findings to spread more effective practice.

Comprehensive Programmes and 'Systemic' Change

There are several developments in the United States which have set out to create 'comprehensive' programmes, based on the various separate components that have been shown to work on their own. The argument is that single developments at one time-point are unlikely to be successful on their own. This was very much the strategy behind the so-called American 'Follow-Through' programme in the 1970s that was intended to carry forward the gains made at preschool level by the national Headstart programme into the elementary school. The evidence from studies of the long-term impact of preschool shows that it may have lasting effects, but these on their own will not transform the prospects for students from disadvantaged backgrounds.

As an example of such programmes. 'Success for All' (SFA) has been operating in some Baltimore elementary schools since 1986 and has since then spread to a number of schools in other states. Rather than a narrow-based programme, the aim is to make use of a wide range of interventions to prevent school failure in the first three grades, before a cycle of failure has built up. It thus includes preschool and kindergarten programmes, teachers working as reading tutors on a one-to-one basis with weaker students, reading programmes, flexible classroom organization, family support teams to promote parental involvement, etc. Within each of these programme areas there is a wide range of initiatives that can be deployed, many of which would be familiar to practitioners in this country, rather than a single fixed model. Inevitably there is an outside 'facilitator' to orchestrate these developments within schools.

The SFA programme has been evaluated by comparing the progress of pupils in similarly placed schools in the same area, and pooling the results from different sites and year-groups using the effect-size technique. The results at third grade (Figure 2.8 below) show the distribution of SFA and control-group scores in a way that echoes Figure 2.1 at the beginning of this paper. Here the SFA students are doing distinctly better than the control group and appear to be skewed slightly above grade level on this reading test.

The SFA and similar developments are still aimed predominantly at school level. One strong current strand in educational debate in the United States is 'systemic reform'. While there is much rhetoric associated with this term, the intent is to extend some of the successful reforms at individual-school level to the system at large. This particularly applies to education for disadvantaged areas and students. A central issue in the United States is the very low levels of funding for schools in disadvantaged areas.

In their most developed form such systemic reforms have some similarity with the 'comprehensive' school-based programmes such as SFA. Thus in Kentucky, where the whole state-school system was declared unconstitutional in 1989, a comprehensive reform programme was instituted covering all aspects of schooling, from its financing through to pupil assessment, including a range of measures aimed at disadvantaged students. A strong theme in Kentucky has been the impact of such reform in disadvantaged areas. Its central tenet is that 'every child can learn – most to high levels' – important in a state with historically low levels of education and low expectations (Steffy, 1993).

49

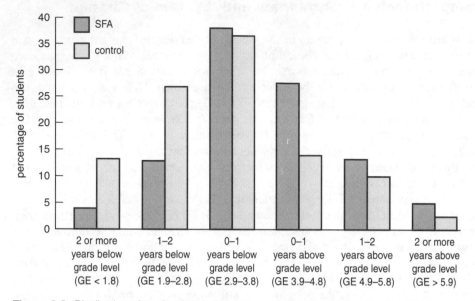

Figure 2.8. *Distribution of grade-equivalent scores on the Durrell Oral Reading Test, third grades in Baltimore 'Success for All' schools (1991)*

Resourcing

Some of the initiatives described in the previous sections do not require additional resources, but rather the redeployment of existing resources, changes of direction or increases in motivation. These might include some aspects of the school-effectiveness and school-improvement initiatives. But many require significant additional resources and some, such as substantial reductions in class size or increased provision of high-quality preschooling, would be very costly developments.

It has sometimes been claimed that there are no clear links between educational expenditure and results or outcomes: for example schools with higher levels of expenditure are not necessarily associated with better results. Clearly there is real problems of comparing 'like with like'. As we saw in Tables 2.3 and 2.4 above, schools in the most disadvantaged areas have slightly higher pre-pupil costs than other schools, but this is additional funding in recognition of the problems they face. Teasing out the effects of such overall differences in funding on school performance is likely to be exceedingly difficult.

However the position is much more simple when it comes to additional programmes with clear additional costs. Their effects can be directly related to the extra resources. When we look at resources in this way there is little doubt that additional resources can be shown to have an impact. And, increasingly, by making use of standardized measures of effectiveness such as 'effect size', it would be possible, in principle, to compare both the effectiveness of these programmes in educational terms and their additional costs. There is thus in principle the

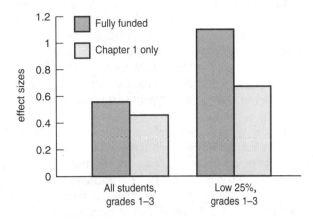

Figure 2.9. *Differences in reading effects between fully-funded and Chapter 1-only schools, Baltimore City*

Note: Includes all students who were in Success for All or control schools since first grade.

Source: Adapted from S. Slavia *et al.* (1992) *Success for All: A Relentless Approach to Prevention and Early Intervention in Elementary Schools.* Arlington, VA: Educational Research Services.

emerging basis for a 'costs and benefits' analysis. We are still some way off this possibility in this country, but it is likely to be a growth area as evidence builds up.

However such analysis is developing in the United States. We have referred to the comparative results from very different initiatives such as class-size reduction and reading tuition. Figure 2.9 taken from Slavin *et al.* (1994), shows the way that costs and benefits can be compared within the same programme. This chart compares the results for two sets of elementary schools, one of which received the standard federal Chapter 1 additional funding for disadvantaged students, the other further resources in addition (= fully funded). The point to note is that while the 'effect sizes' for all students show little difference between the two sets of schools, the differences for the lowest-scoring 25 per cent of students is much more marked, suggesting that increased funding appears to make more of an impact for 'high-risk' students.

Conclusions

This paper began by looking at data on all primary and comprehensive secondary schools in urban disadvantaged areas. In terms of overall funding such schools receive some enhanced funding under LMS allocations, but overall this was modest. They also had slightly better pupil–teacher ratios than other schools. However in both cases there tended to be larger differences between different types of LEA than between schools in disadvantaged and advantaged areas within the same LEA type.

In terms of performance at secondary level, while there may have been some closure of the gap between examination results between schools in the most disadvantaged and most advantaged areas, it was still approximately a twofold difference in terms of the age group getting 5+ GCSE A–C. Preliminary results from the first year of secondary inspections confirm the overall picture presented in the original 'Access and Achievement in Urban Education' survey. Inspectors give a significantly lower rating to achievement in secondary schools in the most disadvantaged areas, even when pupils' capabilities are taken into account. They also give a lower rating to the quality of learning resources and the challenge, pace and motivation of lessons.

Overall the pressures on schools in disadvantaged areas are likely to have increased as a result of recent social and economic changes. Key changes here are the increasing proportions of children without adult earners in the household, and the increasing spatial concentration of low-income families.

The second main part of the paper reviews a wide number of different programmes that have been shown to be effective in raising educational performance by disadvantaged pupils, and in some cases their continuing effects over many years. In particular it underlies the long-term effects from high-quality preschool provision and the contribution that parental involvement can make to reinforcing educational progress.

A large number of special programmes have been shown to have a substantial and sometimes lasting impact, for example Reading Recovery. The use of 'effect size' measurement potentially allows comparison between very different types of programme. The STAR programme to test the effects of class-size reduction has shown that very substantial reductions in class size (down to 15 pupils) can have significant impact on the reading progress of young children particularly, though the effects tended to fade out at higher grades. However there may be several more cost-effective ways of achieving similar results, for example using Reading Recovery.

In this country school-effectiveness research has consistently shown differential effectiveness between schools, and identified some of the factors associated with more effective schools. The focus now is to convert this knowledge into school-improvement programmes.

In the United States the evidence that specific developments can make an impact, but tend to fade out once they have finished, has led to programmes that set up a comprehensive package of initiatives within schools to prevent school failure. These operate across the board in a 'belt and braces' manner rather than in a tightly prescribed programme. Some of these projects have shown impressive results. In the United States there are also moves to introduce systemic reforms across the board, particularly in states where the education system is under legal challenge. As yet there is no hard evidence on the effectiveness of these across-the-board reforms.

Again from the United States there is a growing body of research that has examined the linkage between additional programme costs and their effects. Perhaps for the first time these developments are making it possible in the case of these additional programmes to show the educational impact of additional resources.

While the gap between the most-advantaged and least-advantaged schools and areas remains wide, and there are pressures that might widen it further, evidence presented in this paper on 'what works' suggests there are a very large number of initiatives within schools or outside that could help to close this gap. And there are many more that there has not been space to cover. This optimistic message should not be taken to mean that anything will work. Some developments will be far more effective than others. What is also important, therefore, is the careful evaluation of impact so that the more effective programmes and strategies can be identified and developed. In the long term it may well be by linking together a number of different initiatives that the gap in performance will be significantly closed.

NOTE

1 This chapter was first given as a paper to the OFSTED Conference, 'Access and Achievement in Urban Education', 2–3 November 1994.

REFERENCES

Andersson, B.E. (1992) 'Effects of daycare on cognitive and socio-emotional competence of thirteen-year-old Swedish schoolchildren', *Child Development*, 63, 20–36.

Bruner, J. (1980) *Under Five in Britain*. London: Grant McIntyre.

Department for Education (DFE) (1994) *Statistical Bulletin 6/94*. London: DFE.

Department of Education and Science (DES) (1972) *Education: a Framework for Expansion*. London: HMSO.

Department of Education and Science (DES) (1973) *Nursery Education*. Circular 2/73. London: DES.

Department of the Environment (DoE) (1994) *Index of Local Conditions*. London: DoE.

Department of Social Security (DSS) (1994a) *Households Below Average Income, 1979–1992*. London: HMSO.

Department of Social Security (DSS) (1994b) *Annual Statistical Enquiry, 1993*.

Fox, D.J. (1967) *Expansion of the More Effective Schools Program*. New York: Center for Urban Education.

Galton, M. and Simon, B. (1980) *Progress and Performance in the Primary Classroom*. London: RKP.

Glass, G. and Cahn, L. *et al.* (1982) *School Class Size*. New York: Sage.

Goodman, A. and Webb, S. (1994) *For Richer: For Poorer: The Changing Distribution of Income in the United Kingdom, 1961–1991*. London: Institute for Fiscal Studies.

Green, A. (1994) *The Geography of Poverty and Wealth*. Warwick: Institute of Employment Research.

Hannon, P. (in press) Paper presented at the British Educational Research Association Conference, September, 1994. *Literacy, Home and School: Research and Practice in teaching Literacy with Parents*. London: Falmer Press (in press).

Heath, A. (1992) 'The attitudes of the underclass', in D. Smith, *Understanding the Underclass*. London: Policy Studies Institute.

Hewison, J. (1985) 'Parental involvement and reading attainment: implications of research in Dagenham and Haringey', in K. Topping and S. Wolfendale (eds) *Parental Involvement in Children's Reading*. London: Croom Helm.

Holtermann, S. (1992) *Investing in Young Children: Costing an Education and Day Care Service*. London: National Children's Bureau.

House of Commons Education, Science and Arts Committee (1989) *Educational Provision for the Under Fives*. London: HMSO.

Howes, C. (1991) 'Caregiving environments and their consequences for children: the experience in the United States', in E. Melhuish and P. Moss (eds) *Day Care for Young Children: International Perspectives*. London: Routledge.

Jowett, S. and Sylva, K. (1986) 'Does kind of preschool matter?' *Educational Research*, 28(1), 21–31.

Kozol, J. (1991) *Savage Inequalities: Children in America's Schools*. New York: Harper.

Lazar, I. and Darlington, R. (1982) *The Lasting Effects of Early Education: a Report from the Consortium for Longitudinal Studies*. Monographs of the Society for Research in Child Development, 47(2–3), serial no. 195. Chicago: University of Chicago Press.

Lee, T. (1992) Final Report of research project on LMS, Bath University.

McGuire, J. and Richman, N. (1986) 'The prevalence of behaviour problems in three types of preschool group', *Journal of Child Psychology and Psychiatry*, 27, 455–472.

Mortimore, P., Sammons, P., Stoll, L. *et al.* (1988) *School Matters: The Junior Years*. Wells: Open Books.

Noble, M., Smith, G. *et al.* (1994) *Changing Patterns of Income and Wealth in Two Contrasting Areas*. Oxford: Department of Applied Social Studies.

OFSTED (1993) *Access and Achievement in Urban Education*. London. HMSO.

Osborn, A.F. and Milbank, J.E. (1987) *The Effects of Early Education*. Oxford: Clarendon Press.

Pugh, G. and De'Ath, E. (1987) *Parents and Professionals as Partners: Rhetoric or Reality?* London: National Children's Bureau.

Pugh, G. *et al.* (1987) *Partnership in Action: Working with Parents in Preschool Centres*. London: National Children's Bureau.

Rumbold Committee (1990) *Starting with Quality. Committee of Inquiry into the Quality of the Educational Experience offered to Three and Four Year Olds*. London: HMSO.

Rutter, M. *et al.* (1979) *Fifteen Thousand Hours*. Wells: Open Books.

Sammons, P., Thomas, S., Mortimore, P. *et al.* (1994) *Assessing School Effectiveness: Developing Measures to Put School Performance in Context* (OFSTED Research Report). London.

Schweinart, L.J., Barnes, H.V. and Weikart, D.P. (1993) *Significant Benefits: the High/Scope Perry Preschool Study through Age 27*. Monographs of the High/Scope Educational Foundation No. 10. Ypsilanti, Michigan: High/Scope Press.

Slavin, R.E. (1984) 'Meta-analysis in education: how has it been used?', *Educational Researcher* 13(8).

Slavin, R.E. (1986) 'Best evidence synthesis: an alternative to metanalytic and traditional reviews', *Educational Researcher* 15(9).

Slavin, R.E. (1994) 'School and classroom organisation in beginning reading: class size, aides and instructional grouping,' in R.E. Slavin, N. Karweit and B. Wasik (1994).

Slavin, R.E. and Madden, N. (1989) 'What works for students at risk: a research synthesis', *Educational Leadership*, Feb. 1989.

Slavin, R.E., Karweit, N. and Wasik, B. (1992) 'Preventing early school failure: what works?' *Educational Leadership*, Dec. 1992.

Slavin, R.E., Karweit, N. and Wasik, B. (1994) *Preventing Early School Failure: Research, Policy and Practice*. New York: Allyn and Bacon.

Steffy, B. (1993): *The Kentucky Education Reform Act*. Technomic.

Sylva, K. (1994) 'The importance of early learning on children's later development', in

C. Ball, *Start Right: the Importance of Early Learning*. London: Royal Society for the Encouragement of Arts, Manufacture and Commerce.

Sylva, K., Siraj-Blatchford, I. and Johnson, S. (1992) 'The impact of the UK National Curriculum on preschool practice: some 'top-down' processes at work', *International Journal of Early Education*, 24, 40–53.

Wasik, B. and Slavin, R.E. (1994) 'Preventing Early Reading Failure with One to One Tutoring: a Review of Five Programs', in Slavin, Karweit and Wasik (1994).

Webber, R. (1975) *Liverpool Social Area Study, 1971 Data*. PRAG Technical Paper TP14.

Wolfendale, S. (1983) *Parental Participation in Children's Development and Education*. London: Gordon and Breach.

Young, M. and McGeeney, P. (1968) *Learning Begins at Home: a Study of a Junior School and its Parents*. London: Routledge and Kegan Paul.

Zigler, E. and Valentine, J. (eds) (1979) *Project Head Start: a Legacy of the War on Poverty*. New York: Free Press.

Chapter 3

Urban Education Initiatives: The National Pattern[1]

Michael Barber, Tim Denning, Gerry Gough and Michael Johnson

INTRODUCTION

In late 1993 the Office for Standards in Education (OFSTED) published 'Access and Achievement in Urban Education', a report which had a major impact in both publicity and policy terms. Though it generated a degree of controversy, there was widespread recognition that its analysis provided crucial insights into the problems of urban schools in England and that its conclusions required active urgent consideration.

The Report has been followed up with a coherent set of initiatives in OFSTED and the Department of Education (DFE). Among them has been the commissioning of a report, carried out by the Centre for Successful Schools at Keele University, which forms the basis of this chapter and Chapter 4.

While the general case put in 'Access and Achievement in Urban Education' provides the backdrop for the work presented here, two of its conclusions provide a particular impetus for it. In the concluding paragraph OFSTED argued that:

> The responsibility for addressing some of the issues identified can be taken on by the schools themselves. Schools, and other educational institutions can do more to improve their own effectiveness, to plan to ensure that pupils have the curriculum to which they are entitled and can build on the learning they have gained. But most schools in disadvantaged areas do not have within them the capacity for sustainable renewal. The rising tide of national educational change is not lifting these boats. (our emphasis)

Drawing on this view, the report in its main findings reached a second relevant conclusion.

> The quality and standards of much of the work revealed by this survey are inadequate and disturbing. However, there is enough work of a good quality in each sector to mean that the situation is not

irredeemable. Long-term planning, improved dissemination of effective practice, carefully focussed interventions and concerted efforts between services are required to bring about improvement.

This chapter, drawing on the OFSTED report (1994), focuses on urban education across England. The word 'urban' is defined broadly. In general discussion the words 'urban' and 'inner-city' are often treated as if they were synonymous. In fact of course, many of the areas with the problems of urban education are peripheral estates. There are also pockets of urban disadvantage in relatively small prosperous towns or cities, such as Guildford. The assumption is, however, that all areas covered by the study will have average levels of deprivation.

The word 'initiative' is also defined broadly for the purpose of this study. It is taken to mean any concerted effort by an organization external to the school (such as a local education authority or training and enterprise council) aimed at assisting the school to improve its performance. It is therefore assumed that an urban education initiative involves an organization external to the school. Of course it is recognized that some individual schools in urban areas are successfully raising standards as a result of their own efforts, but these are not the focus of this study. However, a separate report from OFSTED itself has examined this aspect of urban education (*Improving Schools*, HMSO, 1994).

The purpose of the report was to identify the scope and extent of urban-education initiatives in England. In order to try to identify as many as possible a questionnaire was sent to every local education authority (LEA), Training and Enterprise Council (TEC) and higher education institution (HEI) involved in teacher education (see Appendix 8). A follow-up letter, reminding each of them of the importance of responding, was also sent. In some cases submissions received long after the closing date were included in order to ensure coverage was as comprehensive as possible given the tight time-scale. Since this area of policy has not previously been researched, it was decided that the questionnaire should be as inclusive as possible. The aim was to use this limited study to provide an initial sketch upon which further studies could be based. The study also provides a background for the continuing stream of studies looking at particular urban-education initiatives.

This chapter highlights the nature of the various initiatives which are in place, describing their main characteristics. The success criteria on which the various initiatives are focused are examined, and evidence to show how progress is being made towards these criteria is explored. Chapter 4 draws some conclusions about urban education initiatives and suggests, in particular, possible ingredients for success.

It should be said at the outset that this study is a limited one in that evidence and insights are gained from documented information and questionnaire data. There have not been visits made by the Keele team to any of the initiatives and thus the conclusions must remain tentative. More specific examples of the process and progress of urban-education initiatives can be seen in following chapters, particularly Chapter 5, which follows on from the research presented here.

GEOGRAPHICAL DISTRIBUTION OF INITIATIVES

Details of 60 initiatives received in response to the questionnaires sent out to every local education authority, training and enterprise council and higher education institution involved in teacher education provide the data for this study. Returns were received from a wide range of different geographical locations in England, from the North-East to the South-West. All of them are listed in Table 3.1. There are, however, one or two major conurbations (where we know there are initiatives) not included, since questionnaires were not returned. We cautiously suggest that although some institutions may not have responded to the questionnaire, the survey covers the overwhelming majority of current initiatives to raise standards in urban areas. The geographical distribution of the initiatives is shown in Figure 3.1.

In some cases there were several submissions from one source as, for example, from the Teesside Training and Enterprise Council which submitted seven initiatives and Kent LEA which submitted three. In other instances there were submissions from agencies where details of individual projects could not be given because of the scale of the operation and the numerous institutions involved. Such initiatives would include the International School Effectiveness and Improvement Centre and the School Improvement Network of the London Institute of Education and the Cambridge University 'Improving the Quality of Education for All' initiative. In some cases, such as the Sheffield 'RAPP Project' and the Staffordshire 'Two Towns Project', submissions were received separately from LEA and TEC for the same project.

The analysis presented here refers only to the 60 initiatives which are listed in Table 3.1. In Appendix 6, we list the projects funded under the Grants for Education Support and Training heading 19/31 [Raising Standards in Inner Cities]. It will be seen from comparisons with Appendix 2 that there is a significant but by no means complete overlap between the GEST-funded schemes and those dealt with by LEAs in response to our questionnaire.

SCHOOLS' PARTICIPATION

In a number of the initiatives included in the study, schools are not specifically mentioned, and the target for improvement is outside the school. Most of the schemes submitted, however, have schools at the heart of the initiative to raise educational standards.

The number of schools participating in individual projects varies considerably. Schools may be selected by LEAs, the TECs or HEIs for inclusion in the initiative. Alternatively, the schools may have volunteered or may themselves have been instrumental in a project's development. Each individual scheme may include selected and/or self-selected schools (see Appendix 4). Fifty-two per cent of participating schools were self-selected, 48 per cent were selected by other agencies. In some cases a project is centred in a single school, in others there are hundreds of schools involved and in one case (ALIS at Newcastle University) there are more than a thousand participating schools to date, though by no means all of

Table 3.1. *School-improvement initiatives included in this survey*

A Level and GCSE Improvement Project (Barking and Dagenham)	High Scope UK 'Young children First', (Liverpool LEA)
Action Research: Critical Success Factors (North Bucks TEC)	Home Instruction for Pre-school Youngsters (Teesside TEC)
African-Caribbean Project (Hammersmith and Fulham)	Impact Mathematics (Haringey)
	Improving Results at KS4 (Kent LEA)
Black Teachers Mentoring Scheme (Goldsmiths London)	Improving The Quality of Education for All (Cambridge)
CASE-Thinking Science (Teesside TEC)	IPP in Education (Teesside TEC)
City Reading Project (Oxford LEA)	Lewisham School Improvement Project (SIP)
Cleveland Compact (Teesside TEC)	Literacy, Numeracy, Curriculum Enrichment etc. (Humberside)
Compact Extension (North London TEC)	
Countering Bullying (Kent LEA)	Mentoring (North Warwicks EBP)
Curriculum Development Focus (Rotherham)	Middlesbrough Community Education Project (Cleveland LEA)
Developing Effective Schools in Greenwich (Greenwich TVEI)	Monitoring ALIS, YELLIS, PIPS (Newcastle University)
Frequent Monitoring Programme (Wandsworth)	
Helping All Pupils to Achieve More (Bradford LEA)	Nettworks 94 (Gloucester LEA)
	Newspapers in Education (Teesside TEC)
North Guildford Project (Surrey LEA)	School Effectiveness and Improvement Centre (London Univ)
Parental Involvement in the Core Curriculum (Tower Hamlets)	School Effectiveness (Warwick University)
Partnership Reviews (Bradford TEC)	School Improvement (Bexley)
Pathways to School Improvement (Bath University)	School Improvement Networks (London University)
	School Measurement and Improvement Strategy (Newcastle Univ)
Peers Early Education Partnership (Oxford LEA)	
Post-16 Compact. (Teesside TEC)	Schools Make a Difference (Hammersmith and Fulham LEA)
Primary School Improvement Bretton Hall (Leeds University)	Strategies to Enhance Performance at GCSE (Barnsley LEA)
Quality Development Initiative (Birmingham LEA)	Successful Schools (Worcester College of HE)
Raising Achievement and Participation Project (Sheffield LEA)	The 'At Risk' Support Project
	The Tilbury Initiative (Essex LEA)
Raising Achievement in Inner City Schools (Lancashire LEA)	Tower Hamlets Partnership (Exeter University)
Raising Achievement Project (Rochdale LEA)	Truancy (Devon LEA)
Raising Reading Standards Project (Lewisham)	Two Towns Project (Staffs LEA)
Raising Standards in Inner City Schools (Gateshead)	Urban Education (Brunel University)
	Value Added (Kent LEA)
Raising Standards in the Inner City (Notts. LEA)	Vocational Education Development Centre (Devon and Cornwall TEC)
Raising Standards Project (Dudley)	
Raising Standards Project (South Shields)	Youth Work for Young People At Risk (Cambridge LEA)
Research Fellowship (Birmingham University)	

● Urban education initiative

Figure 3.1. *The distribution initiatives used in the survey*

these are in urban areas. For the majority of initiatives, 56.5 per cent, there is a target group of ten schools or less, a further 37 per cent have between 11 and 60 participating schools and only 6.5 per cent of the initiatives have more. The numbers of schools involved appears to depend largely upon the purpose of the initiative and the size and nature of the initiating institution. The largest school groupings are observed in schemes originated by HEIs where there is likely to be a national rather than a local emphasis. The London Institute of Education, for example, may be working with ten LEAs or more at the same time. Regional schemes, usually initiated by LEAs or TECs, may include all or most of the schools within the authority and where the authority is large the numbers will be large, as in the case of Birmingham, where 300 schools are involved. On the other hand the focus of a project might be simply on those schools with specific difficulties in a given area or may be only at the pilot stage.

A wide variety of types and phases of school are included in the initiatives. Most of the initiatives concentrate solely on LEA-maintained schools but this is by

Table 3.2. *Pupil target group*

Nature of the target group	Frequency	Percentage
No particular group	22	41.5
Pupils with specific needs/underachieving	13	24.5
All children in area	8	15.1
Specific year group	8	15.1
Pupils going into training education	2	3.8
Total	53	100.0

no means universal and whilst none of the initiatives exclude the LEA-maintained sector, some include representatives from the voluntary-aided, grant-maintained and independent sectors. Of the 60 schemes included in the study, 13 (21.7 per cent) include voluntary-aided, 9 (15.0 per cent) include grant-maintained and 7 (11.7 per cent) include independent schools.

Some schemes are single phase, others cross phase. Nineteen (31.7 per cent) of the projects involve a mixture of primary and secondary schools, 16 (26.7 per cent) secondary only and 7 (11.7 per cent) primary only. Four (6.7 per cent) of the initiatives, such as the PICC Project in Tower Hamlets, bracket together a mixture of nursery and primary schools, 8 (13.3 per cent), such as Investing in People in Cleveland, include post-16 institutions and 4 (6.7 per cent) have an additional, individual emphasis as with, for example, the home–school link of the Tilbury Initiative.

Within the school cohorts involved there may or may not be a particular target group of children. In the case of 25 (41.7 per cent) of the initiatives there is a particular target group, for 28 (46.7 per cent) there is no target group. For the remaining 9 initiatives there is no indication one way or the other. It is common for LEA initiatives to include all schools in their geographical area or to be engaged in pilot schemes which are intended to include all schools at a later date. Where pupils are targeted it is usually by age group or by some special need such as reading difficulty, bullying or poor attendance. An analysis of responses in respect of target grouping is included in Table 3.2.

THE PARTICIPATION OF AGENCIES OTHER THAN SCHOOLS

The range of 'other agencies' working with the schools to raise standards is wide and varied. The major participants are the LEAs, who make a significant contribution to 89.8 per cent of the initiatives included in this study. The other major contributors are higher and further education, 45.8 per cent and 32.2 per cent respectively, the Training and Enterprise Councils, 44.1 per cent, and industrial representatives and 'education business partnerships', 42.4 per cent. An analysis of all responses to question 11 of the questionnaire (about agencies participating in the initiatives) is presented below in Table 3.3 and Figure 3.2.

Several other groups, not included in the questionnaire, are identified as participants, in some cases in more than one submission. These include the following:

Table 3.3. *Agencies other than schools participating in the initiatives*

Agency	Frequency	Percentage
LEAs	53	89.8
Higher education	27	45.8
TECs	26	44.1
Further education	19	32.2
Parents' organizations	8	13.6
Careers service	8	13.6
Charitable trust	6	10.2
Youth service	7	11.9
Industry, commerce, EBPA	25	42.4
Local community organizations	9	15.3
Police	5	8.5
Education welfare	6	10.2
Education psychology	11	18.6
Social services	5	8.5
Other agency	24	40.7
Total	59	100.0

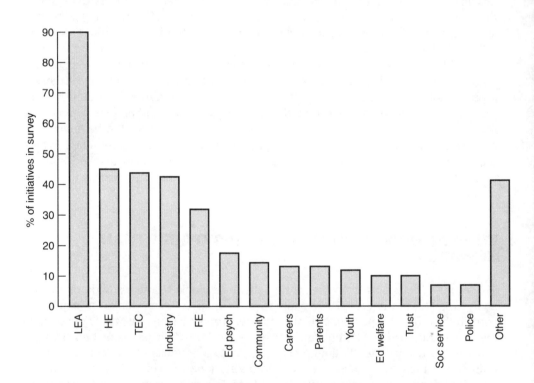

Figure 3.2. *Agencies other than schools participating*

Adult Education – Tilbury, North Guildford, Tower Hamlets, Humberside

City Challenge – Middlesbrough, Teesside

Community Health – Gateshead

Diocesan Education Board – North Guildford

Governors – Bradford, Lewisham, Kent

Independent Consultants – Greenwich

National Authorities such as DFE, HMI

Cambridge University, London Institute

National Foundation for Educational Research – Westminster

National Primary Centre – Worcester

TVEI Extension – Bath

FUNDING

The initiatives identified in this study are largely, though not exclusively, dependent on funding additional to the standard school budget. Ninety per cent of those who responded to the survey are in receipt of additional funding, while 10 per cent are not. Amounts of funding vary considerably although most of them, 58 per cent, have received less than £5,000 in total. Five per cent have received £5,000 to £10,000, 8 per cent between £10,000 and £20,000, 10 per cent between £20,000 and £50,000, 8 per cent between £50,000 and £100,000 and 11 per cent more than £100,000.

FUNDING AGENCIES

For the most part the agencies which have the greatest involvement in initiating and managing the schemes are also responsible for most of the funding. In some cases funding is via a single agency but usually there is more than one contributor.

The major contributors are from the LEAs, EBPs/industry, the TECs and HEIs. Details are presented in Table 3.4. In the case of some LEA-supported initiatives, the additional funding is derived from the GEST scheme under which 60 per cent of the funding comes directly from central government. This direct contribution from central government ought to be recognized.

Other contributors not included in the questionnaire are cited in the survey submissions. They include the following:

City Challenge – Blackburn, Middlesbrough

Cambridge University Department for Education

Economic and Social Research Council (ESRC) – Gateshead, Haringey, London Institute

Hull Task Force – Humberside

Table 3.4. *Providers of additional funding for the initiatives*

Sources of funding	Frequency	Percentage
LEA	41	74.5
School	8	14.5
Charitable trust	5	9.1
University (HEI)	12	21.6
Industry	5	9.1
Other organization	40	72.7
Total	55	100.0

London Docklands Development Corporation – Tower Hamlets

National Primary Centre – Worcester

Safer Surrey Initiative – North Guildford

Department for Employment – North Buckinghamshire, Cleveland,
Devon and Cornwall

It should be borne in mind that the figures in Table 3.4 refer only to the number of initiatives in which the agencies make a funding contribution. The study provides no evidence of the actual amounts of money provided by individual contributors. It is certainly the case that most of the money in total, most provision of time and most revenue, that is to say ongoing funding, comes from the LEAs and that most of the money in one-off grants comes from TECs, EBP/industry and charitable trusts. Contributions from higher education are more likely to be in the form of assistance in kind, in terms of time and expertise contributed.

REPRESENTATION ON MANAGEMENT GROUPS

It was assumed, when framing question 21 of the questionnaire (*Please indicate who contributes to the Steering Group*), that the schools participating in the initiatives in the study would be represented on any management or steering group. The evidence suggests that this is generally but not always the case. The analysis of this question about representation on management and steering groups does not, therefore, include teaching and administrative staff from schools and such data as is included about the schools' contribution is gathered from additional written comments provided in the submissions.

As with the contribution of funding, the non-school agencies which have the greatest involvement in initiating and managing the schemes also provide the greatest contribution toward the management of the initiatives. The major contributions are from the LEAs, which contribute to the management of 47 (88.7 per cent) of the initiatives, HEIs which contribute to 22 (41.5 per cent), the TECs which contribute to 18 (34.0 per cent) and EBP/industry which contribute to 16 (30.2 per cent). It should be noted that these figures are based upon only 53 responses as seven agencies did not complete question 21. Details are presented in Table 3.5 and Figure 3.3.

Table 3.5. *Organizations contributing to a steering group for the initiatives*

Contributors to steering group	Frequency	Percentage
LEA	47	88.7
Further education	10	18.9
Higher education	22	41.5
Parents' organizations	3	5.7
Careers service	9	17.0
TEC	18	34.0
Charitable trust	2	3.8
Youth service	3	5.7
Industry, commerce, EBPA	16	30.2
Local community organizations	7	13.2
Police	2	3.8
Educational welfare	3	5.7
Educational psychology	6	11.3
Social services	1	1.9
Other agency	25	47.2
Total	53	100.0

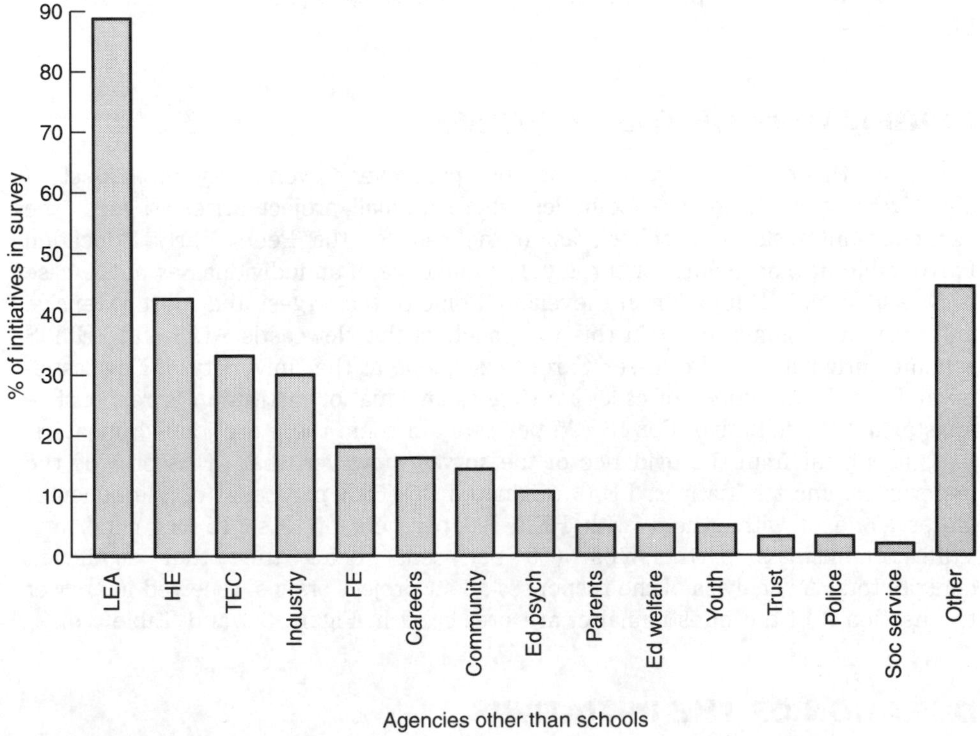

Agencies other than schools

Figure 3.3. *Contribution to steering groups*

Other contributors not included in the questionnaire are cited in the survey submissions. They include the following:

City Challenge – Lewisham

Diocesan Board and local church members – North Guildford

Educational consultants – Lewisham

Governors of schools – Bradford, Middlesbrough

Hull Task Force – Humberside

The local authority – Dudley

London Docklands Development Corporation – Tower Hamlets

Multicultural Service – Sheffield

National authorities (DFE, OFSTED)

School Curriculum and Assessment Authority (SCAA) – London Institute

National Primary Centre – Worcester

Department for Employment – North Buckinghamshire

Most of the initiatives are managed not by a single agency but by a representative or representatives from two or more of the participant groups. More than half of all the initiatives, 53.2 per cent, are managed only by representatives of schools, LEAs, HEIs and TECs.

ORIGINATORS OF THE INITIATIVE

Inevitably the questionnaire did not anticipate every eventuality in respect of initiative origins. There are examples where a small project arises to meet the particular interests of a school, as in the case of the Peers Early Education Partnership in Oxfordshire, or through the influence of an individual, as in the case of Newspapers in Education in Cleveland. Some of the largest and most extensive initiatives have come about in this way, such as the Newcastle ALIS and YELLIS schemes originated by Professor Carol Fitz-Gibbon at the University of Newcastle-upon-Tyne. In a number of cases no single individual or institution is responsible for starting the initiative. For 15 (25 per cent) of them there are joint originators.

It is clear from the evidence of the survey, however, that LEAs provide the impetus for most initiatives. LEAs originated 35 (58.3 per cent) of the schemes either alone or with others, with HEIs (20 per cent), TECs (15 per cent) and 'education/business partnerships' (10 per cent) being the other significant contributors. An analysis of the responses about project origins, received in answer to question 3 of the questionnaire, are presented in Figure 3.4 and Table 3.6.

DURATION OF THE INITIATIVES

More than 90 per cent of the initiatives submitted for the survey have been started since 1988. Details can be seen in Appendix 2. 25.4 per cent of the initiatives are

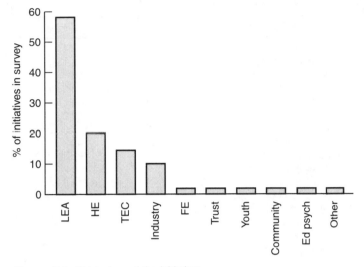

Figure 3.4. *Originators of the initiatives*

Table 3.6. *Organizations originating the initiatives*

Initiating bodies	Frequency	Percentage
LEA	35	58.3
FE	1	1.7
HE	12	20.0
Parents	–	–
Careers service	–	–
TEC	9	15.0
Charitable trust	1	1.7
Youth service	1	1.7
Industry	6	10.0
Local community	1	1.7
Police	–	–
Education welfare	–	–
Educational psychology	1	1.7
Social services	–	–
Other body	7	11.7
Total	60	100.0

(or were at the time of the survey) of no more than twelve months' duration, a further 22 per cent and/were of two years' and a further 22 per cent of three years' duration. This means that as many as 69.5 per cent of the initiatives surveyed have lasted or will last no more than three years. Analysis of the duration of initiatives is detailed in Appendix 2.

Table 3.7. *The aims of the improvement initiatives*

Main project characteristics	Frequency	Percentage
Underachievement	11	18.6
Mentoring/tutoring	3	5.1
School Improvement	15	25.4
Staff development	12	20.3
Environment	3	5.1
Literacy/numeracy	13	22.0
Multi-agency	5	8.5
Raising attainment	24	40.7
Family involvement	18	30.5
Curriculum development	6	10.2
Post-16	8	13.6
Bullying/behavioural problems	4	6.8
Assessment (GCSE/value added)	6	10.2
Attendance/punctuality	3	5.1
Homework	1	1.7
Equal opp/ethnic groups	2	3.4
Improved teaching and learning	1	1.7
Monitoring	1	1.7
Total	59	100.0

THE STATED AIMS AND EXPECTED OUTCOMES OF THE INITIATIVES

THE AIMS

Each respondent to the survey was asked to provide a brief description of the characteristics of the initiative being submitted. Their responses are presented in Appendix 5. Usually included in this initial statement is an indication of the broad aims of the initiative. An analysis of these stated aims is included in Table 3.7.

By the very nature of a survey which seeks to investigate initiatives designed to raise standards in urban areas, the aim of addressing the educational implications of social deprivation and an expectation of underachievement is implicit. Eleven of the initiatives (18.6 per cent) actually mention underachievement in their initial statements. Beyond this, the stated aims of the majority of the initiatives are extremely broad. Twenty-four (40.7 per cent) aim at 'raising attainment', 18 (30.5 per cent) aim to involve the family as partners in children's education, and 15 (25.4 per cent) mention 'school improvement'.

Fewer of the initiatives have more narrowly focused aims. Only two (3.4 per cent), for example, are concerned solely with the interests of ethnic minority groups, 1 (1.6 per cent) targets truancy, 4 (6.8 per cent) include improving attitudes to bullying and behavioural problems among their aims, 3 (5.1 per cent) promote the use of non-teacher adults as mentors in schools, while 8 (13.6 per cent) target improving staying-on rates into full-time post-16 education.

INTENDED AREAS OF IMPROVEMENT

Responses about the areas in which the initiatives were intended to bring about improvement were as wide-ranging as the stated aims of the initiatives. Twelve possible areas were suggested in the questionnaire in which improvement might be expected (question 5). In all cases, even where the project aim was narrowly focused, there were multiple responses to this question, with 7 of the 12 categories being chosen by more than 50 per cent of all respondents and all the categories being selected in some cases. The most popular area of expected improvement was 'higher pupil attainment' (85 per cent) followed in order by higher pupil and teacher expectation (71.7 per cent), greater pupil self-esteem (66.7 per cent) and the involvement of parents (60.0 per cent). A detailed analysis of intended areas of improvement is provided in Table 3.8 and Figure 3.5.

A number of additional areas of improvement were suggested which were not offered in the questionnaire. These include:

- school management and leadership
- teaching and learning
- cross-phase links
- literacy skills
- industrial awareness
- school climate/ethos
- the management of change

An important question posed by the extent and complexity of the anticipated areas of improvement concerns the monitoring and evaluation of the initiatives. Where an initiative has very wide-ranging aims and objectives, monitoring and evaluating its impact becomes an extremely difficult, if not impossible, task. This point is taken up in the next section.

Table 3.8. *Areas targeted for improvement by the initiatives*

Areas targeted for improvement	Frequency	Percentage
Pupil–teacher expectation	43	71.7
Pupil attainment	51	85.0
Pupil behaviour	25	41.7
Parental involvement	36	60.0
Pupil–teacher morale	32	53.3
Pupil self-esteem	40	66.7
Staying-on rates post-16	22	36.7
Curriculum change	30	50.0
Truancy	20	33.3
Bullying	11	18.3
Discipline	13	21.7
Racial awareness tolerance	11	18.3
Other area	26	43.3
Total	60	100.0

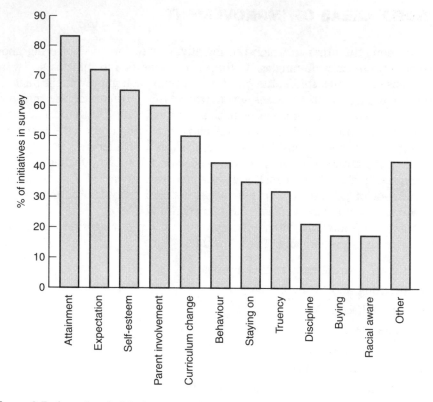

Figure 3.5. *Areas targeted for improvement*

EVALUATING SUCCESS

Given the varied nature of the initiatives included in the study it is not surprising that a wide range of indicators have been considered by participants.

For some it was too early to say. One project in a northern city said that success criteria 'are still under consideration'; another simply that it is 'too early to judge'. The later remark might be acceptable in response to a question about whether performance criteria were being met. It is less so when the question concerns the criteria that ought to be established. It is representative of a significant minority among the initiatives which appear to have been set in motion with little clarity about the specific outcomes that are desired.

In addition to those initiatives where criteria had yet to be established there were others which, for evaluation, depended on 'the implementation of noticeable change' (8.1 per cent) or on the reports of participants. For initiatives of any size and significance such informal approaches to evaluation would seem to be insufficient.

However, the majority of initiatives intended to evaluate success on the basis of internal evaluation or assessment against specified targets or external evaluation or a combination of these approaches. Given the importance of effective evaluation

Table 3.9. *Performance indicators used to measure the success of the initiative*

Performance indicators	Frequency	Percentage
Attendance	25	52.1
Punctuality	14	29.2
Pupil behaviour	17	35.4
Equal opportunities (race)	14	29.2
Equal opportunities (gender)	12	25.0
Parental involvement	24	50.0
Test and examination results	33	68.8
Post-16 stay-on rates	21	43.8
Other indicator (single response)	19	39.6
Other indicator (two responses)	15	31.3
Total	48	100.0

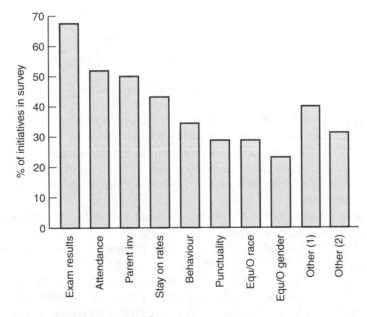

Figure 3.6. *Measurement of success*

in bringing about effective change and in designing the next steps in a process of continuous change, it was disappointing that less than a third of projects intended to use external evaluation (31.4 per cent). In particular, the reaffirmation of success that can result from such evaluation is important in urban-education initiatives.

In addition to examining the approach to evaluation of each initiative, our study also examined the performance indicators that were in use or would be used. The questionnaire asked respondents to state whether they were or were not using a series of indicators. The results are shown in Table 3.9 and Figure 3.6.

It was encouraging to see the extent to which, often in addition to softer, broader aims, clearly measurable indicators were being used. The table also shows that the emphasis in the majority of projects is firmly where it should be, on pupil achievement.

In making judgements such as this it is important to bear in mind that the 60 initiatives included in the study are a disparate group. Clearly if an initiative has a particular objective such as promoting the use of newspapers in Teesside or reducing bullying then its effects ought not to be measured in test results. Nevertheless even in these specific cases there was a strong emphasis on seeking to identify pupil-related outcomes.

EVIDENCE OF SUCCESS TO DATE

The questionnaire asked not only about how success would be evaluated but also what evidence, if any, of success there was to date. It should be borne in mind that a significant proportion of the projects (about 20 per cent) have been only recently established and therefore have little evidence so far. Nevertheless across the country there is evidence that the combined efforts of schools, LEAs, TECs and HE institutions are proving to be beneficial, as Figure 3.7 and Table 3.10 illustrate.

As the table shows, almost a quarter indicate that they have clear evidence that they are achieving their goals.

There are three main sources of information available to initiatives about whether or not they have been successful. The first is anecdotal evidence. As one initiative reported, there is 'feedback from pupils, teachers and mentors'. Another suggests that 'schools which have participated in the project have relayed to us that it has sharpened their thinking . . .' while a third cites 'the reaction of the [teaching] profession'.

A closely related type of evidence is what might be described as market response. Several initiatives claim success on the grounds that significant numbers of schools not yet involved are clamouring to participate. One says for example that 'a further 10 schools have requested involvement', another that 'we have been overwhelmed with requests for involvement'. While evidence of this kind is clearly heartening this may say more about the influence of the availability of additional resources rather than the intrinsic merit of a particular initiative.

A second type of evidence is evaluation. As we have seen, about a third of the projects studied are commissioning external evaluations, while others are undertaking formal internal evaluation. In some cases these have provided clear evidence of success and a re-affirmation of the initiative's mission. One initiative reports that its knowledge of success is 'based upon summative evaluation of TVEI extension and a process evaluation of compacts'. Another attached a lengthy and extremely positive evaluation. In the case of five longer initiatives it is clear that evaluations at an interim stage not only help to discover the extent of success but also contribute to re-directing energy and refining strategy.

The third and most convincing form of evidence is where measurable targets have been set and either met or exceeded. The Two Towns project in

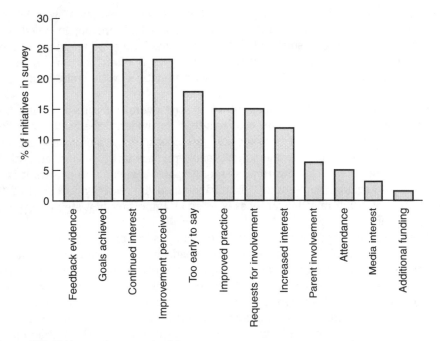

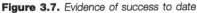

Figure 3.7. *Evidence of success to date*

Table 3.10. *Evidence for the success of the initiative to date*

Evidence for success	Frequency	Percentage
Too early to assess	11	18.6
Achievement of goals	15	25.4
Perception of improvement	14	23.7
Evaluation/feedback evidence	15	25.4
Continued interest and growth	14	23.7
Increased interest and awareness	7	11.9
Increased parental involvement	4	6.8
Requests to be involved	9	15.3
Improved attendance	3	5.1
Increased good practice	9	15.3
Media interest	2	3.4
Obtaining funding	1	1.7
Total	59	100.0

Staffordshire is one example. The Post-16 Compact in Teesside reports that 90 per cent of participants have achieved compact goals, while in Bradford the LEA's 'Helping All Pupils to Achieve More' initiative reported improved GCSE results and SK1 assessment results.

Even in the cases of such apparently incontrovertible evidence it is wise to exercise a healthy scepticism. As in so much educational research, there is the nagging doubt that the improvements might have happened anyway, even without the existence of the initiative. Moreover, there is the question of whether the improvement is greater than in comparable schools which are not involved in an initiative. To make an assessment of this aspect some kind of value-added analysis is necessary. Though it provides important insights it often has an element of doubt. It can also be costly, which may deter initiatives with limited additional funds.

In spite of all these hesitations, however, the overall picture emerging from our survey is a positive one. Success, where it is evident, seems to have four aspects. The first is increased awareness of the characteristics of school improvement in urban areas among teachers, headteachers, parents, governors and others. One initiative reports 'raised awareness amongst staff', while another says it ran a 'well-attended regional conference'. A third noticed 'increased awareness of the issues in school'. Such raised awareness is often an important first step on the road to improvement.

The second aspect is raised morale. This is reported by many of our respondents. One describes the 'impact on heads who feel supported'. Another 'improved teacher and headteacher . . . morale'. 'Improvements . . . in staff morale, motivation, learning, management and teaching skills' are reported by a third. Given that isolation and a downward spiral in morale are ever-present dangers in urban schools, this effect of the initiatives covered in the study is important too. However, on its own it would scarcely provide justification for the investment of time, money and energy.

A third form of reported benefit is of a similar nature. In addition to improved morale, there appear to have been a range of other improvements in the process of education. These include, for example, references to improved teaching skills, better management and enhanced communication with parents. As one submission put it, 'schools who have participated in the project have relayed to us that it has sharpened up their thinking, has motivated them to try new initiatives and to plan for improvement in a systematic way'. Similarly, another submission suggests that there has been 'increased parental involvement' and 'improved home/ school links'. Another notes an improvement in 'the governing body's commitment to improvement and change'. Improvements of this kind are of major significance. While they may not demonstrably improve pupil outcomes, all of them are aspects of an effective school and are therefore indirectly related to improvement of pupil performance.

The final type of success is improved pupil performance. A number of initiatives provided information of this kind. One refers to 'rapidly rising GCSE and A-level performance (though) little evidence of progress in primary schools to date'. Another reports 'achievement of post-16 goals by more than 90 per cent of participants', while a third states that 'KSI outcomes [have been] substantially increased. Reading attainment [has] improved'.

Since improvement in pupil attainment is the chief goal of many of the initiatives, it is encouraging that there is hard evidence of success in some cases. Partly perhaps because of the expense, none of the initiatives report the use of value-added analysis. In the absence of this, it is always difficult to be sure that any improvement that follows the start of an initiative is necessarily a result of it, or indeed is greater than in comparable schools elsewhere. However, in many cases it is possible to conclude that there is marked improvement and that the participants believe the initiative to have been responsible. This kind of evidence is sufficiently convincing in most cases to be acceptable. Value-added analysis is extremely beneficial but even its most committed advocates accept that it too will always be hedged round with caveats.

Issues concerning the continuation of initiatives and suggestions for future progress, related to this research data, are considered in Chapter 4.

NOTE

1 This chapter is adapted from Barber, M., Denning, T., Gough, G. and Johnson, M. *Urban Education Initiatives: The National Pattern. A Report for the Office for Standards in Education, July 1994*. Keele: Keele University.

Chapter 4

Urban Education Initiatives: Future Progress[1]

Michael Barber, Tim Denning, Gerry Gough and Michael Johnson

THE CONTINUATION OF INITIATIVES

A critical issue for every initiative is the extent to which its benefits will continue once the initiative itself has come to an end. A decisive factor in the planning and implementation of educational change is the extent to which preparation is made for the shift from implementation to institutionalization. The past is littered with initiatives which began brightly but faded into irrelevance once the additional time and energy of the 'initiative' phase was withdrawn.

In this study of 60 initiatives the extent of preparation for the end of the 'initiative' varied. In 32.2 per cent the project funding was ongoing or indefinite. The vast majority of these were LEA-led initiatives. About 17 per cent either had no plans for the institutionalization phase or believed it was too early in the project to plan for what would happen once it had finished. Just over 13 per cent hoped that funding would be extended, while about 12 per cent planned a new bid for funding.

Only just over a quarter had actually planned for the continuation of the initiative's benefits once the additional funding was withdrawn. Of these, 12 per cent planned that maintaining the momentum would be a task for the schools alone, while 13.6 per cent expected that the schools would do so with the support of the LEA.

These findings are somewhat surprising, since we had expected to find that those responsible for time-limited projects with restricted funding would give high priority to planning the continuation of the benefits of their initiatives. In fact, not all initiatives lend themselves to continuation, while others such as the HEI-led ones discussed in Appendix 4, assume continued funding activity, with good reason, but cannot be specific about precisely how these ends will be assured.

Nevertheless, examination of some of the comments from those surveyed suggests that much more might be expected in terms of planning for continuation. One suggests that 'It is hoped that the programme can be expanded in 1994/5 . . .'

but with no indication as to how or what will be the consequence if it cannot. Another says 'schools indicate that they will seek to maintain the scheme at the end of compact funding'. A third says the project is open-ended – a 'process not an event' – which is fine in theory but in practice may be so vague as to be ineffective. Several state simply 'None as yet'.

Some answers of greater clarity and precision were given. The Middlesbrough Community Education Coalition Project for example, suggests that 'the steering group when considering bids from schools for support require evidence of how the proposals (a) contribute to raising standards (b) might enable developments to be maintained beyond the funding period. Plans must also be related to the School Development Plan and to school budget allocations'; while Essex County Council's fledgling Tilbury initiative has already emphasized that 'the expectation from the outset has been that the LEA might support research and contribute but not *do* it all. The Heads recognize that a contribution from school time and funds is required long term. The LEA will clearly aim to maintain a supportive framework within which the schools will be working into the future'.

Similarly, the Sheffield LEA/TEC Raising Achievement and Participation Project (RAPP) points out that 'funding from RAPP is at best seed-corn funding requiring real school commitment'. It also has a 'requirement for extended feedback to the steering group beyond the project timetable'. Moreover, like a handful of other projects in the study, it has plans for a dissemination event and proposes a new round of bids for an extended group of schools.

Overall the study suggests that while some of those responsible for urban-education initiatives have given a great deal of thought to the issue of the embedding of any gains in the institutions, a considerable number, perhaps as many as a third, had no clear plans for the inevitable moment. It would seem to us that even where there were realistic grounds to hope for continued funding, serious thought ought to be given to the question of how best to ensure that the gains that resulted from any initiative could be sustained.

PROMOTING PROGRESS IN INNER CITIES: LESSONS FROM THE STUDY

The final part of the report for OFSTED drew together the most significant conclusions from the analysis of urban-education initiatives. These are outlined in the remainder of this chapter in order to highlight the issues and possibilities related to promoting future progress in urban education. The propositions below have been outlined using the research data gathered in this study as well as a wealth of first-hand knowledge and experience gleaned from other urban-education initiatives and studies (including feedback from OFSTED on their visits to GEST-funded initiatives). Inevitably there are some limitations. However, we have substantial confidence in them.

Proposition 1: There is a great deal of concern at local level about urban education and this has generated a wide variety of initiatives designed to address urban education problems.

Given the nature and extent of education reform in recent years, it is not surprising that the chief focus of both educators and researchers in education has been on policy-making at central-government level and on the implementation of those policies. As a result, the extent of policy initiatives at local level through LEAs, TECs and HEIs may have been under-estimated. Our research shows a wide variety of initiatives bringing together different collaborating agencies and targeted at a wide range of educational objectives.

Proposition 2: Loose collaboration rather than formal structures provided the pattern for the organization of urban-education initiatives, but LEAs will remain the most important players in the game.

The survey evidence shows that LEAs still play an important role in improving the quality of education in urban areas (see Figures 3.2 and 3.3). In doing so they depend less on their greatly reduced formal powers and much more on the quality of their relationship with schools and on what might be called their moral authority as representatives of a given city or area. They also depend on their ability to act as the co-ordinator of a network. Obviously LEAs vary significantly in each of these respects, but where they do have credibility their role remains critical.

It is certainly positive to discover the extent of collaboration between LEAs, TECs, EBPs and HEIs in supporting initiatives in schools. Projects as varied as the major school-improvement project in Tilbury, one promoting education in the arts in Sunderland and one on 'Mentoring' in North Warwickshire all involved two or more of these players. All of them depend, however, on the extent to which they recognize that schools themselves must play a central role in the improvement strategy. It may well be that the model of future development of educational initiatives will increasingly involve voluntary collaboration between agencies and schools rather than formal structural arrangements. If so, however, it seems likely that in relation to urban school initiatives the LEA will be 'primus inter pares'.

Proposition 3: Management structures need to reflect the loose nature of collaboration and to place initiative firmly with the schools involved.

The replacement of traditional structures with looser collaboration has already been referred to. It has coincided with a shift in the point of accountability across the education system from LEAs to schools, whether GM or LM. One result of this shift has been to place the responsibility for school improvement firmly in the hands of the schools. Initiatives to raise standards in urban areas need to reflect and indeed make use of this development. They cannot operate successfully by directing the schools against their will: they must instead ensure that the wider initiative is consistent with and ultimately integral to the development plans of individual participating schools.

This means that management structures need to be designed to bring together all those involved in the initiative in a co-operative mode. The trend is towards steering groups working on a consensus model of decision-making, or in the case of smaller projects towards even less formal approaches to decision-making.

Proposition 4: The scope and range of projects does not coincide with the extent of urban educational need: rather it reflects initiative in the LEAs, HEIs and/or TECs in a given area.

In Chapter 3 we described the kinds of project that are being undertaken and showed their location. This analysis shows that the extent of local activity bears little relationship to the extent of deprivation. Rather it depends on a range of contingent factors such as the policy and approach of the LEA, the research profile and interests of the local university and the quality of relationship between the various educational organizations in a given area.

This raises an important strategic policy issue: should national policy give priority to compensating those areas where need is extensive and local initiative is lacking? Or should it be aimed at providing incentives for and the encouragement of local initiative?

This study indicates that the latter approach is more likely to be effective for three reasons. Firstly, it would be more consistent with the pattern of existing successful projects which place the initiative with the schools. Secondly, it would avoid the danger of central intervention acting, in effect, as a disincentive to local developments. Thirdly, the most intractable problem of all initiatives (how to ensure that their influence outlives any additional funding and support) is more likely to be soluble where the initiative has been built on the basis of the schools' own development strategies.

One incentive to local development may simply be the publication of information about, and where appropriate, the celebration of existing successful locally-led schemes. In this way this report and the other actions OFSTED has taken to follow up 'Access and Achievement in Urban Education' may in themselves have a positive effect.

Proposition 5: There is a lack of clarity in some projects about success criteria.

The survey instrument used for this study specifically requested information about success criteria. In fact, as shown in Chapter 3, the answers to this question were disappointing. Given the need for value for money and the inevitable restrictions on the overall levels of funding for local initiatives, as well as the significant progress in management practice across the education system, we had anticipated greater clarity in the answers to this question. The lack of effective success criteria, however, should not be confused necessarily with lack of success.

The absence of success criteria in some initiatives makes it difficult for participants to know and understand the impact of their work, and means that they depend on subjective judgement or anecdotal evidence, neither of which are likely to be accurate about the past or a good guide to future planning.

Proposition 6: Clear measurable targets for the progress of urban-education initiatives are essential.

Many of the initiatives surveyed do have clear measurable targets. These are valuable for three reasons. Firstly, they enable progress to be monitored effectively. Secondly, they enable participants to build the confidence and self-belief which are central to educational progress. If, by contrast, targets are unclear, then participants are unable to be certain whether their activity is paying dividends. Thirdly, only with clear targets can effective accountability to those who are contributing time and money be ensured. This in turn is the key to further funding for, or development of, any initiative.

It is on the whole easier to set clear targets for secondary education because of the existence of public examinations. A fully-operational national assessment system would assist target-setting in primary education. In the meantime a range of standardized tests are available and can be used for this purpose. The importance of being able to monitor and evaluate progress should not be underestimated.

Proposition 7: Significant amounts of money are, in some cases, being spent relatively ineffectively.

There appear to be, among the projects surveyed, a number where a great deal of time, energy and money has been spent with the best intentions, but to little demonstrable effect. These projects are characterized by a lack of clarity about success criteria, an absence of external evaluation or effective monitoring, a lack of clarity about aims and a scattergun approach to the use of time and investment.

While such projects may be marginally beneficial in the sense that doing something is usually better than doing nothing, there is no doubt that the same levels of investment could have brought far greater benefits if the initiatives had been more carefully structured. In particular, initiatives need to recognize the shift of accountability over recent years from the LEA to the school. Initiatives which attempt to wrest control of a school's destiny from the school are unlikely to succeed.

Proposition 8: **Small amounts of additional funding, spent well, can make a huge difference.**

There are a series of paradoxes involved in the provision of additional funding for urban-educational initiatives. One is that although there is an evident need for extra funding, most urban schools are already funded at above-average levels in per capita terms. Another is that there is a danger of, in effect, using additional funding as a reward for poor performance. There is a substantial tradition of this stretching back over 30 years in this country. A third is that if additional funding is the decisive factor in bringing about improvement, then it may prove difficult to sustain the improvement when the funding is withdrawn.

The resolution of these paradoxes is possible given careful planning. The evidence of the survey suggests that where additional resources are carefully targeted they can bring about significant and sustainable improvement. They do so where they are used to provide flexibility at the margin, where they act as a catalyst and where they are used to assist with the implementation of innovation. Above all they are effective when used to bring about a change in culture and to assist the school in putting in place the in-school processes which enable improvement from within.

They achieve this when:

- the planning of expenditure integrally involves the schools themselves;
- outside consultants, with high credibility, are bought in to provide insight and analysis and to give the initiative status;
- significant numbers of teachers in the schools are involved in planning and consultation;
- there is limited but significant expenditure on symbolic change (such as establishing high-quality displays of pupil work and other achievements in entrance halls);
- they are focused on attempts to change pupil (peer group) attitudes or staff attitudes and expectations;
- provision is made for professional development opportunities related to the goals of the project.
- the additional expenditure becomes an integral part of a school's development strategy.

Additional funding is less beneficial when:

- it is spent on a range of unrelated one-off activities, however beneficial each individual one might be;
- the target schools are not thoroughly involved in decisions about it;
- it is spent on what can only be a temporary addition to mainstream staffing.

The evidence we have gathered suggests that there is already considerable awareness of the complexity of ensuring that additional resources are well spent.

Given the extent of the urban-educational challenge and the limited resources available to bring about change it is important that all those involved in initiatives of the kind examined in this study learn from the best.

Proposition 9: **External attention and recognition can help inspire a school.**

There is evidence from the survey that the simple fact of being part of a project which brings advice to the school and recognition of its efforts is in itself positive.

Given the extent of pressure upon them, headteachers and teachers in urban schools are often so involved with their own work that they lack effective contact with outside organizations or colleagues in other schools. Participation in a wider initiative can help to break down this sense of isolation which was noted in 'Access and Achievement in Urban Education'.

There is evidence in the research literature (Fullan, 1991, for example) to confirm that the external consultant/adviser can be a valuable promoter of educational progress, but only where he/she has high credibility in the school.

Proposition 10: **Participation in an initiative is not an alternative to getting the in-school factors right.**

As we have suggested above, the initiatives with the greatest chance of bringing about sustainable improvement are those that assist schools in creating the conditions for improvement from within.

It should be emphasized that participating in an initiative is not an alternative to a school taking responsibility for its own improvement. Instead it is a means of assisting it to improve, and may act as a catalyst which helps it to change and improve more quickly.

Proposition 11: **For the monitoring and evaluation of an initiative to be effective it needs to take into account schools not involved.**

One way to measure whether or not an initiative has succeeded would be to compare schools involved with similar schools that are not involved. Where academic performance is the goal of the initiative this is best done through some form of value-added analysis.

However, it is also necessary to check that progress in schools involved in an initiative is not at the expense of progress in those not involved. Given the limited nature of this study it has not been possible to ascertain whether the initiatives studied have diverted resources – time and money – to those schools which are included in a way that has been detrimental to other schools in the locality. Nevertheless, our attention has been drawn to this possibility and it clearly is an issue which those developing initiatives should bear in mind.

Proposition 12: **Co-operating agencies as well as schools can benefit from urban school-improvement initiatives.**

While the focus of the initiatives we have studied is clearly school improvement, or some aspect of it, it is clear that the collaboration can provide benefits to other participating agencies. For example, a university can accumulate data and experience which will contribute to its research and publication profile. TECs, for example, can gain through understanding better the links between schools, FE and employers. LEAs can learn lessons applicable to all their schools and gain in terms of their public profile.

These wider benefits ought to be taken into account by those at local level who are considering investing in urban-education initiatives. The investment may reap benefits far beyond those immediately specified in the project goals. Furthermore, given the potential for mutual benefit schools should see their role in such projects as being active partners, rather than passive beneficiaries.

Proposition 13: **The emphasis of urban-educational improvement is on secondary schools in spite of the fact that there is more to play for in primary education.**

Our data shows that most urban-educational initiatives involve both primary and secondary education (and sometimes further education as well). However, of those that concentrate on a single phase over two-thirds are secondary-oriented. Out of 60 projects, 16 are solely secondary, while only 7 are solely primary. We also know that in some of the cross-phase initiatives primary schooling is to some extent an after-thought. Yet the evidence suggests that in terms of the potential for improvement there is, as Peter Mortimore said to the Select Committee on Education (Hansard, 22 June 1994) 'more to play for' in primary education. Given the importance of clear target-setting in urban-educational initiatives, it may be that the greater difficulty of setting hard targets for achievement in primary schools is a factor. It is interesting that the improvement strategy of England's largest urban education authority, Birmingham, has begun with a primary emphasis and an attempt to establish clear targets across the sector.

Proposition 14: **Planning the end of an initiative needs to come at the beginning.**

There is plenty of evidence in studies of educational change that innovation is more likely to bring about permanent benefit where plans have been made for it to become institutionalized. Our evidence in this study suggests that in a significant number of cases there has been insufficient planning for the time when the formal initiative comes to an end. In the best initiatives this crucial phase has been prepared for from the outset. While such advance planning needs to avoid inflexibility, since all initiatives inevitably involve unexpected developments, nevertheless it is essential in providing an overall direction. It is important that the development planning in the schools involved also anticipates the end of any additional funding and/or support. It is precisely for this reason that schools involved in initiatives need both to be integrally involved in the planning process and to take 'ownership' of the changes they bring about.

Proposition 15: Some university departments of education are in a position to make a major contribution to improving education in urban areas.

The survey reveals important evidence of universities playing an important role, not just in researching school improvement, but in assisting urban schools in making it happen. In general this role is being developed in collaboration with LEAs although there are significant numbers of schools and groups of schools working with universities on their own initiative. Sometimes this is linked to initial teacher–education partnership activity but by no means always (see Appendix 7). It would seem wise for those involved in the development of urban-education policy at either local or national level to take into account this growing contribution from higher education.

Proposition 16: Educational consultants are making a contribution to urban educational improvement, which is under-estimated by this survey.

Given the tight timescale and the difficulty of finding a national list of educational consultants, it was not possible to survey all educational consultants. Nevertheless there is evidence in the survey responses from LEAs and TECs, for example, that consultants are a factor in the urban-educational initiatives covered by this study. They have been involved in various tasks including training, advice and evaluation. They are, however, unlikely, by their nature, to be making a funding contribution or to be the initiators of urban-educational initiatives.

NOTE

1 This chapter is adapted from Barber, M., Denning, T., Gough, G. and Johnson, M. *Urban Education Initiatives: The National Pattern. A Report for the Office for Standards in Education, July 1994*. Keele: Keele University.

REFERENCE

Fullan, M. (1991) *The New Meaning of Educational Change*. London: Cassell.

Chapter 5

Urban Education Initiatives: Three Case Studies

Michael Barber, Tim Denning, Gerry Gough and Michael Johnson

INTRODUCTION

In July 1994 Keele University's Centre for Successful Schools completed for OFSTED a report entitled 'Urban Education Initiatives: the National Pattern' (included here in an adapted form as Chapters 3 and 4). This report identified the pattern and nature of urban-education initiatives across the country.

This chapter outlines a follow-up study which focuses on three of the sixty education initiatives covered in the first report. They have been chosen to provide variety in terms of geographical location, target phase and stage development. The order reflects their stage of development; Tilbury is just beginning, Hammersmith and Fulham is well on the way to completion and the GEST-funded project in Nottingham is complete.

The case studies are based on observation and interviews conducted with staff involved in co-ordinating the initiatives, including, in two cases, the appropriate Chief Education Officers, and staff involved at the school level. In the time available it was not possible to visit all the schools involved in each of the projects but an attempt was made to gain a representative insight. Available documents, such as evaluation reports, were also drawn on where appropriate.

CASE STUDY 1: TILBURY IN ESSEX

Outline

The Tilbury Initiative is a school-improvement project due to run for three years starting in 1994, and involving all the primary schools and the secondary school in Tilbury. Tilbury, an urban area situated in Essex on the Thames estuary, has many of the characteristics of urban deprivation more usually found in inner cities, including high unemployment, crime and large proportions of families on low incomes.

The initiative was established by the Essex LEA following HMI Reports on two of the schools in the town and the OFSTED Report 'Access and Achievement in Urban Education'. Up to £200,000 has been made available for the initiative. A proportion of this had already been committed through GEST and other grants. The project is still in its early stages but the evidence to date suggests that there is strong commitment to it from the schools and the LEA and that it has tremendous potential to improve schooling in the town. The LEA, along with partners in the private sector including the Training and Enterprise Council (TEC), has submitted a bid to the Single Regeneration Budget (SRB) which focuses on education and training in the 14–19 age group and on adult education. The success of this bid means that Tilbury could, by combining the present initiative and the SRB-funded project, put in place a strategy to reconstruct and develop the educational culture and the quality of educational provision of the whole town.

Origins

The Tilbury initiative has its origins in reports by HMI on the secondary school in the town (St Chads) and on one of the junior schools (Tilbury Manor Junior School). Both reports identified a combination of serious underachievement and low expectations. The headteachers take the view that the main effect of the reports was to make public problems they had already identified. Some months later when OFSTED published its national report, 'Access and Achievement in Urban Education' (October 1993), Tilbury was one of the areas covered and, for that report, all of the schools in the town had been visited at least briefly.

These reports prompted the headteachers of all the Tilbury schools to begin to meet on a regular basis to discuss their common concerns, which included a recognition that the local community had very low expectations, and a belief that the LEA had, prior to the reports, not sufficiently acknowledged the levels of disadvantage and educational need in the town. These meetings were attended by Tony Porter who was then, and remains, the Essex LEA's Senior Education Officer for the area which includes Tilbury, and who has played an important role in promoting the interests of the town at LEA level.

During the time between the reports on the individual schools and the 'Access and Achievement' report discussions developed slowly. Headteachers recognize that there were suspicions among them. There were fears that there were (unspecified) hidden agendas and recognition that, while the town shared many problems, each of the schools was at a different stage of development. Whilst they could agree that they wanted additional funding and support from the LEA there was much less agreement on anything approaching a common strategy. These problems remained for some time after 'Access and Achievement' too. While all the headteachers now take the view that trust has been developed and a common strategy has emerged, they agree that this took longer than they would have hoped. Both they and representatives of the LEA, however, believe that though the strategy took nearly two years to emerge, the time devoted to building a collaborative and trusting culture among them was well spent, and will provide a firm foundation for the period of the initiative.

Time has also been an essential element in the process of recovering from the crushing blows of the individual school HMI Reports and the 'Access and Achievement' report itself. There is no doubt – at least from the Tilbury evidence – that the publication of such reports can have a devastating effect on morale both in the schools and in the community as a whole. The local press for a front-page article on one of these reports chose the banner headline 'Dunce Town'.

The heads of the schools on which there were individual HMI Reports suggest that it has taken over a year to re-build morale. It is also true that some staff have never recovered. Other schools in Tilbury feel that the fleeting visits they received during the time OFSTED was researching 'Access and Achievement' provided an inadequate basis of evidence for a report which appeared to brand all the schools in the town equally. However, this should not be construed necessarily as an argument against the publication of reports. The headteachers and the LEA acknowledge that the reports gave Tilbury's needs a much higher profile than ever before. The headteachers used OFSTED's judgements as a basis for constructing a case for additional funding and support from the LEA, as well as for planning school-level development. They also believe that a sense of solidarity developed both among themselves and among staff within each of their schools. Thus, there was a paradoxical coincidence of lower morale and a determination to face up squarely to the problems they encountered. The only way, as it were, was up.

Meanwhile the reports also galvanized the LEA and ensured a sense of urgency in that quarter. There was a change of political control (from Conservative to Liberal/Labour) during the period between the HMI reports on the individual schools and the 'Access and Achievement' report. However, the evidence suggests that the LEA's determination to assist in tackling Tilbury's problems predates that change, and that all parties have supported it.

The combination of improved collaboration across the schools in Tilbury with a willingness to assist at LEA level, and a determination by both school and LEA to act, provided the foundation for what has become the Tilbury Initiative.

The Nature of the Initiative

Two reports, approved by the Essex Education Committee in 1993–94, brought together a range of proposals, identified in consultation with the schools, which would together form the basis for the Tilbury Initiative. Taken together the proposals would involve an expenditure of £300,000, a substantial proportion of which was new money. Overall the initiative aims to bring about change in four broad areas: levels of achievement, levels of self-esteem among pupils, management development and the learning environment.

The regular meetings between the Essex Education Officer, Tony Porter, and the headteachers became in effect the initiative's steering group. Other elements of the LEA's service centres, such as the Essex Development and Advisory Service (EDAS) development were to be drawn upon as and when it seemed appropriate.

Early in 1994 a meeting was held for all school governors in the town. Over half of all the governors attended, demonstrating the heightened levels of concern for education in Tilbury following the OFSTED Reports. It should be said at this stage that throughout the period parents, on the whole, were strongly supportive of the schools and their staff, although there is some evidence to suggest that there was a slight increase in the number of parents who chose secondary schools outside Tilbury after the report on St Chads.

The meeting provided an opportunity to build commitment for the initiative across the community. During 1994 the heads also began to raise awareness of the Tilbury-wide developments among their staff. In September 1994 a steering-group meeting was opened up to senior managers from each of the schools and discussion focused on developing specific targets and success criteria within the agreed broad aims of the initiative. The meeting also involved the participation of an external consultant with extensive knowledge of what strategies appeared to work in similar initiatives elsewhere. Immediately following the meeting, the schools were each engaged in discussions of how they might individually contribute to the initiative and what targets might be appropriate for them.

The steering group has begun to identify measurable targets related to each of the four aims of the initiative. For example, in the area of pupil achievement they have agreed to develop literacy targets right through from five to sixteen. This has involved discussion not only of what targets might be appropriate but also how literacy development might be measured. There has been an agreement that all the primary schools will now use the Hertfordshire reading test in order to ensure consistency across the schools, in spite of the misgivings of some of them about the narrowness of the test. This is a good example of the kind of collaboration which is possible now but which a year or two ago would have been inconceivable.

Other practical developments are now in hand in relation to other aims of the initiative. St Chad's, for example, has involved its pupils in preparing a plan to improve the learning environment which has already been partly implemented. Consideration is currently being given to the provision of management development training across the schools, possibly accredited by a local higher education institution. 'Investors in People' will be implemented in all of the schools. In the area of pupil self-esteem a new behaviour policy – 'Discipline for Learning' – is being introduced across the schools. This began as an initiative in one of the schools but has now been adopted by all of them as a result of the common strategy, and there has been some joint training. On a similar basis a school which had developed training for its lunch-time supervisors has now opened the training up to staff from other schools.

Plans are also in place to maintain a high profile for the initiative among all staff and the wider community too. Early in the new year a public launch of 'the primary classroom', based in the secondary school, is planned. The 'primary classroom' will be an outstandingly resourced facility used on a timetabled basis by each of the primary schools in turn. It will be staffed by a range of staff from the secondary school and the primaries and is designed to enhance the links between schools both for pupils and teachers.

February 1995 has been designated for the staff of all the schools to be brought together for a professional development day as part of the promotion of the initiative and to build the professional network among Tilbury teachers. On that evening there will be a reception for governors from the schools. Plans are in hand to appoint a part-time initiative co-ordinator with knowledge and experience of urban-school improvement.

Overall, therefore, although the initiative is still in the early stages, and has taken longer than any of the participants would have wished to begin to make a practical impact, there is already evidence that it will lead over the three-year period to significant improvement in levels of educational achievement. Certainly the evidence we gathered during the fieldwork for this report suggests a powerful determination among the staff of the schools and the LEA to bring about change for the better. Once the success criteria have been more clearly identified, the schools will be in a position to build a spiral of success based on the evidence that they hope will accrue from genuine progress.

CASE STUDY 2: THE 'SCHOOLS MAKE A DIFFERENCE' INITIATIVE IN HAMMERSMITH AND FULHAM LEA

Outline

The 'Schools Make a Difference' (SMAD) project is a secondary-school improvement initiative in the London Borough of Hammersmith and Fulham. It has been running for a period of two years which will end in December 1994 when internal and externally commissioned evaluations of its effectiveness will be published.

The broad purpose of the project is 'to lay the foundation for raising achievement, attainment and self-esteem', to address the issues of underachievement and low expectation, to provide a framework within which schools are enabled to improve the learning environment and to enhance pupil-learning opportunities. All eight of the secondary schools in the borough have been involved in the project and, although its impact has been greater in some schools than others, the evidence suggests that there has been great commitment to it. It is seen as having made a considerable contribution to raising expectation, achievement and morale.

Origins

The SMAD project has its origins in the evaluation of secondary-school provision carried out by the officers and inspectors of the Borough of Hammersmith and Fulham Education Authority in 1990, in the wake of the abolition of the ILEA. The evaluation identified an urgent need for the development of a strategy to raise educational standards in the borough. There was a view that the inner-city children were being failed because 'they were not achieving what they deserved to achieve' and there existed the political will to put some additional resources into the secondary sector. A paper suggesting wide-ranging measures, based upon the most recent and reliable school-effectiveness research, was prepared and presented to the members by the newly-appointed Director of Education and the Chief Inspector. It is very much to the credit of the elected members of the Authority that they recognized the priority status of educational provision and accepted the recommendations of the Director for implementation of the project. Over the projected two-year duration of the project a sum in the region of £500,000 was made available over and above the standard school funding.

Organization

The steering group set up to have oversight of the project comprised LEA officers and inspectors, headteachers, teachers, parent and governor representatives and the CRE education officer, who was involved because of the range and significance of the minority ethnic communities in the borough. As a first step they appointed an 'animateur' to manage the project and there followed intensive discussions with the eight headteachers about the nature of school improvement and the implementation of good practice. After these initial meetings schools were invited to bid for inclusion in the project and to submit proposals detailing their improvement strategy. These proposals were shared with the Strategic Management Group which comprises the eight headteachers and the project manager and which advises the steering group and takes responsibility for strategic decisions. The group's initial task was to devise criteria for agreeing funding for school proposals. Where necessary the project manager worked with the schools to refine and amend the proposals so that they all met the agreed criteria of the project framework. It was a feature of the project that the right schools worked collaboratively when there were many other external forces driving them to compete.

Each school had appointed a project co-ordinator who would receive an honorarium for the duration of the project and who, in some cases, though not all, was included as a member of the school senior-management team in recognition of the importance of the initiative in the school. These co-ordinators, who met regularly, formed the third tier of management and were responsible for convening school-based working parties and for the day-to-day organization and administration of the project.

Funding Distribution

The funding allocated for the project covered the salary of the project manager and the salary enhancement of the co-ordinators. For the rest, the capital allocation was divided equally among the participating schools whatever the size, whilst the revenue allocation depended on the merit of the bid, the size of the school and the perceived level of need. Each school has received a single payment of £28,000 which was designated for capital costs and a roughly equivalent sum of revenue for the implementation of specific school initiatives.

The Nature of the Initiative

The SMAD initiative has a number of 'guiding principles', the most important of which is the view that it is appropriate to have high expectations of children and young people in inner cities. It was considered essential that all staff in schools be involved in, and committed to, the school's development and that they work together to create a learning community. Lessons need to be well-structured and challenging. They should make demands on children which consistently reflect high expectations in achievement and progress. They should be appropriate to the needs of the pupils and allow a high degree of engagement of the pupils in the learning process. The pupils should be encouraged to believe that schooling is worthwhile and they should be able to see a connection between learning and the outside world.

The school climate must be conducive to effective teaching and learning. This involves not only the physical environment but also the demeanour of those involved in the learning process. Good behaviour is seen as a necessary condition for effective learning and pupils, as well as teachers, must accept responsibility for their own behaviour and for regulating conduct in the school.

It was a central part of the SMAD philosophy that all plans had to be part of a school development plan and connected as much as possible with any previous initiatives such as TVEI. The following were the main features common to all schools.

Support for the Schools   Headteachers, co-ordinators, senior management teams, working parties and all the teachers concerned with the implementation of the SMAD initiative have had access to relevant INSET. This has included visits to observe good practice in other parts of the country, and additional support has been purchased from consultants with proven expertise in school effectiveness and school improvement, in particular from the London Institute for Education and from freelance consultants, as well as the universities of Cambridge and Nottingham. Support in monitoring the progress of the programme has been contributed by the officers of the LEA.

The Learning Environment   All the schools involved in the project were provided with resources to improve the learning environment and, consistent with the guiding principles, they all involved the whole school community, including the pupils, and in some cases parents, extensively in the planning of these improvements. Although the flexibility in the system allowed for individual schools to react to their own specific needs, thus enabling one school to provide lockers, another carpets, and a third a multi-cultural archive area, there was a degree of commonality in practice. It was deemed necessary to establish flexible learning centres in four schools (the others had developed them previously with TVEI money). As a result of the project, all the schools had pupils' study areas, refurbished toilet areas, extended capacity to display work and more attractive and welcoming entrance foyers.

As well as improving the physical environment, every school has sought to address the broader issues of school climate and, particularly, the management of behaviour. Here again it has been the practice to involve the young people as widely as possible in the process. The prospectus from one of the schools visited states that 'the whole school community has worked together to produce our behaviour policy'. It is intended that involving the pupils in this way encourages positive pupil–teacher relationships built on mutual support and trust. Seven out of the eight schools also made use of pupil attitudinal surveys, which were analysed by the Centre for Successful Schools at Keele University.

Curriculum Extension and Enrichment An important ingredient of the project has been the focus on curriculum development and enhancement. A proportion of the revenue funding in most of the schools has been used on the development of flexible-learning and differentiated-learning strategies which encourage the pupils to take greater responsibility and move toward becoming independent learners. Implicit in this development is the staff expertise to deliver a flexible-learning environment, which has meant the provision of staff training and time in which to prepare the ground.

A range of programmes and learning opportunities has been provided outside the normal school curriculum. Extension lessons in subject areas, particularly the core subjects, for support with reading or for the completion of homework have been made available after school for volunteers. Attendance at such classes seems to legitimize an ethos of achievement and mitigate, to some extent, the anti-learning culture in some sections of the peer group. Even more popular are enrichment classes, attended by pupils from all age groups, in a wide range of educational, social and recreational areas. A great deal of flexibility is possible in these classes and each school has tailored them to the needs of its pupils. In one school, for instance, the opportunities on offer include calligraphy, photography, a culture club, a mural club and a year-7 society. In another school there are classes for art, craft and drama, and a computer club.

Specific to year 11 in each of the schools have been revision centres and course-work clinics. Schools opened during the Easter holidays and in the October and February half-terms to give year-11 pupils – and in some cases lower year-groups – the opportunity to seek help with their course-work and examination-revision strategies. Staff support for this venture has been encouraging, and pupil attendance, monitored in one of the schools visited, indicated that over 75 per cent of year-11 pupils attended for at least one day and many came more often. Many of those least expected to attend arrived promptly and worked with enthusiasm.

Evaluation

The evaluation of the SMAD project is seen as complex because its introduction was not 'tied down to hard outcomes'. Within the broad framework of improved attainment and achievement, the money was spent on what the schools perceived as priorities for them. For the members of the LEA there was a large element of trust that the measures taken would yield the promised improvement. Constant feedback has been gathered by the project manager and a monitoring role was undertaken by the officers of the Authority but it was felt that in addition an 'outside check' was necessary and the project is therefore being evaluated by an independent educational consultant of national reputation.

Perceptions of Progress From the point of view of the senior management teams and the SMAD co-ordinators in some of the schools the project has been highly successful. In none of the schools has it been without impact. In some cases there was initial doubt about the intentions of the project: 'I rather thought it was yet another acronymed initiative saying that if you do what we want we will give you some money.' Some staff found it difficult to accept that somebody was actually giving money for them to be released from teaching in order to go and prepare things. But this suspicion has been dispelled, at least in the schools that were visited. 'Once that initial thing was over it has been seen very clearly as something which has been supporting the aims of the school. It's a school initiative based on school priorities which we have control over.'

The capital funding, which provided for environmental and structural improvements, has brought benefits to each school in a different way. The planning process involved all the members of the school community and generated a sense of community spirit. '. . . on the capital side everybody had a say in what was going on and people were really interested because, for the first time, you were going to put down on a piece of paper what you wanted and you knew that by September a good percentage of it was going to be there'. The improvements impacted on the quality of life in the school and thence on the pupil behaviour. The introduction of carpeting in one school, for instance, was an initial cause of concern to the cleaners but elicited the comment from one member of staff, 'I have been really surprised at what effect improving the environment has had on behaviour'.

Improved behaviour in this school has then been seen to produce benefits in the classroom: 'It's now a much calmer school. The learning environment is, therefore, a great deal better.' What was achieved in one school by carpets was achieved in another by supplying every pupil with a locker and in another by providing appropriate study areas.

There is a clear perception that the development of young people as autonomous and independent learners, with all that implies for flexible learning and the emphasis on curriculum enrichment and extension, is the most important determinant of the success of the project and, at the same time, the most difficult part to evaluate. 'That's really where the change in culture has got to start, it's actually getting the youngsters to recognise that they have a responsibility for their own learning . . . carpets look nice and are easy to see but the classroom is the crunch area. How do you actually check on what's going on?' The extent to which schools had taken advantage of development in these areas was expressed as 'patchy' between and within schools: '. . . some people are brilliant and enthusiastic, dying to try new things, and others are cynical.'

Revision centres and course-work clinics conducted during half-terms and the Easter holidays have been successful to the point of surprising many of the teachers involved. The sessions were '. . . wonderfully well attended, and the response from students you would have thought wouldn't have come within miles of the school during the half term was fantastic'. The only reservation expressed about the clinics was 'the very large investment of money in a single cohort of students'. There was a concern that, without additional funding, it would be difficult to envisage their continuing beyond the end of the project.

The SMAD project was held in high esteem within the schools visited. Although the staff questioned were at pains to point out that it was not a panacea, they were convinced that 'areas of the schools are going to flourish as a result of the project'. '. . . We are going to have part of the budget to keep the momentum going' and . . . 'we are at that stage where we don't give money unless it's seen as something we need to do'.

The perception of the CEO and the project manager is that SMAD has evoked 'a variety of levels of interest and commitment'. In some schools it has been a virtually unqualified success, in others the level of development, in terms of internal structure and philosophy, has made it difficult for the school to take full advantage of the situation. In these schools the environmental improvements have made an important difference but the scale of difficulty has been such that SMAD has been unable to add significantly to the ethos and they find it hard to use the help effectively.

The fact that the senior management of the schools want the Authority to continue to act as a catalyst for the project and are prepared to commit funds from their delegated budget for that purpose is seen as testimony to the overall success of the project. Another powerful performance-indicator is that the CEO intends that the lessons learned from the project will be 'mainstreamed' across the Authority. SMAD is not the only influence which is pushing schools in Hammersmith and Fulham in the direction of looking at their own effectiveness. Many external influences are now driving schools in the same direction, but SMAD has built up a certain momentum and it is the general view that its ethos and philosophy will remain. Those most closely concerned with its progress see SMAD as 'money well spent'.

CASE STUDY 3: NOTTINGHAM CITY

Outline

Nottinghamshire LEA received GEST funding under the inner-city education heading for the two years 1992–3 and 1993–4. The total funding for its inner-city project was £310,000 in the first year and £315,000 in the second. Of this about £70,000 per annum was devoted to the Reading Recovery scheme. The remainder of the funding was shared between nine inner-city primary schools in Nottingham, which were selected from a large number of bids from primary schools in the city.

When the GEST grant ceased in 1994, the LEA was able to build on the initiative through City Challenge. Under that programme the LEA is due to receive £600,000 over three years for an area which includes ten primary schools and three secondary schools. Five of the ten primary schools were also involved in the GEST-funded project and will therefore ultimately have been involved for five years in urban school-improvement initiatives.

The evidence of both an evaluation completed in December 1993 by the County's Advisory and Inspection Service and pupil progress records suggests that the project has been notably successful. The City Challenge scheme has only just begun and it is therefore too early to comment on its impact.

Origins

The origins of the GEST-funded project lay in the LEA's determination to raise standards in the City of Nottingham. The LEA was aware that the city had a number of distinctive educational challenges resulting from typical inner-city social problems such as high levels of unemployment, homelessness, crime and family breakdown. The educational consequences of these social circumstances include low levels of expectation, high pupil turnover and high levels of a variety of special educational needs. In addition the City of Nottingham has a significant proportion of people from minority ethnic communities and children whose home language is not English.

The LEA's performance-monitoring at secondary level revealed under-achievement in much of Nottingham City. Unlike many, the LEA took the view that a serious strategy to improve urban education ought to prioritize primary education. It believed the additional funding under GEST attached to a carefully prepared strategy would be able to bring significant progress if it was concentrated in a relatively small number of primary schools. The strategy focused, under the GEST scheme's rules, on junior education. The success of the LEA's bid enabled the project to begin in April 1992.

The Nature of the GEST-Funded Project

The project was overseen by a steering group which included senior education officers, advisers, two headteachers from among the nine primary schools and the project manager. The project manager was seconded part-time to the post from his post as headteacher at one of the nine schools at the recommendation of all the heads involved.

Co-ordination and implementation of the project was the responsibility of the project manager and seconded deputy heads in each of the schools. Participants considered the role of the deputy heads to have been a decisive factor in the project's success. In each case the deputy was relieved of all class-teaching duties by an additional experienced teacher and took responsibility for project implementation at school level. The additional flexibility in staffing that this provided in each school was vital. It meant the project was a consistently high priority. It allowed the deputy to relieve other staff of their teaching responsibilities as and when required without recourse to supply teachers. It was therefore the key to greatly enhanced professional development.

In a previous LEA-funded professional development project schools had made their own decision over whom to second. The lesson of that had been that teachers without management responsibilities had not had the clout either at project level or at school level to ensure successful implementation. The seconded deputy role, by contrast, was considered to have been tremendously successful. The combination of the overall project manager and the seconded deputy role ensured effective implementation of the improvement strategy.

Each of the nine schools implemented programmes, or modules as they called them, under the three headings:

- recovering achievement
- behaviour management
- home/school partnership

However, the schools had a high degree of flexibility over precisely what they did under each of the headings. The project funding meant that each school received an additional £25,000 for each of the two years. At the margin, on LMS budgets of £400,000 or so this provided significant opportunities for development.

It was also the case in a number of the schools that it was enhanced through LMS budget underspends, which had arisen in some schools partly as a result of the transitional element in Nottingham's LMS formula. The combination of the two sources of funding provided the possibility for genuine transformation.

Some examples of developments under each of the three headings are now looked at in turn.

(i) Recovering Achievement The most significant feature under this heading was what the schools described as target grouping. All the participants we spoke to in the project schools were powerful advocates of target grouping. Unlike traditional setting or streaming, target grouping was only used for part of the school week and in the case of at least one school only for part of each school year. There appeared to be two main features of it. The most common was for a year group to be split into ability groupings in the National Curriculum core subjects for a part of the school week. Headteachers claimed that this had beneficial effects in allowing a better match of teaching to the pupils' capabilities without the detrimental effects of traditional setting and streaming. The evidence of pupil outcomes, the careful measurement of which was a striking feature of the project, appeared to confirm their case.

The second aspect of target grouping was the targeting of specific groups chosen on the basis of evidence of noticeable underachievement. For example some schools had targeted Moslem girls as a group in science, a subject in which they appeared to be underperforming. In these cases the target group were taught for a particular period in the week in a relatively small group. The success of target grouping depended on the flexible use of staff, including in some cases non-teaching staff, and on careful monitoring of pupil outcomes.

The schools involved in the project believed that in addition to improving outcomes, they had improved the quality of teaching, raised teacher morale and promoted much more intellectually challenging teaching and learning. The schools had decided collectively that the next step was to look at pedagogy within the target grouping sessions. They were keen in particular to draw on the 'School Matters' evidence (Mortimore *et al.*, 1988) that showed that directive teaching of whole classes and specific groups within classes is an important and effective strategy in certain circumstances. They believed they were advancing from the traditional Plowdenesque primary philosophy to a new and powerful mix of informal and more directive approaches.

Indeed, the headteachers we spoke to in the project schools believed that target grouping was affecting their educational philosophy as a whole. They recognized that they were challenging the prevailing primary orthodoxy in Nottinghamshire and believed they were setting a new agenda for high achievement in urban areas. The evidence we saw suggests that they have a powerful case.

Underpinning the whole approach to teaching and learning was a much greater emphasis on the monitoring of pupil outcomes than is the case in many inner-city primary schools. Standard tests were used regularly in English and Maths and discussed among the staff. The information yielded affected decisions about teaching, the curriculum, grouping of pupils and the development of staff. The hidden message conveyed to all staff was that pupil performance and understanding the progress of individual children and specific groups of children were of the highest priority. In science, where the schools had not found a test which met their needs, the school's science co-ordinators had set about designing their own test. In the schools we saw, the use of information technology also appeared to be effectively integrated into teaching and learning.

Overall, on the basis of the evidence we saw, it seemed that the schools involved in the Nottingham GEST scheme had made major advances in primary practice. Their emphasis on target-grouping, directive teaching and performance monitoring appeared not to be at the expense of the benefits of traditional primary practice. For example, in all the schools we visited classroom displays were outstanding and pupils were encouraged to take initiative and to manage their own learning either as individuals or in groups. One was tempted to conclude, 'I have seen the future and it works'.

(ii) Behaviour Management Under this heading the schools had implemented a wide variety of changes. Each of the schools we visited had carefully constructed rewards systems which rewarded both individuals and classes for good behaviour and attendance. In one school, particularly good work resulted in the class being given another piece in a large jigsaw on the wall. Once it was completed, they had an afternoon where they, as a class, chose what to do. In another school, each week the year group with the best record of behaviour in the playground had an additional day's entitlement to use of the astroturf pitch at break times.

Each class in each of the schools we visited also had a classroom charter of eight or ten rules for classroom behaviour. These had been negotiated between teacher and children and thus varied from class to class, though not surprisingly the main themes were very similar. There were also 'charters' for the public spaces such as the corridors and playgrounds.

The schools recognized that both rewards systems and charters needed to be kept under review. They were conscious of the danger of them becoming 'part of the furniture' and thus losing their impact. They also believed that the process of arriving at the charters was as important as the existence of them.

The behaviour-management programmes had also led to changes in the use and management of play time. In one of the schools the seconded deputy, who had taken special responsibility for behaviour policy, saw lunch time as his busiest time. There the playground had three zones, one with various pieces of play apparatus and another with tables and chairs for sitting quietly. For children who chose the latter option, crayons, paper and games were provided. The third zone was a traditional play area for football (enjoyed by girls and boys) and other such activities. Different years took turns to have first use of each zone.

Another school had invested in much better playground furniture and equipment. Consistency among all staff was considered to be an important aim. As a result not only teaching staff but also lunch-time supervisors had been trained to play their role in managing behaviour more effectively. Overall the schools placed great emphasis on behaviour management, believing it to be a pre-condition of successful teaching and learning.

(iii) Home/School Partnership We saw less evidence of progress in this area, partly because the evidence is less tangible. Perhaps the most striking feature was the production by the schools of videos aimed to encourage learning in the home. Paired reading has also featured in the project. The videos had been produced in more than one language. The evaluation reports from the LEA's advisory service states that 'this was an imaginative approach that has already proved successful as a means of motivating pupils'. Overall the home–school partnership strand has contributed positively and successfully to the development of improved links with parents.

CONCLUSIONS

The concentration of funding and careful planning had ensured that the project had made a significant impact in the schools. There was clear evidence of marked improvement in pupil outcomes across the nine schools as a result of the project. Various strategies were in hand to disseminate some of the lessons that had been learned. The schools had held an 'open day' for other primary teachers in the LEA and over 500 had taken advantage of the opportunity. The LEA had evaluated the project, enabling the advisory team both to comment on and learn from experience in the schools. The CEO is considering making further use of the project's lessons. In addition to the City Challenge-funded project which has just begun, the authority plans a value-added development at primary level which would build on the project's experience and Nottinghamshire's well-know work on value added at secondary level.

REFERENCE

Mortimore, P., Sammons, P., Stoll, L., Lewis, D. and Ecob, R. (1988) *School Matters*. Wells: Open Books.

PART TWO

Policy into Practice

Chapter 6

The Role of Partnerships and Networking in School Improvement[1]

Louise Stoll

INTRODUCTION

The role of school becomes heightened in a society where there is considerable concern about the incidence of violence, the influence of the media, changing family structures, and changes in employment practices which raise the critical issues of structural unemployment and strategies to address its impact. Many of these issues are especially challenging in the inner city, and schools in such areas face particular difficulties. Currently, league tables of schools' results take no account of background factors related to deprivation that are known to be associated with children's achievement and development in school (Goldstein, 1992; Thomas and Mortimore, 1994). Support from parents, shown to be a key characteristic of a school's effectiveness (Mortimore et al., 1988; Fullan, 1991; McGaw et al., 1992), is often much more difficult to achieve in situations where there is a preponderance of families in which single parents or both parents work, there is a poor understanding of the English language in the home, or there is an intergenerational tradition of a lack of involvement in children's schools and schooling. Furthermore, increasingly, many of these schools find themselves taking on roles that would normally be served by other agencies. Indeed, there are those who believe that, given the constraints with which many schools have to work, they can do little to redress the balance.

Research, however, shows that individual schools can make a substantial difference to the lives of their pupils by promoting greater achievement, progress and social development. Most importantly, the research demonstrates that the effectiveness of a school is not determined simply by the quality of the pupil intake to the school. Schools receiving socially disadvantaged pupils can be very effective just as, sometimes, those with advantaged pupils can fail to develop their potential fully.

The findings of research studies in Britain and throughout the world have given us considerable understanding of what makes a school effective. For example, characteristics of more successful schools include teachers' high expectations of pupils, a variety of teaching and learning techniques, regular feedback from teachers to pupils, pupils' involvement in their own learning, positive relationships between teachers and pupils, parental involvement and support, and teachers who collaborate and reflect on their practice. Practical studies of school-improvement efforts have also enlightened us as to the processes successful schools go through on their route to becoming more effective. These include all constituent groups – the headteacher, teachers, pupils and parents – sharing a common vision, clear goals, teacher empowerment and development, a focus on teaching and learning, and the promotion of schools as learning communities. Leadership plays a critical role in the development of such a culture.

School-improvement literature is also replete with examples of the importance of external support to successful school change (Rosenholtz, 1989; Coleman and LaRocque, 1990; Louis and Miles, 1990; Baker *et al.*, 1991; Fullan, 1991; Comer, 1992; Glickman *et al.*, 1992; Dalin, 1993; Hopkins *et al.*, 1994; Stoll and Fink, 1994). Local Management of Schools (LMS) in Britain and similar trends in many other countries towards decentralization and greater autonomy for schools, therefore, raise serious questions for school improvement. Support provision has traditionally been very much the domain of local education authorities (LEAs). LMS, however, has not only led to a reduction of LEA control, but also to diminution of support and resources.

There are strong arguments that the school cannot 'go it alone' and specifically needs connections with outside agencies. Michael Fullan views the seeking of outside help as a sign of a school's vitality: 'It is the organizations that act self-sufficient that are going nowhere' (Fullan, 1993, p. 86). Essentially, the school should neither see itself, nor be viewed, as an island. It needs to be the centre, rather than the unit, of change (Sirotnik, 1987), and its success depends to a significant extent on its interactions with its environment (Dalin, 1993).

Over the years, many schools have built productive relationships with a variety of partners, including parents, governing bodies, their LEA, local community members, social services agencies, psychological services, businesses and industry. Schools have also engaged in a range of partnerships with higher-education institutions related to initial and ongoing teacher development (Rudduck, 1991; Hake, 1993; Allsop, 1994). The Learning Consortium in Canada, a partnership between four school districts, the University of Toronto Faculty of Education and the Ontario Institute for Studies in Education, has focused on a variety of initiatives that link classroom, teacher and whole-school development (Watson and Fullan, 1992). Watson and Fullan conclude that strong partnerships are not accidental, neither do they arise purely through good will or *ad hoc* projects. They require new structures, activities and the rethinking of the way each institution operates as well as how they might work as part of a network. LEAs, for example, severely affected by the reduction in their powers, have had to carve for themselves new roles that emphasize not only leadership but also their willingness and ability to work with schools and other partners (Audit Commission, 1989). Some have been more successful than others.

From the school's perspective, the decentralization thrust of LMS has been more than balanced by an increase in central control and accountability in terms of a National Curriculum and associated assessments, monitoring by external inspection and publication of league tables of raw academic results, truancy and attendance. Changes have occurred frequently and have been very time-consuming to master, leaving, many would argue, reduced time and energy for ongoing attention to the process of teaching and learning, greater stress and less spontaneity (Pollard *et al.*, 1994). For headteachers, LMS has had further ramifications in its push for them to focus on issues of financial management rather than educational leadership.

A recent surge of school-based interest in school improvement has developed, to a large extent, as a response to the changes that have faced schools since the 1988 Education Act. As schools have begun to surface from underneath these and many other externally-imposed changes, they have realized that they still have an important agenda of their own. This agenda focuses on empowerment rather than control, self-accountability, and the use of the most effective teaching and learning strategies. Interestingly, the incentives for increased competition between schools have largely been resisted in favour of networking and clustering opportunities, as schools have searched for ways to increase collaboration between colleagues within school and beyond with other partners, all towards the goal of improved effectiveness.

In this chapter, I will examine how, through partnerships and networks, one higher-education institution is working with schools in a variety of ways to investigate, implement and evaluate the most effective learning, teaching and organizational development practices, and to support them in developing their internal capacity for managing and taking charge of change. I shall discuss the rationale that underpins this work, look at its aims and core activities and give some examples of partnerships and networking that offer schools a variety of types of support. Finally, I shall raise issues for consideration by those who work in such partnerships.

INTERNATIONAL SCHOOL EFFECTIVENESS AND IMPROVEMENT CENTRE (ISEIC)

During the period of all of the changes in Britain, school-effectiveness researchers have continued to search for factors correlated with pupil progress, development and achievement in different contexts; more sophisticated measures to demonstrate the value added by schools; and answers to questions of consistency and stability of school effects and differential effectiveness. Separately, school-improvement researchers have analyzed the processes that lead to improvement. In the last couple of years, these two groups of researchers have started to move together in their thinking and have realized that they have a considerable amount to offer to each other (Reynolds *et al.*, 1993; MacBeath and Mortimore, 1994; Stoll, in press). This is none too soon for practitioners in search of support for improvement efforts.

At the Institute of Education at the University of London, we have established an International School Effectiveness and Improvement Centre (ISEIC). Our aim is to draw on, extend and link the two bodies of knowledge in order to support schools in systematic programmes that:

- improve the quality of teaching and learning;
- improve pupils' academic performance, attendance, self-image and attitudes towards continuing education and training;
- ensure progress for pupils of all backgrounds;
- develop improved educational indicators;
- promote the concept of lifelong learning within schools for adults as well as children;
- develop the internal capacity of schools for managing change and evaluating its impact;
- encourage effective working relationships within schools; and
- enhance relationships between schools and their partners – pupils, parents, governing bodies, local education authorities, the business community and higher education.

We work to achieve this by engaging in four activities: developmental work, research, teaching and dissemination.

Developmental Work

A major function of the ISEIC is developmental work with schools engaged in effectiveness and improvement projects. Activities include:

- **action research** with individual schools, groups of schools, and local education authorities to develop the appropriate culture to support and evaluate their school-improvement activities. Schools are aided and studied as they investigate and implement the most effective teaching and learning strategies in order to raise pupil attainment, achievement and morale (Stoll, in press);
- **development of a team of Associates** around the country who provide consultancy support to schools engaged in improvement efforts;
- **support for school self-evaluation** through access to relevant information about pupils' achievement and development. ISEIC helps schools to examine their results from a 'value-added' perspective, so that they can determine the extent of pupils' progress from one year to the next (Thomas and Mortimore, 1994);
- **different programmes of school improvement** are designed. Successful work from other countries, notably the United States and Canada, has been adapted for English schools;
- **a nationwide School Improvement Network** brings together people engaged in school improvement to share ideas and further refine improvement strategies. Network members also receive

listings of people involved in school improvement, newsletters, and summaries of research findings (Hillman and Stoll, 1994); and

- **support material** is being identified and developed, and a resources centre for school effectiveness and improvement will be established and located within the Institute's library.

Work is also commencing on development programmes specifically oriented towards the roles of a variety of partners in the school-improvement process, for example school governors.

Research

A vital function of ISEIC is to continue to expand the knowledge base about school effectiveness and the challenge of school improvement. In this work we also attempt to collaborate with a variety of partners that include other higher-education institutions, LEA personnel, educational consultants, and government agencies. A range of current and recent research projects include:

- **exploration of differential school effectiveness** to establish whether it is possible to talk in terms of whole-school effectiveness or whether and why some secondary-school departments are more effective than others (Sammons *et al.*, 1994a; Thomas *et al.*, 1994);

- **a study of the stability** of primary school effects over time (Sammons *et al.*, 1993);

- **examination of processes** which foster a wider range of outcomes, including pupil satisfaction, than have been investigated to date;

- **study of schools engaged in improvement activities** in the areas of school-development planning, developing a 'moving school' culture, and teaching and learning, and the impact of outside interventions on such efforts (MacBeath and Mortimore, 1994);

- **exploration of appropriate models to establish the value added** by schools to be incorporated into the school inspection process (Sammons *et al.*, 1994b); and

- **exploration of the most effective methods of school development planning** (MacGilchrist *et al.*, 1994; Mortimore *et al.*, in press).

Teaching

Through a combination of existing and newly established courses, educators at all stages of the profession are able to participate in a wide variety of pre-service and in-service courses related to school effectiveness and improvement, a specifically designed masters course in school effectiveness and school improvement, research degrees, and accredited diploma courses for teachers involved in school-improvement projects.

Dissemination

An important function of networking is dissemination. ISEIC uses national and international conferences, public lecturers, workshops, books, articles and brief summaries of key research studies and their findings to disseminate our own and other colleagues' research and development findings.

In the remainder of this chapter I will focus in more detail on two of the practical development strategies in which we are engaged to assist schools in improving themselves: the 'school improvement network' and one of our partnership action projects.

SCHOOL IMPROVEMENT NETWORK

The School Improvement Network (SIN) was established to provide a forum in which people with a variety of interests and backgrounds could meet to share and discuss experiences, debate issues of mutual concern and solve common problems. At the initial meeting in October 1993, an evaluation form asked participants what they felt the key priorities of such a network ought to be. Responses suggested that they sought support through meetings, contacts and partnerships, access to information and the latest research findings, consultancy and training, and a voice that would contribute to the national education debate. Specifically, of 66 respondents to this open-ended question, three-quarters (73 per cent) were interested in the sharing of good practice, successes and failures; just under a third (30 per cent) wanted in-depth discussions of issues, to 'tease out' the principles of good practice, and to critique and analyze ideas; a quarter (24 per cent) desired a written information exchange; and a similar number (23 per cent) requested that results of national and international research studies be shared.

From this and other feedback, we further developed the School Improvement Network (SIN). Currently, SIN membership includes:

- **three full-day meetings each year**, two of them at the Institute and one elsewhere in Britain, co-hosted by a member-LEA or another partner. At these meetings, keynote speakers share recent research findings, raise key issues and pose questions for small-group discussion. Participants also attend workshops run by educators involved in school-improvement efforts. Members are encouraged, where possible, to attend with a colleague, with the purpose that discussion and joint reflection between peers should lead to issues being followed up after the meetings. These meetings have been attended by teachers, middle and senior managers in schools, LEA personnel, representatives from teaching unions; parents', governors' and other organizations; government agencies; higher-education staff; and private consultants. Over 200 people attended in July 1994. All three meetings held thus far have also been rated as useful by more than 90 per cent of the participants. Each subsequent meeting is also adapted as necessary, on the basis of evaluation feedback.

- **School Improvement Network News (SINN)**, a regular newsletter which describes projects and initiatives around the country, focuses on key research findings, suggests improvement ideas and useful books and articles, and highlights relevant events. Members are also invited to submit brief reports or notices;

- **Research Matters**, a bulletin that summarizes the research on specific aspects of school improvement and raises questions with the purpose of inviting readers to reflect on and discuss the issues. One LEA, for example, has sent out the first bulletin, 'Understanding School Improvement' (Hillman and Stoll, 1994), to all of its schools as part of a school-improvement initiative;

- **a database list** of all members that includes specific improvement interests and contact locations.

By October 1994, one year after our first meeting, nearly 200 schools or individuals, 15 LEAs, and several clusters of schools had joined the network. From feedback, it appears to us that such a network enables educators to combat isolation and realize that others share their concerns, and promotes deeper thinking about teaching, learning and organizational issues.

SIN participants have also been asked in what ways they think higher education can support school improvement. Responses indicate that educators look to higher education to 'feed in' research findings in an accessible form; to help them make the links between theory and practice; to offer staff development, act as facilitators, and provide an impartial outside view as 'critical friends' (Costa and Kallick, 1993); and to offer expertise in the areas of data collection and analysis, monitoring and evaluation of school improvement and school effectiveness. ISEIC's partnership action projects provide opportunities for Institute of Education staff members to engage in such work.

PARTNERSHIP ACTION PROJECTS

Increasingly, schools and LEAs have started to work with partners in higher education institutions on improvement projects in the action research mode (for example, Hopkins *et al.*, 1994; Ribbins and Burridge, 1994). As a consequence of interest in school-effectiveness research findings, as well as those from school-improvement studies, others are beginning to mesh the two (for example, Stoll and Fink, 1992; 1994). No two approaches are identical, nor are the schools and LEAs that are involved, and therefore no blueprint for improvement can be offered. Nonetheless, the partners involved from schools, LEAs and higher education continue to try to identify the strategies that lead to improvement and promote pupil progress, development and achievement.

I will focus on one example of such a project, within an urban London borough, the Lewisham School Improvement Project. It involves the Institute of Education as one partner.

Lewisham School Improvement Project

Background and Origins Lewisham LEA in south London serves a diverse population, socially and ethnically. The north of the borough is characterized by areas of high deprivation, where unemployment levels are well above the national average. The south, in contrast, contains areas of middle-class, professional home owners as well as large council estates. There are 92 schools, of which 69 are primary, 13 secondary, seven special and two nursery.

Local management was introduced in Lewisham's schools in April 1992. The Institute of Education had already worked with the LEA, headteachers and deputies in the previous 22 months to help schools prepare for new and extended management responsibilities. All the system's schools were required and supported to develop school-management plans within a common LEA planning framework.[2]

In summer 1992, in further centrally-provided training, Institute and LEA staff revisited the school-management planning process. While schools and the LEA were seen to have introduced Local Management successfully there was widespread recognition of the need to address the key school-effectiveness questions, 'Has it (LMS) made a difference?' and 'How do we, or could we, know?'.

A group of Lewisham headteachers and advisers attended the Institute of Education's 'School Improvement: the Search for Quality' conference in October 1992. From this they identified the value of a planned and systematic approach to school improvement and the idea of a three-way partnership (higher education, LEA, and schools) exemplified by the programme within the Halton Board of Education, a member of Ontario's Learning Consortium (Stoll and Fink, 1992). Consequently, Lewisham LEA approached the International School Effectiveness and Improvement Centre (ISEIC) at the Institute and two of its associate directors worked with LEA personnel and headteacher representatives to develop a coherent programme for school improvement.

Aims The project, which commenced in the spring of 1993, has four aims:

- to enhance pupils progress, achievement and development;
- to develop the internal capacity of schools for managing change and evaluating its impact at whole-school level, classroom level and pupil level;
- to develop the capacity of the LEA to provide data to schools that will strengthen their ability to plan and evaluate change;
- to integrate the above with the system's ongoing in-service and support services to form a coherent approach to professional development.[3]

Strategies At all stages and in all components of the project, schools and individual teachers have volunteered to take part. The project has four main components:

1 *'Leaders Together' in-service*   Headteachers and deputies from about half the LEA's 92 primary, secondary and special schools have attended a five-day series of workshops at which Institute staff have helped them to explore concepts of school effectiveness and school improvement and introduced them to the research base. The workshops have sought to enable school leaders to monitor and evaluate more vigorously the educational effectiveness of changes taking place in their schools, and develop coherent school-improvement programmes that address the issues of school culture, teaching and learning, the management of change, and staff development. Participants have worked in pairs to solve school-based problems during and between sessions, and networking opportunities between schools have been encouraged.

Reactions to this programme have been positive. In response to a follow-up evaluation, heads and deputies have described more involvement of staff in the school-management planning process, developments in teacher observations, greater clarity in objectives and in approaches to change, a sense of understanding about key school-improvement issues, more constructive collaboration between heads and deputies, and an increased focus on 'learning': 'Debate on the teacher as learner has been opened.'

2 *Pilot schools*   On the basis of individual school bids, ten of these schools have formed a group of pilot schools. 'Ground rules' for participation in this part of the project have been based on findings of school-effectiveness and improvement research, and include:

- a focus on achievement in its broadest sense, emphasizing teaching and learning;
- a manageable focus linked to the school's management plan;
- shared leadership and teacher ownership;
- representative teams co-ordinating the project in their school;
- the role of teams as facilitators of change;
- management of the project to rest with the school;
- systematic monitoring and evaluation;
- support from the LEA and Institute; and
- agreement to disseminate findings to colleagues throughout the school system.

Each school selected a cross-role team of three to six teachers and administrators who have also been introduced to school-effectiveness and school-improvement research findings and assisted in preparing for a change-agent role within their schools. Each team has developed their own school focus for development and improvement. Evaluations of the four-day in-service demonstrate that participants believed that their learning had been enhanced in a variety of ways:

'. . . in terms of thinking, reflecting, opening my eyes to possibilities which I felt had been closed off.'

'It has made me read more, think more and have the confidence to relate information gained to and with others.'

'I am more prepared to speak, listen and become involved.'

The particular improvement foci determined by individual schools include developing structured group work as a means of improving individuals' achievement; raising achievement in non-fiction writing, the under-achievement of black boys, reading and specific curriculum areas. Strategies incorporated developing and trying out new teaching and assessment techniques, teachers observing each other, the use of teacher diaries, open meetings, invitations to external 'critical friends' to provide feedback, student surveys, integration of school-improvement plans into the school-management plan, and in-service sessions run by school-improvement teams for staff members.

The initial set of pilot-school progress reports in April 1994 recorded that involvement in the project has had a positive impact on morale and has led to improved communication, reflected in more effective staff meetings, a greater focus on teaching and learning, and increased reflection.

In one primary school with a focus on raising achievement in non-fiction writing, teachers keep journals in which they record thoughts about the teaching and learning of non-fiction writing in their classes. Colleagues read each other's journals and respond to them. They also respond to others teachers' entries in their own journals. Through this process they seek, give and receive ideas and advice, and reflect on the writing process. Several strategies that teachers consider make a difference to writing achievement have been identified, and in a progress report the deputy head has noted that staff have become more analytical about considering the success of a teaching strategy for groups of pupils rather than globally for the class.

Attitude-to-writing surveys have been completed by all pupils, as have writing samples, which have been analysed by staff using National Curriculum attainment-target criteria broken down into component strands. Comparison of writing samples from one year to the next will occur, and within year groups movement up levels of attainment in other subjects will be compared with writing progress to see if the improvement in writing has been greater than improvement in other areas of the curriculum.

The deputy head has described her school's progress in terms of Joyce's (1991) doors to school improvement. Of the doors related to access to research findings and school-specific data, she wrote:

Staff are reading more widely than previously, discussing literature and applying what they have read to their own teaching . . . . Staff are now very in tune with the idea of using a computerised database to analyse pupil achievement . . . a school-wide computerised record-keeping system will give individual teachers the capacity to analyse their classes' achievement and can give all curriculum co-ordinators more information to analyse success and areas of concern.

3 *Indicators development* A voluntary group of 15 teachers, headteachers, LEA advisers and officers have been working to identify and develop LEA and whole-school indicators of change, development and achievement. Against the background of the introduction of the Special Educational Needs Code of Practice, the group has chosen to concentrate on pupils with special needs. They are developing indicators which will be available to the LEA's schools when evaluating their effectiveness in respect of individual pupils' progress, whole-school systems and value for money.

4 *Dissemination* There is a programme of dissemination within and beyond the LEA that includes feedback at headteachers' and deputy heads' conferences, special school cluster meetings, the Institute of Education's School Improvement Network meetings, and research conferences, nationally and internationally. More significant has been wider involvement of staff in pilot schools. In two secondary schools the original teams of six have expanded and now involve over 20 teachers. In the special school the whole staff (teaching and non-teaching) have taken part in in-service led by the school team, and every teacher has chosen to have their work accredited through the Institute. In the five pilot primary schools, the teams have led in-service or structured their staff development around school-improvement themes.

Beyond the ten pilot schools, many heads and deputies have planned staff-development programmes on the basis of the school-effectiveness/school-improvement agenda and in some cases have been able to involve their governing bodies. The LEA is also committed to an Investors In People programme for central staff whose main role is support for schools. Through this programme it has been possible to engage these staff in a consideration of school-effectiveness and school-improvement issues.

Monitoring and Evaluation The evaluation of change has been at the heart of the project from its outset, and the question 'Has it made a difference?' is a recurring theme. The intention is for the project itself to exemplify appropriate evaluation procedures and to demonstrate effectiveness as well as encouraging and supporting schools to evaluate their own effectiveness. ISEIC staff have worked with LEA and school staff to develop and support evaluation strategies.

The LEA collects borough-wide data that includes examination results, attendance and truancy, exclusions and staff-absence data. Secondary schools have been provided with base-line data, analysed by gender and ethnicity on a school and borough-wide basis, which can assist them in evaluating their own effectiveness. The available data will also enable evaluation of the project's effectiveness in the pilot secondary schools against borough averages, against other matched schools and longitudinally.

At present, however, the capacity for monitoring and evaluating effectiveness in primary schools is limited and pilot primary schools are being assisted to develop appropriate indicators. An alternative approach is also required in the pilot special school. Its intake varies significantly from year to year, both in numbers and relative levels of achievement and disability of individual pupils, who enter in small cohorts. For this reason, evaluation will occur through tracking of individual pupils' progress.

The Halton Effective Schools teacher survey (Stoll, 1992) has been adapted for completion by staff in all pilot schools and in a group of matched schools. This will be repeated within the next two years. The schools themselves also provide regular progress reports, addressing issues relating to success criteria, base-line data and progress to date.

Interviews are being carried out in the ten schools and with key members of the LEA, including the Director. LEA Link Advisers are also completing questionnaires on their perspective of progress in individual schools with which they are involved.

Improvement Themes   Although this project is still in progress, some improvement themes have already emerged. Many of these tend to confirm the findings of other improvement studies. In particular, the process of initiation and implementation of such a project appears to be smoother when:

- the focus for improvement is core to the school. In most cases this translates itself as a focus on a specific target of the school's development plan, although other research demonstrates that what is written in a plan does not always get off the paper (Stoll and Fink, 1994; MacGilchrist *et al.*, 1994). Within the framework of this project, schools were encouraged to relate their improvement project to the ongoing work as set out in their management plan;

- there is an emphasis on classroom practice. Teachers derive meaning from their work in the classroom and thus have a natural commitment to classroom processes over school processes (Fullan and Hargreaves, 1992). In this project, whilst much of the in-service was targeted towards organizational and cultural understandings and strategies to support teachers throughout the change process, this was not the central focus;

- there is leadership within the team or small group co-ordinating the project within the school. This leadership can rotate, but what seems to be important in the presence of one person who takes on the role of active initiator and momentum builder. Sometimes, this person has been a member of the school's Senior Management Team (SMT), although this has not always been the case, In the successful schools, however, there has always been support from the SMT;

- other staff beyond the small team have become involved early on in the process. This has depended on the ability of the school-improvement team to communicate, spread ideas, seek feedback and engender the interest and commitment of other colleagues. In some schools this had been achieved through the establishment of larger working parties or committees. Other schools, in contrast, have used more informal means. All staff are already involved in some small schools;

- **the headteacher is committed** and empathetic to the project. All heads in this project have elected to participate and have been involved in in-service. Nonetheless, a few have found it difficult to relinquish control of decision-making. Where heads have taken an active interest and have supported the project team, implementation has proceeded much more smoothly and effectively.

This project is ongoing and therefore it is not possible to determine its long-term impact. Already, however, senior officers visiting schools report that agendas have changed from financial management and problems to the central issues of teaching and learning, and school-management planning has strengthened, with many schools beginning to engage in the process of 'corporate' planning (MacGilchrist *et al.*, 1994).

Challenging Issues As we work with the schools through the School Improve-ment Network and our action projects and try to understand the factors that lead to improvement and effectiveness, we face various challenging issues:

- **The 'non-volunteers'.** School involvement in networks and action projects is usually voluntary and, particularly in the case of the latter, often requires a commitment of time and resources on behalf of the school, with limited LEA capacity for resources to be offered as an incentive. There remain, therefore, schools that do not choose to be involved, some of whom may be least aware and most in need of such support and stimulation. The challenges are how to raise awareness of and engage interest in and commitment to school effectiveness and improvement.

- **Accountability versus empowerment.** Glickman (1990) talks of twin pillars of accountability and empowerment. When schools have embarked on improvement efforts they appear to have a better understanding of the need for an importance of collecting base-line data against which they can measure increased effectiveness. Certainly, schools involved in our action projects now use more data in their planning and are beginning, if they were not already doing so, to address issues of differential effectiveness. There is clearly, however, a tension between encouraging school ownership of improvement while persuading schools of the importance of assessment and evaluation processes they may not fully understand as being essential to self-evaluation and accountability.

- **The means–end dilemma and the complexity of evaluation.** A related issue is that whilst it is often difficult to measure the outcomes of school improvement initiatives, it is vital to keep them in mind. We have observed that some schools, albeit with the best of intentions, become 'bogged down' in the improvement process for its own sake. This has been borne out in our research (Stoll, 1992; Mortimore *et al.*, in press). We find it necessary to remind schools frequently that they should develop appropriate success criteria that they monitor on an ongoing basis and evaluate.

- **School improvement as a 'bolt on'.** The advantages of action 'projects' include the bringing together of people with the same focus; support and status; limited extra resources, and the Hawthorne effect. By describing such programmes as 'projects', however, there is a possibility that schools see their involvement as a bolt-on activity rather than informing and being fully integrated within the school development or management process. Where the project is linked to centrally-provided funding there is a danger of it having a finite life span and thus becoming an event rather than a process (Fullan, 1991). While the School Improvement Network offers alternative 'doors' into school improvement, occasional attendance at meetings could also easily become events unless they become part of a bigger picture that is focused on continuous improvement. This points to the importance of strategies that will help schools maintain and build on the process.

- **Concurrent external agendas.** At the same time that the schools are involved in specific school-improvement endeavours, they also have to maintain their focus on all of their other work commitments, respond to various external directives, for example changes in curricula, and devote time to national assessment procedures. Advanced knowledge of, preparation for and, sometimes, the aftermath of OFSTED inspections has already proved to have a strong impact on schools engaged in improvement projects (Stoll *et al.*, 1994). The immediate reaction to schools' receiving notification of an inspection often is that all efforts must be devoted to preparing for it and that nothing else can be considered until it is over. Indeed, we have observed 'development paralysis' in some schools, often for many months. This reaction has obvious implications for short-term improvement projects.

- **Will one size fit all?** For schools that face particular difficulties or for educators that 'find themselves working in historically ineffective settings' (Reynolds *et al.*, 1993) or 'stuck' schools (Rosenholtz, 1989), it is necessary to consider whether the sort of support that is usually provided within the scope of improvement projects helps such a school sufficiently that it will be able to set its own priorities for change, take ownership of the change process, and focus on teaching and learning. Other facets of the school's culture may need attention before people will feel able to participate in such a project. These include clarification of rules regarding pupil behaviour, the physical environment, communication, collaboration and recognition (Stoll, 1992). This seems to be an earlier stage of improvement that some schools appear to need to go through before they can concentrate on the real agenda. In other words, it is necessary to take care of the roots or there is little chance that branches will grow (Hargreaves and Hopkins, 1991). Unquestionably, this is one of the greatest challenges for school improvers, to identify the support processes necessary to help move a 'stuck' school.

CONCLUSION

There is no one route to school improvement. Each school has its own unique context and culture. Some schools, particularly many of those in urban areas, may work within a context that presents considerable challenges in terms of school improvement. We have plenty of research evidence, however, that demonstrates the difference individual schools can make to the lives of their pupils. We also know that educators in schools benefit from collaboration, partnerships and networking with colleagues outside. At the International School Effectiveness and Improvement Centre various models of partnership and networking have been developed. These are under constant refinement as we endeavour to find the most effective ways to support schools in the provision of the best possible learning opportunities for pupils and adults alike.

NOTES

1 With thanks to Kate Myers and John Harrington for their contribution to an earlier paper in which some of these ideas were first discussed.
2 Lewisham LEA adopted the title 'school management plan' (rather than 'development plan') to emphasize the need to maintain and sustain as well as develop.
3 The project mirrors and has informed the parallel evolution of the borough's Quality Assurance and Development Team (QAD) which has moved from an inspectorate to service role in which members work in partnership with schools and other local-authority services to provide school-improvement strategies, assisted school self-review, and professional, management and curriculum development.

REFERENCES

Allsop, T. (1994) 'The Language of Partnership', in M. Wilkin and D. Sankey (eds) *Collaboration and Transition in Initial Teacher Training*. London: Kogan Page.
Audit Commission (1989) *Losing an Empire, Finding a Role: The LEA of the Future*. Occasional Paper 10. London: HMSO.
Baker, P., Curtis, D. and Benenson, W. (1991) *Collaborative Opportunities to Build Better Schools*. Illinois: Illinois Association for Supervision and Curriculum Development.

Barth, R. (1990) *Improving Schools From Within*. San Francisco: Jossey Bass.

Coleman, P. and LaRocque, L. (1990) *Struggling to be 'Good Enough': Administrative Practices and School District Ethos*. Lewes: Falmer Press.

Comer, J. (1992) *A Brief History and Summary of the School Development Program*. New Haven, unpublished paper.

Costa, A.L. and Kallick, B. (1993) 'Through the lens of a critical friend', *Educational Leadership*, 51(2), 49–51.

Dalin, P. (1993) *Changing the School Culture*. London: Cassell.

Fullan, M. (1991) *The New Meaning of Educational Change*. New York: Teachers College Press.

Fullan, M. (1993) *Change Forces: Probing the Depths of Educational Reform*. London: Falmer Press.

Fullan, M. and Hargreaves, A. (1992) *What's Worth Fighting For in Your School?* Buckingham: Open University Press.

Glickman, C.D. (1990) 'Open accountability for the '90s: between the pillars', *Educational Leadership*, 47(7), 38–42.

Glickman, C., Allen, L. and Lunsford, B. (1992) *Facilitation of Internal Change: The League of Professional Schools*. Paper presented at the annual meeting of the American Educational Research Association, San Francisco.

Goldstein, H. (1992) 'Editorial: statistical information and the measurement of education outcomes', *Journal of the Royal Statistical Society A*, 155(3), 313–315.

Hake, C. (1993) *Partnership in Initial Teacher Training: Talk and Chalk*. The London File Papers from the Institute of Education. London: Tufnell Press.

Hargreaves, D.H. and Hopkins, D. (1991) *The Empowered School*. London: Cassell.

Hillman, J. and Stoll, L. (1994) 'Understanding school improvement', *Research Matters*, No. 1. London: Institute of Education.

Hopkins, D., Ainscow, M. and West, M. (1994) *School Improvement in an Era of Change*. London: Cassell.

Joyce, B.R. (1991) 'The doors to school improvement', *Educational Leadership*, 48(8), 59–62.

Lewisham Education (1993) *QAD – Quality Assurance and Development Team: The Nature of Service*. Unpublished paper. Lewisham Education.

Louis, K.S. and Miles, M.B. (1990) *Improving the Urban High School: What Works and Why*. New York: Teachers College Press.

MacBeath, J. and Mortimore, P. (1994) *Improving School Effectiveness: Research and Intervention in Scottish Schools*. Paper presented to the Annual Conference of the British Educational Research Association, Oxford.

MacGilchrist, B., Savage, J., Mortimore, P. and Beresford, C. (1994) 'Making a difference', *Managing Schools Today*, 3(9), 7–8.

McGaw, B., Piper, K., Banks, D. and Evans, B. (1992) *Making Schools More Effective*. Victoria: Australian Council for Educational Research.

Mortimore, P., Sammons, P., Stoll, L., Lewis, D. and Ecob, R. (1988) *School Matters: The Junior Years*. Wells: Open Books (reprinted in 1993 by Paul Chapman).

Mortimore, P., MacGilchrist, B., Savage, J. and Beresford, C. (in press) *School Development Planning Matters*. London: Paul Chapman.

Pollard, A., Broadfoot, P., Croll, P., Osborn, M. and Abbot, D. (1994) *Changing English Primary Schools?: The Impact of the Education Reform Act at Key Stage One*. London: Cassell.

Reynolds, D., Hopkins, D. and Stoll, L. (1993) 'Linking school effectiveness knowledge and school improvement practice: towards a synergy', *School Effectiveness and School Improvement*, 4(1), 37–58.

Ribbins, P. and Burridge, E. (1994) *Improving Education: Promoting Quality in Schools.* London: Cassell.

Rosenholtz, S. (1989) *Teachers' Workplace: The Social Organization of Schools.* New York: Longman.

Rudduck, J. (1991) 'Universities in Partnership with Schools and School Systems: Les Liaisons Dangereuses?', in M. Fullan and A. Hargreaves (eds) *Teacher Development and Educational Change.* Lewes: Falmer Press.

Sammons, P., Nuttall, D. and Cuttance, P. (1993) 'Differential school effectiveness: results from a reanalysis of the Inner London Education Authority's Junior School Project data', *British Education Research Journal*, 19(4), 381–405.

Sammons, P., Thomas, S., Mortimore, P., Cairns, R. and Bausor, J. (1994a) 'Understanding the Processes of School and Departmental Effectiveness'. Paper presented to the annual conference of the British Educational Research Association, Oxford.

Sammons, P., Thomas, S., Mortimore, P., Owen, C., Pennell, H. and Hillman, J. (1994b) *Assessing School Effectiveness: Developing Measures to Put School Performance in Context.* London: Institute of Education and Office for Standards in Education.

Sirotnik, K.A. (1987) *The School as the Center of Change* (Occasional Paper No. 5). Seattle, WA: Center for Educational Renewal.

Stoll, L. (1992) *Making Schools Matter: Linking School Effectiveness and School Improvement in a Canadian School District.* Unpublished doctoral dissertation.

Stoll, L. (in press) 'Linking School effectiveness and School Improvement: Issues and Possibilities'. In D. Reynolds, J. Gray, C. Fitz-Gibbon and D. Jesson (eds) *Merging Traditions: The Future of School Effectiveness and School Improvement.* London: Cassell.

Stoll, L. and Fink, D. (1992) 'Effecting school change: the Halton approach', *School Effectiveness and School Improvement*, 3(1), 19–41.

Stoll, L. and Fink, D. (1994) 'Views from the field: linking school effectiveness and school improvement', *School Effectiveness and School Improvement*, 5(2), 149–177.

Stoll, L., Myers, K. and Harrington, J. (1994) *Linking School Effectiveness and School Improvement Through Action Projects.* Paper presented to the annual conference of the British Educational Research Association, Oxford.

Thomas, S. and Mortimore, P. (1994) *Report on Value Added Analysis of 1993 GCSE Examination Results in Lancashire.* Unpublished report, London: Institute of Education.

Thomas, S., Sammons, P. and Mortimore, P. (1994) *Stability in Secondary Schools' Effects on Students' GCSE Outcomes.* Paper presented to the annual conference of the British Educational Research Association, Oxford.

Watson, N. and Fullan, M. (1992) 'Beyond School District-University Partnerships', in M. Fullan and A. Hargreaves (eds) *Teacher Development and Educational Change.* Lewes: Falmer Press.

Chapter 7

Urban Deserts or Fine Cities?[1]

Tim Brighouse

Unless we start in the classroom and the school there is no hope for our cities and our society. It is there, not in city hall, still less Whitehall, that the keys to the most intractable problems of our own and our future generations lie. What are those problems? What are those keys?

First and foremost the problems are in what generally we used to call the 'inner-cities', but what we have now re-named the 'city'. Or perhaps, as I hear a councillor's voice saying 'Do not forget the outer-ring estates' and another voice saying 'and sometimes there are pockets of poverty and hopelessness in other places, even the most salubrious neighbourhood like the one I represent', we should simply call it 'urban' education.

The remembered councillors' voices – a tribute to the value of local democracy – provide a sharp reminder not to generalize. What constitutes the urban problem? Words like 'poverty', 'unemployment', 'crime', 'vandalism', 'under-achievement', immediately come to mind; as do phrases such as 'socioeconomic disadvantage', 'low aspirations', 'low staying-on-rates', 'parental neglect' and 'parents with no experience of higher education', but they are at the macro level. In the schools you will sometimes hear in the staffroom 'what more can you expect from children with backgrounds like these? and you will despair. No longer in the home, however, will you hear the claim 'I have had a word with the gaffer on the line and there is a job for you at 16 in the local works, so just keep your head down and your nose clean for another year or so'. It is here in the home and in the classroom, and in the inter-play between the two, that the key to unlock this problem lies.

Let us turn to the classroom first. Too often HMI, backed by researchers, have summarized the issue as one of teacher expectations which they have seen as consistently too low. It is more complicated than that. Professor Michael Barber's matrix (Figure 7.1) reveals it as the interface between expectation and self-esteem.

Most of us can find the words to put into box B since there is a strong correlation between high pupil self-esteem and low teacher expectation in the leafier suburbs where home support is strong and where the skills of autonomous learning are learned early. 'Complacency' is the word I would use for Box B and it is a running sore but not a fatal wound. It is a suburban issue.

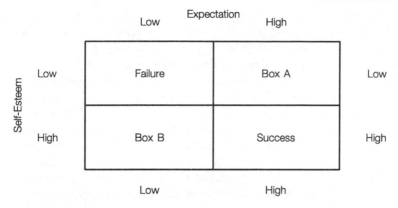

Figure 7.1. *The Barber matrix*

It is in Box A, however, that the trickier and more intractable puzzle lies. Where the learner has low self-esteem and the teachers' expectations are too high, 'despair, anger, frustration, demoralization' set in. It is my contention that there are very high quantities of that in the inner-city and outer-ring estate schools. Remembering my councillor friend's voice, I accept that even in relatively affluent areas there are pockets of this, but of course they lie amongst a peer-group culture which is more likely to include an underlying and more explicit quest for achievement. Nor am I advancing the proposition that it is a condition exclusively experienced by children from backgrounds suffering deprivation or poverty. I am simply claiming that there is a high correlation between the two. Moreover, for those teaching in a school where there are large numbers of such children – perhaps now it is safe to forget the words of the second councillor and say in the inner-city or the outer-ring estate – it is more difficult to shift the value system attached to self-esteem towards learning and to raise expectations.

There are two more complications for the teachers in this situation. First, as the age of the pupil changes so does the challenge. At three, four and five they will not have heard the 3,000 to 4,000 stories which the educated middle class have told their children. Small wonder that children deprived of such a head start in life often have speech difficulties and a poverty of language which, without the most skilful professional intervention, can persist. At ten, eleven, twelve and thirteen these already disadvantaged children are into adolescence – no longer children and not yet sure what sort of adults they will become. They are surrounded by a commercial culture, by drugs, drink, crime and despair. The bravado of the developmental stage camouflages the lack of self-esteem. So, at the different ages in the different communities there are different challenges. Secondly, the values of the most vociferous homes – although they are not a majority – are stridently anti-educational. From despair and poverty they sometimes cry words to the effect that 'It's your job to teach them not mine. I don't even like the child, I don't care about the school. It didn't do me no good.'

Here in the home parental involvement in education has been the subject of a cruel trick. Instead of being encouraged to share a proper partnership with

119

teachers as joint educators, parents have been sold a choice which poverty precludes them from exercising, and a sharing of power in the government of schools for which their own lack of education ill prepares them.

I shall return both to the detail of the classroom and the home and to a map from which we can navigate towards a solution to these issues later in this chapter. Firstly, however, the historical context requires some exploration.

It is not as though there was a golden age as far as urban education is concerned. What has changed is the context in which education happens. In the great Victorian city, creations of grime and smoke, the schools were close to the factories. However mean the streets, the back-to-back housing contained families where the father earned a modest wage, but just sufficient to let him hope that the next generation might do better. And at least the daily drudgery provided gainful and secure employment for his three score years and ten. His wife might extend his wages with piece work in the factory or the home. Their children's education should be as Robert Lowe, the architect of the first national curriculum and the first period of payment by results had determined, 'just sufficient to give them that sense of awe for higher education which the leaders of our nation demand'. The grammar schools in such cities provided a thin vein of hope to those few of exceptional general intelligence. Hence the misplaced reverence – misplaced because their clientele is now so different – for the great grammar schools of Birmingham, Manchester, Leeds, Sheffield and Bradford.

Nowadays the permanent modest unskilled jobs have gone. Your neighbour speaks a different language and worships another God. Your mind is far away with images of elsewhere – hill villages in a warmer climate for some, suburban tree-lined comfort for others. Or you are old and on a vandalized grey concrete damp estate remembering street parties as you cower nervously at the first sounds from the approaching shouts of the local gang, desperately hoping that they are off to the 'hotters' display of stolen cars and that they will not pause to vandalize your home.

At the macro and strategic level it is not too difficult to analyse the causes of these phenomena. First, there is a chronic and acute shortage of permanent jobs for the unskilled and semi-skilled, especially for those for whom strength and motor skill are important; secondly, there is economic migration from the south to the continents of the north. Thirdly, we are attempting to live in a multi-faith, multi-ethnic and multi-cultural society where democratic traditions are hard won. If our aim is health, harmony and wealth within a continuing democratic frame-work – and that seems a reasonable agenda – we also need a clear strategy for action. And yet there is no strategy, simply a set of gestures.

Through City Challenge, Urban Aid, Inner-City Partnerships, the European Social Fund, the European Regional Development Programmes, the Single Regeneration Budget and City Pride, those who view the cities from afar fling money at the problem in time-limited dollops – the equivalent of food parcels to the Third World. At the very moment when local government should have had its purse strings loosened and its discretion increased within a broad and agreed strategy for the city, the reverse happens. Nanny state knows best. And between the 1981 Census and the 1991 Census we see the appalling consequences on every side, whether of poverty, homelessness, crime, unemployment or decay. The great cities have become worse.

To reverse that trend requires local, not national decisions, and the involvement as participants as far as possible of those affected. The communities themselves have to be empowered to find their own solutions if our cities are to be regenerated. A sense of powerlessness is the enemy of democracy.

Within this framework of local involvement there are three strands to the regeneration. They are:

- sharing what employment there is more equitably;
- extending the infrastructure to the rebuilding and refurbishment of all public buildings and linking higher-education research programmes to a focus for regional employment and economic regeneration;
- transforming the education system in a hike of standards of educational performance.

I shall deal with the first two briefly – they connect with the third, which is the main focus of this chapter.

SHARING EMPLOYMENT

So far as jobs are concerned, all of us in the personal services, whether in health, care or education, need to examine the balance of the professional and the para-professional jobs in favour of the latter. With Michael Barber I wrote a pamphlet, which was the beginning of a plea for a long overdue re-thinking of the future of the teaching profession. To do that properly, however, as we argued, you have to examine first the potential and unrealized role of classroom assistants (or teaching assistants as we call them) and occasional visiting experts (or teaching associates as we name them). The role of such permanent and extra staff in the classroom will offer more employment prospects for those who live locally and whose inter-personal skills are an example of what Howard Gardner would call the area of personal intelligences. They will need training, which is why the former Secretary of State for Education, John Patten's initiatives for their training alongside teachers should be not resisted but widely welcomed.

If we could shift out thinking (as indeed we have in the pre-five field) towards adult/child rather than teacher/pupil ratios, we would be making significant progress – not least in the issue of creating a more equitable share of employment, as well of course as in re-thinking and up-skilling the role of the teacher towards defining what in pedagogical terms the teacher brings which others cannot. It is not too fanciful to say that the school of the 21st century ought to have adult/child ratios, which incorporate the teaching assistant and the teacher, of 1 to 7 or 8, but maybe teacher/pupil ratios of 1 to 22 or 23.

The same argument of course applies in other parts of the education service – for example in the work of educational psychologists, the education social workers and the youth service, but also in other fields such as health and social services.

EXTENDING INFRASTRUCTURE

As for the infrastructure, no longer should pure and applied research be the subject of at best scorn and at worst neglect. There should now be a government drive to ensure that research strengths within certain departments of universities in our older industrial areas – for example, Birmingham, Glasgow, Leeds, Liverpool, Manchester, Sheffield, Belfast, Nottingham and Leicester – are encouraged and supported within a regional economic development plan and a strategy designed to ensure that major industries expand in those areas. To do this would be to link our brain power and pre-eminence in research with the future social well-being of areas where there is the greatest need for employment. There is no sign of our country seeking to attract in any coordinated way the best combination of pure and applied research and business interests in order to solve regional and especially city problems. Secondly, there needs to be a costed plan to bring up to standard all the schools – and other public buildings – to the highest standards. 'Surround them with things which that are noble' echoes the mocking voice of a Victorian educator. The block to realizing this goal is entirely of the Treasury's making. Great public works, especially at a time of high chronic structural unemployment, are surely to the benefit of every one. It is, however, on the transformation of the education system and standards of educational achievement that this chapter concentrates. It is intended to be at the practical rather than theoretical level, emphasising teaching, learning and parental involvement. Inevitably, I shall refer to Birmingham because it is the city I know best. It has all the ingredients of urban decline. First and foremost there is poverty – half the Birmingham population lives on or below the poverty line. Unemployment is high – 47 per cent of the male population in some areas: the prospects for employment in unskilled and semi-skilled jobs at the best are in temporary or short supply and therefore, offer no long-term security, however modest the rewards.

In 1992, in the first Greenwich Lecture, Peter Mortimore outlined eight practical strategies for improving urban education. He advocated the separation of pre- and post-16, the rationalization of the academic year, the abolition of GCSE, an extension of primary education to age twelve, the introduction of structured learning programmes and enhanced programmes for under-fives. The following year, Gillian Pugh explored, in detail, policies for the pre-fives.

School-improvement strategies, together with a coherent language and musically rich set of provisions for youngsters from birth through to five, seem to me essential and wholly practical and realizable policies for the part-resolution of our urban education problems. Either without the other would be frustratingly unsuccessful. In Birmingham we have set our sights on both.

RAISING STANDARDS

The detail of each is important, for we believe that in small detail and the particular, great enterprises can wax or wane. The attempt here is to offer some broad brush strokes on a larger canvas. Suffice it to say that the picture includes a determination to set up a coherent forum at local level for provisions from birth to age two involving preschool workers, health visitors, housing advice agencies and voluntary agencies. We shall set targets for the number of nursery rhymes, jingles and stories which children should hear by their fourth birthday. We aim to hold out our hands to the voluntary and statutory sectors to join in an unbreakable partnership and guarantee to secure care and education provisions in social settings for three, four and five-year-olds which will be distinguished by their quality and will give those youngsters the best possible start to life.

Concerning school improvement, we have charted seven crucial processes – leadership, management and organization, creating an environment fit for learning, staff development, collective review, teaching and learning and parental involvement – by which we shall map individual actions in an endeavour to improve against previous best. Fundamental indeed from classroom to LEA is this principle of competition based on 'previous best'. We call it 'ipsative' rather than 'normative' competition. It is the principle on which we disagree with the government. It contradicts the market-place. It ways to OFSTED 'Don't always compare quality of lessons and learning with national or LEA norms. All that does is reinforce complacency among those above the norm and despair among those below. Moreover, it regresses to the mean!' Far better that everybody competes, if they must compete, to improve at a faster rate against their previous best. In the school-improvement programme we have already established circles of primary heads according to their length of time in post, a factor which, of course, widely affects the rate of school-improvement. These networks or circles are committed to improving against previous best. We have set up a secondary network of support for the same goals and are about to discuss with special-school heads their contribution towards helping all their children realize their right to as normal an experience of schooling as possible. So they will be invited to set targets for integration.

To keep our shoulders to the wheel we are to establish three forms of guarantee, one for the early years, another covering the secondary years, but at the centre – as the key piece of the jigsaw – a 'primary guarantee'. It will have targets of input, school experience and outcomes.

The three targets of input include a commitment to real increases in resources for the primary sector over three to five years. It is a commitment made in the knowledge of the implications for other parts of the budget, but meets OFSTED recommendations in 'Access and Achievement in Urban Education'. It should be an example for national policy. A second target of input covers 'guarantees' of service to the schools from the education social workers, educational psychologists, advisers and other services. Never again shall we leave schools to manage as best they can because a member of staff has left post or fallen sick. Finally, a target promises schools timely expert outside support when appropriate. School improvement is uneven and the guarantee acknowledges that, by offering support at the moment it is needed in the particular circumstances of the school.

The targets of experience and outcome seek to shift the National Curriculum simply by city-wide emphasis. For example, we think residential experiences can act as catalysts for learning for many children; they can also transform teacher/pupil relationships. So a residential experience is suggested as a guaranteed offer as part of the primary guarantee. Similarly the expressive arts provide for some youngsters the vital springboard for confidence and success which they transfer to other learning. Unsurprisingly, therefore, we propose simply to guarantee in a Birmingham primary school to tell parents what their child is good at in the expressive arts in the penultimate years (when there is still time to do something about it) of the infant and junior years. There is one other environmental-education experience affecting scientific thinking and citizenship, but the rest is unapologetically concerned with language and numeracy. Each school will themselves set targets – low, middle and upper targets – for improvements against previous best for each successive year-group for standards achieved at age seven and eleven in literacy and numeracy. The literacy targets are placed within 'guaranteed' experiences for each youngster of public performance and writing for an audience.

That is the guarantee – a simple document which by emphasising a few things, attempts to change the climate of a city to support the efforts of its schools and in due course the expectations the nation should have of this vital sector of education. Similar guarantees will be worked up for the Early Years before five and the Secondary sector.

To reinforce the centrality of language and numeracy we are discussing the establishment of Commissions, analogous to the great reports of the Central Advisory Committees of the past and the more recent reports on particular topics at a national level – on the issues of literacy and numeracy. There are plenty of enthusiasts at the leading edge of these activities within Birmingham and as the largest urban authority in the country we see it as our duty to fund reports designed to give pointers for future direction and expanding success for teachers whose achievements we ought to be celebrating rather than denigrating.

TEACHING AND LEARNING FOR THE FUTURE

Nobody should underestimate the exhaustion of teachers arising from the very real national mismanagement of the teaching profession these past six years. To read the editorials of newspapers during this period is to see a modern-day version of the Emperor's clothes. The pre-Dearing version of the National Curriculum was lauded to the skies by *The Times*, the *Independent*, the *Guardian*, the *Telegraph* and the *TES*, during 1988, 1989, 1990 and even 1991. How different it is now. About the only doubting voice that could be heard consistently, because of its humour, was on the back page of *The Times Educational Supplement*. Those of us who chose exile because we did not wish to be Cassandras, Catos, or Jeremiahs, welcome the change of tune, but a bit of self-criticism on the part of others would not come amiss. It is after all the case (since the introduction of the National Curriculum and the crazy insistence within the LMS formula of average rather than real teachers' salary costs) that we have lost about 40,000 teachers to early retirement at a cost to the nation over ten years of upwards of two billion pounds from the public exchequer in extra pension costs. Thank goodness for the recession, which held teachers in the profession. Let us now capitalize on that benefit by turning the spotlight on the crucial importance of teachers.

The debate in the next few years must be about successful teaching and learning within successful urban schools in that order. The teaching and learning first, the successful schools second. Unless the focus is precise we shall fail just as all previous attempts at school improvement have failed at least at the macro level of the system. Any analysis of those false starts reveals the centrality of there being a focus on teaching and learning.

Michael Barber's matrix (Figure 7.1) sets the scene for two tasks, one relatively straightforward and the other more difficult and, as he would say, part of the unknown universe of teaching. The former is to speculate about the ways in which children's self-esteem can be raised within the value systems we wish for our society. After all it is quite possible for someone to have high self-esteem but within an alien or anti-social value system – for example in the shadowy world of crime, drugs, or of commercialism where self-interest is raised to a level where it overrides and sacrifices the interests of the community. The second, however, concerns the skill of the teacher in always edging upwards the expectation of the learner. Some people call it pitch – that subtle ability to match exactly the materials and the challenge to the learner's need – to let them see that what is apparently out of reach can suddenly be brought within their grasp. Others approach it by discussing more loosely the very precise art of differentiation.

I believe we can take this debate on by reviewing the nature of teaching and learning at its cutting edge. As a teacher I was never very good at that bit of teaching. Oh, I could do the crowd control bit; I learned and practised more and more about classroom management, about behavioural management – how to start lessons, plan lessons, organize materials and so on. And I understood that I was a different role model for all the children in my class and a different role model to the *same* child sometimes at different times of his/her life. I wished too that I had been better at doing two, three or four things at once because I understood that the essential basic skill of a teacher involves being able to do more than one thing simultaneously. Nevertheless, I mastered the craft of the classroom, but I was adrift in its art and its science.

It seems to me there are three basic elements to teaching and I have tried to set them out diagrammatically in what I would call the golden cracker of teaching (Figure 7.2).

There are three parts to the cracker. The first involves the teacher getting to know the child, the second involves the child practising skills, doing exercises, being occupied in consolidation of learning, and the third is what I have called the

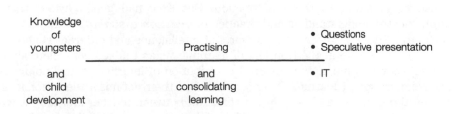

Figure 7.2. *The golden cracker of teaching*

alchemists' stone – the teacher's skill in intervening to stretch the pupil's learning. Let us consider each end of this cracker. The first, as I have said, is getting to know the youngsters. You would think that would go without saying. Almost universally it is the case that when there is a 'colleague' for whom the rest of the staff have no regard, it is because that colleague is ungenerous and uninterested in children. A glass for that teacher is always half empty, never half full.

Much time is taken up in getting to know more and more about the children we teach – their likes, their dislikes, their families, their friends, their hopes and ambitions, their strengths, their weaknesses and their preferred learning styles. For make no mistake about it, we all have different ways of learning.

It is one end of the golden cracker: for most of us it is our meat and drink, an ever-changing kaleidoscope. It is a much richer soap opera of interest than any we watch on television. Within it is the vital connection to the other end of the cracker. To mark the learner's mind we need to know its intricacies, its preferred learning style, its different sorts of intelligence – motor, linguistic, spatial, musical, logical, scientific, personal. We need to know that the pupil's mind stands ready to do a deal with the other end of the cracker – the teacher's extraordinary skill as an alchemist to the mind in the amazing capacity to transform mental slavery into freedom. At this end of that cracker lies the golden cusp of the teacher's skill, her ability to open the mind. It is that part about which we talk so little.

It was brought home to me forcibly in a Birmingham school one day. It shall stand proxy for one of the many excellent schools in the city. Indeed, I have described it as one lively vessel among a flotilla of richly different craft which constitute a fleet determined to weather the storms of urban schooling and navigate to the calmer waters where self-esteem and expectation are brought into harmony. The teachers do it daily. They know about the preferred learning styles of the youngsters they teach.

This particular school forced its excellence to my attention during an hour-long visit. It was their questioning which was outstanding: each and every teacher was engaged in intensive, subtle, sensitive, but insistent questioning and speculation among the groups of children I visited. They knew more about questioning than I shall ever know. I envy the children in that school: there is no easy ride for any of them, of course. There is simply the promise of the priceless confidence which comes from endlessly surprising themselves in what they can do and understand.

These teachers had examined together some of the four key elements of questioning and intended to collect evidence on practice. I refer of course to the issues of *pause*, and of the *balance* of memory to non-memory questions – to those of fact and to those of opinion. But they had gone beyond that to a sophisticated understanding and practice of *question distribution* and an analysis of *types of questions* for different sorts of intelligence and different stages of self-esteem. They were at the frontiers of learning. When I talked with them about the issues, they told me of the powerful contribution of information technology to the next generation of learning. I confess I shared their optimism there, for it is easy to see the qualitative change in conversation between teacher and taught when it is focused on a third party, especially when, in the case of IT, that third party has almost an inter-active intelligence of its own. 'You see, it is not very clever. It has only been programmed to react to our putting it in without a pause' is an example we all understand from our initial IT training.

So we debated into the twilight in the Birmingham school the other end of the cracker. We talked of how the teacher's presentation, whether at whole-school assembly or whole class, can be full of ambiguity and challenge at different levels. We called it 'speculative presentation'. We talked of the studied inconsistency of the teacher when dismissing a class, using even the criteria which might enable different tables to depart from the room as an opportunity for opening the mind. We agreed there is a taxonomy to be made about this. Included in that taxonomy is the potent potential (as yet uncharted, literally part of the unknown universe) of IT, more revolutionary in its potential contribution to learning than the book since it touches all different types of intelligence, including literacy.

The teachers in this inner-city school were as excited as others in an outer-ring equivalent. Together the teachers in these schools have found what they called the golden cusp of teaching. At one end of the cracker they had brain-stormed the understanding of children, their preferred learning styles, their subtle differences in states of self-esteem, and at the other the golden cusp of pedagogy. In between, the everyday occupation of the children, the crowd control, the necessary practice of skills and understanding, the 'times-tables', the work-sheets, the rites and rituals of school life. While that happens, as they enthusiastically explained to me, the tension between the one end of the cracker and the other continues to shower us all with the sparks of true learning – the sudden and indescribable moments when children grow before our eyes.

We were all agreed – these teachers and I – that what we really were creating in Birmingham from the classroom was an education agenda quite consciously different from the national one. We have a strategy and at the heart of it is a debate about teaching and learning which will run and run.

From these teachers' confidence in their teaching comes a willingness to involve parents as joint educators. Everywhere the notice 'no parents beyond this point' may have been physically removed: but in some places they are still in the minds of some teachers and of many parents.

So for these teachers there is excited talk of 'family homeworks', 'community story-telling for extended reading skills' – and a range of practical measures which makes parental involvement a reality rather than rhetoric. There is the challenge for the LEA also to lead that aspect of parental involvement and we intend to rise to that challenge through the 'Guarantees', pre-school workers, newsletters and educational tasks for summer-holiday parent/child activity, expertly designed to counter the annual setback to children's learning which accompanies the long summer holiday.

From this axis of teachers being at the forefront of their profession and parental involvement we can be confident that this time in Birmingham we have an agenda for pre-five reforms and school improvement which will work. Birmingham has similar challenges as hundreds of cities in other parts of Europe and the United States. Scattered all around within these communities, however, there are the ingredients of hope. They are the schools.

Birmingham is fortunate: there is one common factor of agreement and determination. We are going to capitalize on our teachers and the hopes of all our parents for the next generation. Together we are applying the lessons of research and we are backed by formidable political will. The pride of the City, which was the cradle of local government and municipalization, does not admit any outcome other than a certainty that we shall succeed.

NOTE

1 Adapted from the Greenwich Lecture, May 1994. 'Urban deserts or fine cities? – education, the alchemists' stone.'

Chapter 8

Collaboration for School Improvement: The Power of Partnership

Michael Barber and Michael Johnson

The 1970s and 1980s have seen a steady decline in the fortunes of the British economy which has led to considerable change in the country's educational needs and priorities. The closure of long-standing heavy industries and the weakening of the manufacturing base has meant that unskilled and semi-skilled employment no longer offers job security. Education and training have become a prerequisite for employment, and those without education and training face an uncertain future.

Nowhere is the need for change more acute than in the inner cities, where there has been no tradition of continuity in education beyond the statutory leaving age. The educational potential of the pupil population has not changed, but the structural stability of the communities and families from which the schools draw their populations has weakened. There are diminishing employment prospects. Young people who would have left school in the past to take jobs in local industries and business find that such jobs have disappeared. They need to understand the changes taking place in their communities and be aware of the need to acquire the appropriate skills for contributing to the society in which they will live in the twenty-first century.

Underachievement and low expectation have long been endemic to the inner cities. Some local education authorities became increasingly conscious of the need to raise both expectations and the skill level of the workforce. In Stoke-on-Trent in 1989 the question that concerned Philip Hunter, Staffordshire's Chief Education Officer, was how the problem could best be addressed. Was it within the capability of the education system to do something about the fact that in some schools less than 20 per cent of the population stayed on in school beyond sixteen and less than 3 per cent went on into higher education? At the same time, Tim Brighouse, the newly appointed Professor of Education at Keele University, was contemplating how the most recent research in school effectiveness and school improvement could best be put to use for the benefit of young people in the local context.

It is hard to remember that until late in the 1970s many people, in the United Kingdom at least, accepted the given wisdom that schools could not much change life-chances and that 'heredity' or the influences of 'society' would be the predominant determinant of children's behaviour, aspirations and attainment. With the publication of Michael Rutter's *Fifteen Thousand Hours* in 1979, however, views began to change. The research findings of Rutter and his colleagues not only indicated that schools did make a difference to pupils' attainment but also pointed to particular strategies by means of which schools could improve.

> Schools do indeed have an important impact on children's development and it does matter which school a child attends. Moreover, the results provide strong indications of what are the particular features of school organisation and functioning which make for success (Rutter, 1979).

Rutter's findings ushered in a decade of research into school effectiveness and school improvement. Peter Mortimore, Barbara Tizzard, John Gray, David Reynolds, Tim Brighouse, Sally Tomlinson, David Hopkins, Peter Holly and many others in this country and North America have built on the work of Rutter to reach broad areas of agreement about ways in which schools can materially change the achievement and attainment of their pupils.

Towards the end of 1989, discussions between Tim Brighouse and Philip Hunter, the CEO of Staffordshire, explored the possibility of a collaborative initiative in secondary education in the northern part of Stoke-on-Trent. The intention was to bring together an education partnership comprising the local education authority, local universities and colleges, the careers service, the local business community and the Training and Enterprise Council to support a pilot project which would seek to promote, in three secondary schools, the processes identified in the research findings as important for raising achievement. Funding for the project was sought successfully from the Staffordshire TEC and The Paul Hamlyn Foundation.

The research identifies a number of characteristics which are associated with successful schools. The achievement of quality in teaching and learning is about purposeful leadership at all levels within the school and the creation of a school climate and environment conducive to learning. It involves extending and enriching the school curriculum. It demands teacher commitment, good pupil/teacher relationships and raising the level of expectation the teacher has of the pupil. It requires a school to review and reflect on its own performance and re-create itself as a community where teaching and learning are seen by all the pupils as legitimate activities and the principal purpose of the school. It means involving parents as partners in their children's education. In *The Quality of Schooling: Frameworks for Judgement* (1990), Gray suggests that 'As a rule schools which do the kinds of things the research suggests make a difference, tend to get better results (however the measures are assessed)'. Brighouse (1993) cautions us, in *The Potteries: Continuity and Change in a Staffordshire Conurbation*, that 'Research on school effectiveness tells everyone all the characteristics evident in successful schools. What research does not reveal as obviously is how a school can become a place where those characteristics appear'. It was to try to apply these theories that the Two Towns Project was born.

ORIGINS OF THE TWO TOWNS PROJECT

The purpose of the Two Towns Project was, therefore, to raise ambitions, expectations and achievement in Burslem and Tunstall, two of the constituent towns of Stoke-on-Trent. The discussions initiated in late 1989 by Tim Brighouse continued through the spring of 1990 and the project was officially launched at a meeting at Haywood High School in September of that year.

Tim Brighouse and Philip Hunter believed that a collaborative school-based initiative would affect for the better the educational culture of the whole community. The three county high schools, Brownhills, Haywood and James Brindley, which serve the towns of Burslem and Tunstall were at the heart of the project. The idea was to implement an initial five-year programme of measures to bring educational success to these city schools. This would be followed by a period of re-definition of goals and the dissemination of practice throughout the county. The goal for teachers was 'to ensure that their pupils do not adopt fixed views of their own abilities but, rather, come to realise that they have considerable potential which, given motivation and good teaching in an effective school, can be realised' (Mortimore *et al.*, 1988). The strategy was to harness the energies of teachers, pupils and parents of the three schools to improving attitudes and performance and for their efforts to be supported by the LEA, post-16 colleges, the careers service and local universities, with funding from the Paul Hamlyn Foundation and the Staffordshire Training and Enterprise Council.

Co-ordination of the project was, and continues to be, provided by a steering group chaired by Philip Hunter. This group includes representatives of all participants, with administration provided by the project co-ordinator at Keele. Its role is to determine policy and monitor the progress of the project. A second tier of management, the 'project group', also serviced by the co-ordinator at Keele University, includes representatives of schools, colleges, careers service, universities and the Staffordshire TEC, and is responsible for implementing the decisions of the steering group.

Against a background of comparative failure, where, in 1988, no more than 19 per cent of the school population stayed on in education beyond sixteen and less than 5 per cent reached higher education, the steering group set targets for the project to meet. These were as follows:

1 To improve pupil participation in education post-16 by 50 per cent over the first five years of the programme.

2 To improve GCSE examination results by raising the pupil average score for each pupil by 1 point over the first five years of the programme (using the GCSE grades point system where Grade A = 7 and Grade G = 1).

3 To increase attendance rates by 5 per cent over the whole programme.

Above and beyond these indicators, however, was a much broader and more ambitious agenda, including a strategy, more difficult to monitor and evaluate, which sought to win hearts and minds, to instil the belief that it is possible to promote an achievement philosophy and to improve the educational progress and academic success of all pupils in the urban context. The aim was to create a climate where commitment and achievement are celebrated and in which it becomes possible for teachers, pupils and parents to enjoy success, initially in the three high schools and ultimately in the community as a whole.

From the outset there was a drive toward quality in each of the schools. School processes and values have been reviewed and revised and translated into appropriate systems to deliver the desired outcomes. Internal management has been restructured to support the project through, for example, the appointment of project co-ordinators and identified staff responsible for linking with partner institutions.

THE IMPACT OF THE PROJECT IN THE SCHOOLS

In terms of the agreed performance-indicators for the schools, the project targets had already been met by the half-way point of the initial programme.

1   Full-time post-16 education participation rose from 22 per cent in 1989 to more than 46 per cent in 1992 – a rise of 109 per cent (see Figures 8.1 and 8.1a), and by 1993 the stay-on rates were well over 50 per cent.

2   The numbers of pupils achieving five or more GCSE grades A to C rose from 10 per cent in 1989 to 19.8 per cent in 1992, – a rise of 100 per cent (see Figures 8.2 and 8.2a). By 1993 the figure had risen to 22 per cent.

3   Attendance has improved beyond the target 5 per cent in all schools. It can be seen, therefore, that targets that seemed in 1990 to be over-ambitious proved ultimately to err on the side of caution.

The three schools have taken note of the research findings at Keele and elsewhere of characteristics evident in successful schools and have engaged in systematic collective review of their practices with cross-school and cross-phase in-service training. Staff have worked together with enormous commitment to develop an ethos of high expectation which will create lasting, long-term benefit to the regional community by contributing to the adaptable, multi-skilled work force necessary to move away from the traditional dependence on the mining and pottery industries and provide the kind of educated work force to drive the more varied economy of the future.

'Records of Achievement' have been used for each individual pupil, with a consistent policy of rewards for good attendance, effort and progress at all levels. The schools have taken imaginative and ambitious initiatives to improve the quality of teaching and learning. They have made fundamental changes in organization, introducing extra posts of responsibility to oversee the project and to create a school climate conductive to pupil achievement and positive behaviour patterns. Every opportunity has been sought to involve parents in the schools and as joint

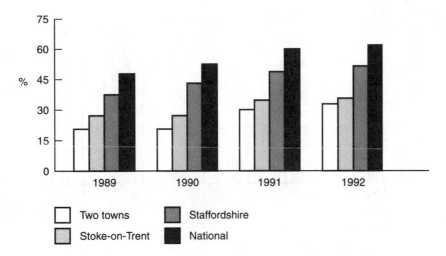

Figure 8.1. *Percentage of pupils staying on*

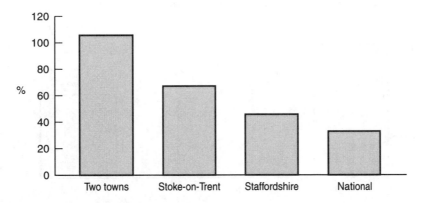

Figure 8.1a. *Percentage increase in stay-on rate, 1989 to 1992*

educators of the children. From the outset, there has been a determination to move forward simultaneously with the interests of all three groups involved in raising standards – not only teachers but also pupils and parents.

Major initiatives currently undertaken include:

- providing opportunities for volunteers to take extra lessons for extension or compensation outside the normal curriculum;

- extended school library hours with staff available to provide facilities for pupils wishing to stay on and work after school;

- arrangements to keep schools open with volunteer staffing during holiday periods, particularly at Easter, to enable pupils wishing to do so to continue to study for examination success;

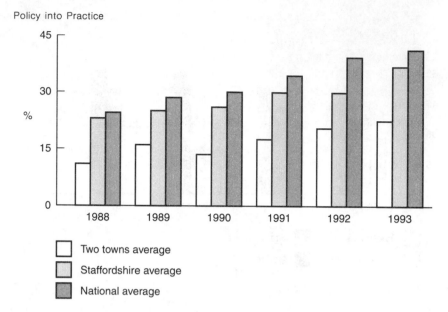

Figure 8.2. *Percentage of pupils achieving five or more GCSE grades A to C*

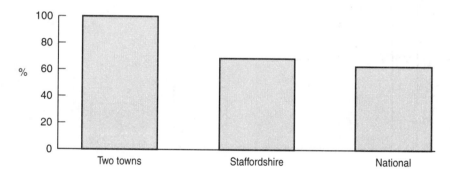

Figure 8.2a. *Percentage increase in numbers achieving five or more GCSE grades A to C, 1988 to 1993*

- personal tutoring schemes where staff accept responsibility for small groups of Year-11 pupils and give on-going help and advice with study skills, examination preparation, revision technique, course-work presentation, 'records of achievement', etc.

- the development – with the help and experience of the post-16 colleges – of flexible-learning packages to facilitate supported self-study for the pupils;

- individual action-planning – provided in co-operation with the county careers service – to ensure that each pupil is given guidance in seeking out career opportunities, is aware of the qualification implications, and has a set of achievable short-term targets;

134

- taster courses and college experience made available in the post-16 colleges to allow pupils to sample the next step in the educational process;

- residential experiences provided in collaboration with Keele and Staffordshire Universities to give year-11 pupils in the three schools a taste of university life and teaching at first hand.

It is crucial to the Two Towns Project that the parents and the school work together and share the same aims and aspirations for the children. The schools have consequently attempted to keep parents constantly informed of developments in the life and work of the school. The number of opportunities for the parents to visit the schools has been increased and creche facilities provided to encourage those with small children to attend. Systems have been introduced to monitor the numbers of parents accepting such invitations. Termly newsletters are sent out to keep parents in touch. Each school has developed a 'day-book' which monitors progress in every aspect of the children's school life and which is regularly taken home for the parents to read and comment on. It is a measure of the quality of processes in the school and the shared commitment among staff that the day-books have been consistently maintained and play a central part in ensuring that parents and teachers have a shared understanding of what is expected of the pupils. Courses have been run in collaboration with the colleges and universities to advise parents on strategies for dealing with their children during their school years.

The Two Towns Project is a partnership not only between the pupils, parents and staff of the three high schools but also between them and the careers service, the post-16 institutions, the post-18 institutions, the local primary schools and the business and industrial community. The three high schools are highly dependent upon the work done in primary schools, particularly in respect of literacy and numeracy, and they have actively sought to forge links with their primary partners to focus on achievement, concentrating on these key areas. With hindsight, many of the participants in the project now believe that the primary schools should have been integrally involved at the outset.

At the other end of the age range there have been growing links with colleges and universities whose commitment and support for the work of the schools has been a significant factor in the success of the project. Keele and Staffordshire Universities have shown, by their public expression of interest in the schools' activities, by their presence at school functions, by their endorsement of the schools 'records of achievement', the importance of encouragement, enthusiasm, and empathy from external agencies for raising the self-esteem of pupils, parents and staff. The issues raised in implementing the project, as well as the improvements gained, are more clearly illustrated through a case-study example.

CASE STUDY – BROWNHILLS HIGH SCHOOL: AN IMPROVING SCHOOL

The systematic use of rewards as an integral part of a behavioural management strategy or in the context of an 'assertive discipline' scheme is a comparatively new innovation in many schools. At Brownhills High School in Stoke-on-Trent, staff have been carefully developing a rewards system for more than four years. 'Praise postcards' are distributed when a pupil has done a piece of work that demonstrates improvement or quality. A teacher fills in the details on a card which the head signs and posts to the parent at home. The praise postcards are symbolic of the efforts at Brownhills to shift the culture of low aspirations which formerly dominated the school and the community. Through awards evenings, displays of work and constant insistence on high expectations across the staff, the culture is indeed changing dramatically. There is hard evidence of success: in 1988, 4 per cent of the cohort gained 5 GCSEs at grades A–C. Four years later 13 per cent did so; in 1994 the figure was 22 per cent.

Some observers have commented to the headteacher that 22 per cent is probably the sort of level with which to be satisfied, in a school in a disadvantaged urban area with high unemployment and a tradition of low educational expectations, she dismisses such complacency: 'You can't look at cohorts as so-called bad years, you have to think about your knowledge of the group: what are the barriers to their success and how can they be removed?' Her sights are set on continuous improvement through to the end of the century. If by then her success rate had doubled, she would still be demonstrating her quiet but firm commitment to improvement.

Nor does any year get described as a particularly good year by the head; that can cause complacency, she suggests. The job of school management is never to panic – whatever the pressures – and always to aim very high.

It is clear from talking to staff that her commitment and steadfastness has been communicated to staff. A senior member of staff, a maths teacher with management responsibilities, says that the staff are constantly stumbling across new ideas. The climate in the school means they have the courage to implement them. For example, he has recently implemented a voluntary system of additional tutorials for small groups of pupils. Twelve staff volunteered to give extra attention to the needs of sixty pupils. The demand came from the pupils. The staff responded, and the evidence suggests that the pupils involved performed noticeably better at GCSE than peers of similar ability.

The English department has involved artists-in-residence in their literacy strategy. Pupils are constantly encouraged to read and review books. In technology, participation of pupils in a 'science and technology' week at the local college raises aspirations and encourages staying on. Another member of staff, meanwhile, runs a community-education project from the school which, among other things, teaches parents how to support their children's education. Here they learn what the demands of course-work on young people will be and how they can be encouraged to read and to study. 'It is all part of changing aspirations in the community,' he said. A few years ago a pupil told him she wanted to be an estate agent. 'Why not become a chartered surveyor?' he said. She had never heard of one of those then, but recently he heard that she had become just that. In Brownhills like other successful urban schools the real meaning of high expectations lies in details such as these.

Pupils are the first to acknowledge that the peer-group culture has changed. They say they are proud to attend Brownhills and that the atmosphere in the classroom has changed dramatically over five years. The head places great emphasis on discipline. 'If that's wrong,' she says, 'you can never get the classroom experience right.' Rather than a system of punishing offenders, they tackled the aspects of school which seemed to create the opportunities for trouble. The rewards system – praise postcards included – was overhauled. Lunchtime caused problems and provided opportunities for some pupils to skip the afternoon, so the school moved to a continuous day. There are always lessons in progress now. Each year-group in turn has a forty-minute break during which they must stay on the premises. School finishes early – at 3.05 p.m. – but is followed by 90 minutes of additional voluntary extension activities including an oversubscribed homework club.

The head recognizes that the school's success depends on the quality and commitment of her staff. The improvement strategy consciously involved all of them from the beginning. 'They have to give a lot,' she comments, 'but the growing evidence of success provides its own rewards.' She acknowledges too that participation in the Two Towns Project with other local schools, the LEA and nearby universities was crucial. It provided a source of ideas and encouragement to take risks. 'It enabled us to do in three years what might otherwise have taken ten,' she suggests. The increasing attention the school's success is bringing provides further encouragement. She particularly appreciated the phone call from the CEO when this year's GCSE results were published.

The popular image of school improvement is one of a charismatic head wielding authority and driving staff and pupils on. The Brownhills' experience belies that picture. Here school improvement is to do with commitment to high expectations, an openness about performance data, a pragmatic approach in which taking risks is encouraged and constant attention to the details, like the use of praise postcards.

EVALUATION OF THE TWO TOWNS PROJECT

At school level, the project has been subjected to evaluation on three occasions since its inception in 1990. An early report to point the way for the project was carried out in 1991 by W.S. Walton, formerly Chief Education Officer of Sheffield. An interim evaluation was carried out in 1992 by Quality Learning Services in Staffordshire and Gordon Hainsworth, formerly Chief Executive for Manchester. A final evaluation was conducted in 1993 by a Keele University team, including a headteacher and two teachers from the Haggerston School in Hackney to ensure external validation.

THE CONTRIBUTION OF THE PARTNER INSTITUTIONS

The Two Towns Project has derived great strength from the fact that it has functioned as a loose network, led by and focused on the three high schools. But substantial contributions have been made by the local education authority, the local universities and colleges and the Staffordshire careers service. The nature of the contribution of each of these is summarized below.

- The active participation of the Chief Education Officer of Staffordshire and his part in the initiation of the project has given it status and credibility within the school and the local community. The availability of the officers of the authority throughout the project has been a valuable support in getting things 'delivered'.

- The influence and moral authority of the LEA, rather than its statutory powers, have drawn together the partnership network.

- The collaboration of the LEA with the Staffordshire TEC has resulted in substantial funding for the project.

- The expertise of universities and colleges in and knowledge of the process of educational change and development was central to the underlying philosophy of the project.

- Keele University's first material contribution to the project was to negotiate funding by entering into agreement with the Paul Hamlyn Foundation. The Foundation has provided the salary for a project co-ordinator who has been based at Keele and provided with accommodation and support services there. The Foundation funded residential experiences which have been organized and delivered at the university.

- One of the lessons of the Two Towns has been the need for universities to have particular criteria for local students who traditionally would not be expected to enter university. Keele and Staffordshire Universities' response has been a review of admissions procedures and the implementation of a guaranteed entry to local youngsters who can demonstrate that they are of serious intent and committed to study. Students admitted by this route – the Staffordshire Access Scheme – since October 1993 have been closely monitored and the evidence suggests that they are succeeding in higher education.

- One of the early lessons learned from the Two Towns Project was that a residential experience at an institute of higher education might raise significantly the aspirations of the pupils who attend. Each September since 1991 the universities have hosted a three-day residential experience, funded by the Paul Hamlyn Foundation, for 150 year-11 pupils. This event is supported by all the members of the partnership. The young people attend workshops and seminars with staff and students from the post-16 institutions and the universities, the careers service and management teams from local and national industry. They visit university departments, live in student accommodation and enjoy the social life of the campus.

- A student tutoring programme has been piloted in local schools since October 1992. It has been funded by a small grant from British Petroleum and Community Service Volunteers. Student volunteers from universities and colleges have worked alongside teachers to act as role models for pupils at secondary level or to support the development of reading and speaking skills in the primary schools, particularly with children from ethnic minority groups. As from October 1994 additional money from the Staffordshire TEC will facilitate the expansion of the tutoring scheme into all the Two Towns high schools and three of their primary feeder schools. The benefits from the scheme for the school children are already becoming apparent, as are a variety of spin-off benefits for the universities and colleges.

- A function of the Two Towns co-ordinator at Keele has been to monitor the project's performance-indicators and undertake the research which informs the debate on school-improvement measures in the schools and colleges. The research profile of the education department at Keele has been significantly influenced by this work and a 'Centre for Successful Schools' has been developed around the project. The Centre has undertaken work related directly to the project, identifying ways, for example, in which a failing school can reverse the downward spiral and become a place where characteristics evident in successful schools appear. Surveys were carried out, by questionnaire and interview techniques, of the attitudes held by all students in their last year of compulsory schooling, seeking, in particular, to establish their attitude to staying on in education post-16. Similar surveys have been conducted to research the attitudes to education of parents from the three schools. Adapted versions of these surveys are now in widespread use.

- University involvement in community projects is normally perceived as a contribution by the university to the community. The benefit for the university tends to be measured in public-relations terms. In the case of the Two Towns Project much more significant gains have been made from the University's point of view. There has been an influence on the teaching and the quality of experience gained by associate teachers on the university Post-Graduate Certificate of Education course. Even more significant has been the direction it has given to the university's educational research. A variety of developments have resulted from, or been inspired by, the university's involvement in the Two Towns Project.

- The Staffordshire Careers Service has shown a consistently strong commitment to the project. Representatives have been provided for the steering and project groups and there has been a careers presence at every Two Towns function. Its most important contribution has been to ensure that each year-10 and year-11 pupil in the three schools has been provided with an opportunity to work on an 'individual action plan' to record career aspirations and the steps to be taken, in terms of personal development and obtaining qualifications, for these ambitions to be realized. The plan involves individual support in setting short- and long-term targets.

LESSONS LEARNED FROM THE TWO TOWNS PROJECT

1   There is a great deal of research evidence about the characteristics of effective schools. It would seem from the Two Towns Project that urban schools which target their resources and energy on strategies for developing these characteristics are more likely to raise children's aspirations and achievement.

2   Loose collaboration rather than formal structures has successfully provided the pattern for the organization of The Two Towns Project.

3   Management structures succeeded because they reflected the loose nature of collaboration and placed the initiative firmly with the schools involved.

4   Clear measurable targets were essential.

5   Relatively small amounts of additional funding, spent well, made a huge difference.

In the case of the Two Towns Project the following features appeared to be important:

- the planning of expenditure integrally involved the schools themselves;
- outside consultants, with high credibility, provided insight and analysis and gave the initiative status;
- significant numbers of teachers in the schools were involved in planning and consultation;
- There was limited but significant expenditure on symbolic change (such as establishing high-quality displays of pupil work and other achievements in entrance halls);
- there were focused attempts to change pupil (peer-group) attitudes or staff attitudes and expectations;
- provision was made for professional development opportunities related to the goals of the project;
- the additional expenditure became an integral part of a school's development strategy.

GENERALIZABLE LESSONS LEARNED

1 Participation in an initiative is not an alternative to getting the in-school factors right.

As we have suggested above, the initiatives with the greatest chance of bringing about sustainable improvement are those that assist schools in creating the conditions for improvement from within. It should be emphasized that participating in an initiative is not an alternative to a school taking responsibility for its own improvement. Instead it is a means of assisting it to improve, and may act as a catalyst helping it change and improve more quickly.

2 Co-operating agencies as well as schools can benefit from urban school-improvement initiatives.

While the focus of the Two Towns Project is clearly school improvement, or some aspects of it, it is clear that the collaboration can provide benefits to other participating agencies. For example, a university can accumulate data and experience which will contribute to its research and publication profile. TECs, for example, can gain through understanding better the links between schools, FE and employers. LEAs can learn lessons applicable to all their schools and gain in terms of their public profile.

These wider benefits ought to be taken into account by those at local level who are considering investing in urban education initiatives. The investment may reap benefits far beyond those immediately specified in the project goals. Furthermore, given the potential for mutual benefit schools should see their role in such projects as being that of active partners, rather than passive beneficiaries.

The Next Steps

The achievements of the Two Towns Project to date underline the need for the partners to reaffirm their commitment to present policies: to maintaining and improving standards of examination performance and school attendance; to curriculum extension; to ever closer links with primary and post-16 partners; to providing individual counselling and career advice; to enhance and enrich learning experiences; and to the increasing involvement of parents. Targets for the next phase of the project should include the following: a pre-school programme building on the lessons of the 'Headstart' programme in the USA (it is hoped that the pre-school agencies would be better co-ordinated), closer involvement of the primary sector, and enhancement of the status of pupils who do not necessarily 'stay on' in full-time education but who, nevertheless, pursue interests which have structured learning post-16 as an integral ingredient.

Consideration will be given to which aspects of the project are replicable elsewhere. What are the implications for the rest of the education system? Staffordshire LEA will make use of the Two Towns experience in its strategy for education across the country, to improve schools and encourage a gradual turnaround in peer-group and parental pressure in favour of a climate of achievement. The involvement of the universities with the LEA and the TEC in support of local schools has proved a powerful influence and there is a need to establish how this influence might be spread more widely.

REFERENCES

Barber, M.B., Collarbone, P., Cullen, E., Owen, D. (1994) *Raising Expectation and Achievement in City Schools: The Two Towns School Improvement Project*. Keele: Keele University.

Brighouse, T.R.P. (1993) 'Education in Stoke-on-Trent: The Two Towns Project' in *The Potteries: Continuity and Change in a Staffordshire Conurbation* (ed. A.D.M. Phillips). Stoke-on-Trent: Butler and Tanner.

Fullan, M. (1989) *The New Meaning of Educational Change*. London: Cassell.

Goddard, D., Hainsworth, G., Love, R. (1993) *The Two Towns Evaluation Report*. Keele: Keele University.

Gray, J. (1990) 'The Quality of Schooling: Frameworks for Judgement', *British Journal of Education Studies*, 38(3).

Johnson, M. (1994) *The Two Towns Project – Raising Expectation and Achievement in City Schools*.

Mortimore, P., Sammons, P., Stoll, L., Lewis, D. and Ecob, R. *et al.* (1988) *School Matters*. Wells: Open Books.

Rutter, M. *et al.* (1979) *Fifteen Thousand Hours*. Wells: Open Books.

PART THREE

Policy and Practice in American City Schooling

Chapter 9

Implications of Restructuring and Site-Level Decentralization upon District-level Leadership

Robert L. Crowson and William Lowe Boyd

INTRODUCTION

Despite a decentralization and central-office downsizing that has been generally regarded as 'radical', Chicago's public school system is still claimed by many to be determinedly top-heavy and unduly bureaucratic. By mid-1993, nearly four years after the inauguration of Chicago's power-to-the-people reform, individual schools were still winning Foundation-sponsored awards for 'breaking bureaucratic rules' (e.g., extending the hours of the school day or conducting their own repairs to poorly-maintained facilities) (Wisby, 1993; also Seibel, 1992).

Simultaneously, faced with an expected deficit of about $400 million for 1993–4, the city's system was under heavy political pressure in the spring of 1993 to cut added 'waste', to streamline further, to abolish sub-district offices, and to transfer additional authority in lump-sum budget fashion to the schools (Spielman and Vander Weele, 1993).

While unusual in its emphasis upon parent/community governance at the school-site, Chicago's school system is not unique as an experiment in organizational restructuring. Edmonton, Canada and Miami (Dade County), Florida have long been considered pioneers in the development of school-based management and in a reallocation of preciously centralized powers to those persons (particularly teachers) in closest touch with the student/parent clientele (see Chapman, 1990; Brown, 1992; Fernandez, 1993). Cincinnati, the New York City Schools, and Detroit are other large-city districts well known for decentralizing initiatives; while Kentucky has gained notoriety for its thrust statewide toward school-based decision-making within the framework of a top-down structure of state requirements and goals (Murphy, 1993a, 1993b).[1]

Curiously underdeveloped in decentralization, whether city or state, is a clarification of the role and authority of district-level administration. Typically, the district role has been defined only in the negative, as a rather top-heavy component now ripe for some deep pruning (Fullan, 1993) or even dismantling.

However, in Chicago and elsewhere, there is now increasing interest in a new understanding of the district-level in restructured schooling. Murphy (1993a) urges new conceptualizations of superintendent and central-office leadership around the active support and facilitation of bottom-up improvement. Smith and O'Day (1991, p. 256) assign districts the dual responsibility of (a) removing hindrances to school-based innovation (e.g., rigid time requirements, uniform class sizes), but simultaneously (b) ensuring that resources (federal, state and local) are 'integrated and administered in a way that maximizes opportunities for the needy.'

Elsewhere, Otterman (in a superintendent's initiative for Cincinnati speaking theoretic volumes) offers a privatization of many central-office services around the firm removal of 'entrenched layers of middle management' (see Bradley, 1993). Elmore (1993), however, warns that a dichotomy between centralized and decentralized schooling is not a pedagogically important issue, and furthermore such a dichotomy fails to recognize that some functions at each level of government should probably be tight, others loose. Finally, Brown (1992) observes that while this locus-of-authority debate rages, the possibility is real in many localities for a *re*-centralization of the schools, if public expectations of instructional improvement are not soon met.

Beyond this unresolved balancing of 'top' and 'bottom' in the district-level organization of schooling (and an accompanying discussion of the threat of re-centralization in district management), education's policy analysts are finding logic anew in a search for some overall 'coherence' and somewhat less fragmentation in school reform. One view, top-down, is a vision of 'systemic' change which emphasizes national standards, state curricular frameworks, a structure of state and district incentives/supports for the schools in reaching state goals, and a thorough process of monitoring and/or assessment of goal compliance (Smith and O'Day, 1991).

A contrasting, bottom-up, view finds little to be gained in a renewed search for overall coherence from the top. From an historical perspective, the argument here is that the schools have shown a long and glorious tradition of deflecting and co-opting previous efforts toward restructuring; and there is little evidence that even a 'user-firendly' effort to systematize *in support* of school-site innovation will prove to be at all effective (Tyack, 1993). Furthermore, the push, if anything, should not be toward state or district coherence so much as toward an even further focus downward, to classrooms, teachers, and learners. Where there is any added structuring to be engaged in, it should be an aggregation of institutional and managerial supports upward from the core technology of schools (teaching and learning), not downward from state or federal 'frameworks' (J. Murphy, 1991; Elmore, 1993; Sarason, 1993; Newmann, 1993).

It is amid the above backdrop of suggestions for the central-office role under restructuring, plus some major differences in the best approach to 'coherence' in public education, that this paper attempts additional conceptualization of district-level leadership. Where there is an illustration of some key points and the use of some 'case-like' data, the exemplar is usually taken from Chicago. The authors recognize, furthermore, that each school district, large to small, has its own special history and organizational characteristics. Conceptual models can be useful as broad frameworks for restructured roles and relationships; however, they always become more problematic and of reduced utility in the particular.

BACKGROUND

Turn-of-the-century reformers found the inadequacies of urban education well documented in such exposés as *Laggards in our Schools* (Ayres, 1909). These were rooted in unduly decentralized and locally-politicized organizations (Crowson and Hannaway, 1988). School buildings mainly under the control of ward bosses, large numbers of teachers and administrators with inadequate professional preparation, inefficient systems of management and resource allocation, unclear lines of authority/supervision from district-wide governing down to classroom/student – these were thought to be the key 'problems' of an extremely loose, ward-based structure of city-school administration (see Cronin, 1973; Tyack, 1974; Spring, 1990).

An administrative hierarchy was the early-century goal, one that started with the 'best' people on the local school board and proceeded downward through a professionally-trained superintendent into a school organization structured along corporate lines (Callahan, 1962). Strong, professional administration was advocated, providing clear, top-down responsibility for staff assignments, resource allocations, procedural rules, and curricular objectives.

By no means, in practice, have the public schools ever been as fully centralized and bureaucratized as their critics would later charge. Nevertheless, such critiques as David Rogers, *110 Livingston Street* (1968) gave substance to the sense that the 'corporate model' of top-heavy school administration was firmly in place by mid-century. Indeed, images of over-control from the top have been a popular feature of the extant literature on urban school administration for many years; and by the 1960s a number of cities had already entered into an historic period of experimentation. These were short-lived but much publicized efforts in such cities as New York (Ocean-Hill Brownsville and Two Bridges), Chicago (Woodlawn), Detroit, and Los Angeles. Most had a powerful civil-rights and power-to-the-people touch, often with many conflicts related to reform implementation (LaNoue and Smith, 1973; Gittell and Hollander, 1968).

The Impact of the Central Office

Despite a degree of non-responsiveness, red-tape rigidity, and top-down authoritarianism in large-city school systems, there has been surprisingly little analysis of the pros and cons of central-office-dominated schooling. Among the insights that do emerge from a brief, retrospective analysis of the literature are the following:

Mediator of Interests First, the central office (with its governing board and general superintendent) has typically served the school district in a distinctive environmental capacity. Parsonian (i.e., pattern-maintenance) in its emphasis, the central authority has operated traditionally as the key mediator of competing political interests, citywide, vis-a-vis the public schools (e.g., ethnic, racial and religious issues; labour and business pressures; tax-spender vs taxpayer cleavages) (see Sayre and Kaufman, 1960; Wong, 1992).

Centre of Risk-Management   Second, the downtown office has traditionally served the school system as the centre of risk-management (see Hannaway, 1989; Crowson and Morris, 1991). Frequently the source of restrictive rules, burdensome paperwork, and costly (in time) 'clearances' from administrators above, the 'risky business' of educating an urban population has more commonly been a general superintendent's and a central-office staff's burden over the years than a school-site responsibility. Children stranded for hours by their school buses, sex offenders still on the payroll as classroom teachers, crumbling walls and badly flaking (lead-filled) paint, low test scores, a significant increase in within-school violence, a conflict-dominated renegotiation of the teachers' contract – these are among the many hazards that typically come to rest as 'bad press' at central-office doors rather than the school-site (even, quite interestingly, *after* the onset of decentralization).

Monitor   Third, the central office has served the school district as a system-wide monitor of program implementation. Among the key responsibilities have been those of overseeing the utilization of federal and state grant-in-aid monies as well as supervising the compliance of the schools with state codes and federal guidelines (e.g., desegregation rules). Significantly, the role of monitoring programme implementation has been of central importance because, quite often, the focus of extra state and (particularly) federal assistance has been upon a *redistribution* of resources; toward overcoming allocatory inequalities (e.g., protecting the handicapped, the limited-English-proficient, or the educationally disadvantaged) (Wong, 1992).

Co-ordinator of 'Production'   Fourth, the central office has served as a 'production-coordinator' for the technical core. Thus, some scholars have noted an important paradox in the top-to-bottom co-ordination of the school system. The paradox is that despite a reputation for rule-from-the-top, the central office has traditionally defined much of its role as an organizer (albeit also controller) of the technical core. Hiring and allocating teachers, providing new schools where there is population growth, distributing supplies and textbooks, allocating pupils to schools and classrooms, maintaining the schools; these indicate that policy and administrative decisions have a rationale firmly focused in schools. It is from the 'needs' of the technical core that demands and linkages flow through the system; it is from an overseeing of the tasks of teaching and learning that the system becomes centralized.

Summary

In brief summary, a twentieth-century-long saga of best-system approaches to the organization of urban schooling has left unresolved the relationship between school-site bottom and superintendent's-office top. Indeed, in any discussion of 'top' and 'bottom' organizationally in schooling, warns Tyack (1990), it is an error historically to think of U.S. schools as predominately centralized or decentralized. 'The web of interactive relationships,' notes Tyack (1990, p. 186), 'is far too complex for that.' Such terms as 'fragmented centralization' are far more descriptive of even the most reputedly top-heavy of school systems than terms like 'bureaucratized' or 'centralized' (Tyack, 1990, p. 172).

Although surprisingly little investigated or deeply analysed in the extant literature, the functions that central-office personnel have traditionally served in urban education appear to be four in number: (1) a 'pattern maintenance' representation of the school district vis-a-vis its larger-city environment, (2) a collector and distributor of 'risk' in educational management, (3) a monitor of district-wide programmes and allocations, and (somewhat paradoxically), (4) a top-to-bottom co-ordinator of 'production' at the technical core.

However, beyond a popular press toward downsizing in much of the present-day thrust into decentralization, there has not yet been much carefully focused attention upon the changed role of the central office (i.e. superintendent and district-level leadership) in restructured public education. Is there an important role; and how does it fit into, significantly alter, or 'balance' the traditional roles and relationships of decades past vis-a-vis the superintendency and the school-site?

Accordingly, we consider, below, some of the educational leadership and organizational-change considerations/issues that are just now emerging from the renewed interest in central-office roles under decentralization. Our analysis seeks to blend an awareness of the changed organizational relationships that are already evolving in such 'restructured' cities as Chicago, Cincinnati, and Edmonton, with a continuing awareness and consideration of the historical traditions of central-office involvement in pattern maintenance, risk-management, system monitoring, and 'production' co-ordination.

CONCEPTUALIZING DISTRICT-LEVEL LEADERSHIP AMID DECENTRALIZATION

Despite a long-term fascination with questions of hierarchy, 'linkages', and collaboration in the available literature on public-sector organizations, it is not very encouraging to read Fred M. Newmann's (1993, p. 9) observation that:

> in the abundant research and commentary on educational change, I
> have found no theory that adequately explains both how to change all
> the separate agencies that influence education and how to link them to
> have more cumulative impact.

Indeed, the evidence is that linkages abound even in the most loosely-coupled of organizations, but that these linkages can as easily fragment as 'cohere'.

The private interests of individuals, and the incentives in support of these interests, are usually only with great difficulty brought into a semblance of alignment (see Moe, 1984; Leibenstein, 1987). Structures designed to 'link' (e.g., communications systems) can as easily be used to protect separate bases of sub-group power as they can lead to co-operation and sharing (Crozier, 1964; Feldman

149

and March, 1981). In like manner, organizational rules serve to standardize institutional behavior but they simultaneously create opportunities for idiosyncratic variability in behavior (Gouldner, 1955).

On the other hand, from Max Weber (translated into English in 1947) on, there continues to be, stubbornly, a widespread sense that the key linking device of an organizational hierarchy can be a vital, collaborative force. As Hickson and McCullough (1980, p. 30) conclude: 'Hierarchy makes an organization work.' Through hierarchy the many jobs in an organization are blended together, and the diversity of individuals is held sufficiently in check to keep what is done in one job from being too far out of step with what is done in another. Furthermore, hierarchy typically provides: (a) mechanisms for adjusting performances to uncertain events, (b) a means of resolving conflicts within the organization, (c) an establishment of efficient routines (SOPs) for repetitive work, (d) ways of monitoring and rewarding productive effort, and (e) career ladders for the upwardly mobile (Stinchcombe, 1965).

In recent years, new theoretical approaches to questions of hierarchy have developed around the concept of 'agency'. These attempts to explain anew the strange combinations of organizational exchanges and authoritative relationships to be found in hierarchical systems (Moe, 1984; Ferris, 1992). Agency theory proceeds from one of the oldest traditions in organizational analysis, the study of an 'economy of incentives' (Barnard, 1938); finding in the incentives and self-interest structures of organizations some 'rational' explanations for both the cooperative and seemingly non-cooperative behaviors of individuals (Crowson and Boyd, 1988).

On the other hand, also emerging currently are strong arguments in support of a major redefinition of 'old' concepts of hierarchical systems altogether. An appreciation of the worth of 'community', of a much-enhanced democratization of the workplace, and of a more morally attuned/caring system of 'production' are increasingly to be found now in organizational analyses (see Gutman, 1987; Murphy, 1992; Etzioni, 1993; Sergiovanni, 1993). Delightfully, we find it worthy to return here too to the work of Chester Barnard, who wrote in 1938 of the importance of a broad acceptance of the 'moral responsibility of leadership' throughout the levels of an organization.

Amid our long-running confusion vis-a-vis the functions/dysfunctions and the very form or structure of organizational hierarchies, it is discouraging but not at all difficult to understand Michael Fullan's (1993, p. 143) observation that: 'It has become evident that neither centralization nor decentralization works.' Nor is it difficult to appreciate Willis Hawley's (1993) finding, in his case study of school debureaucratization, that non-bureaucratized organizations will tend to encounter an array of important challenges (e.g., specifying roles, allocating risk and 'blame', establishing leadership authority) that formerly might have been resolved quite well hierarchically.

Hawley (1993, p. 53) concludes that for the destructuring of schools to work, common understandings and agreements must be reached among teachers and administrators that go well beyond mere 'reaction to the "evils of bureaucracy".' Fullan (1993, p. 147) similarly suggests that the answer to school restructuring 'lies in some form of "coordinated codevelopment of schools and the district".'

'School-district codevelopment', advises Fullan (1993, p. 160), must somehow become a successful 'exercise in avoiding overcontrol on the one hand and chaos on the other'.

Although the charge is simple (codevelop in such a way as simultaneously to avoid overcontrol and chaos), a conceptualization and implementation of a new relationship between central office and school-site in restructured schooling remains, to date, a rather elusive goal. The major, still-unanswered question, put even more simply by one of Chicago's school principals, is: Under school reform, just 'what are the things that must be done centrally, what not?' In seeking to gain some insights here, three roles are explored: service role, monitoring role and the superintendent's role. It is through the analysis of issues related to control and reform, at both central office and school site levels, that the implications of restructuring are examined.

1 The Service Role

There is little disagreement among analysts that far less should now be done centrally by way of directing, managing, and controlling the schools, in favour of serving, supporting, and facilitating bottom-up change/improvement (see Murphy, 1993a; Smith and O'Day, 1991; Fullan and Miles, 1992; Newmann, 1993). Although the 'how to' of a service-and-support role is still a bit vague, the general sense is that 'old' bureaucratic values of scale efficiency (e.g., centralized purchasing and allocation), standardization (e.g., of curricula), and a guiding/ protecting (albeit top-down) control of the schools, should give way to new values of facilitation and assistance. The notion of managing and serving a 'system of schools' rather than a 'school system' is the key here.[2] These new service values should include: (a) encouraging the development and the exercise of professional expertise (especially among teachers in-the-schools), (b) providing options (in place of standardization), and (c) encouraging technical efficiency in place of scale efficiency (e.g., emphasizing whatever makes a difference in student learning).

Background By no means, as Gamoran and Dreeben (1986) point out, has service-to-the-schools been a missing value in the past. Many of the activities that the central offices of school districts have always engaged in constitute services to the school-site. Transportation routes and bus contracts negotiated 'downtown' are designed to move children as efficiently as possible to and from their individual schools. Personnel departments remove most of the burden of payroll, tax-withholding, new-employment processing, retirement and health-benefit com-pilations, etc. from the workloads of site-level employees. Curriculum guides distributed citywide are useful in daily lesson planning to teachers and, in environments of high family mobility, tend to provide at least a modicum of uniformity across school curricula.

The distribution of services and the allocation of resources from central office to school-site have also been important sources of district level control. The allotment of desks, blackboards, supplies, teachers, curricular materials, and the like constitute important 'constraints', whereby the school system influences mightily the context of teaching and learning (Gamoran and Dreeben, 1986).

Additionally, the services rendered by the central office can often be easy targets for those charging bureaucratic waste and mismanagement. Consequently, it has not been unusual in city-school systems for a number of the 'services' offered centrally to be duplicated (for either efficiency's or ownership's sake) in the schools. Thus, despite a central registry and distribution of substitute teachers one might find each school maintaining its own cadre of subs instantly on call. Despite a computerized (call-up-your-budget) accounting system, the schools may carefully keep their own sets of books, just in case. Although a district-wide personnel office may seek efficiently to match the allocation of teachers to the enrolment needs of the schools, the schools are not unknown to try to 'stockpile' extra teachers because of the time-lag in securing new faculty placements from downtown (Morris et al., 1984).

It has also long been a tradition in many city systems that site-level access to the services offered by the central office depends much more heavily upon 'who-you-know downtown' than upon standardized access procedures. A scratch-my-back reciprocity between principals and members of the central office has been far closer to the culture of the organization than to a Weberian ideal of official, bureaucratic neutrality. Principals would take great pride in working the system to move the renovation/rehabilitation of their building from 154th on the list to next-in-line.

With this background, it is not difficult to understand the slash-the-bureaucracy mood that has accompanied urban school reform. In a special issue on revitalizing education (in January, 1993), *U.S. News & World Report* concluded that one of the major obstacles to quality education is: 'Public schooling's vast infrastructure, from those who change the light bulbs to the bureaucrats who push the paper, [which] has grown so unwieldy and idiosyncratic that it is more a hindrance than a support to education' (p. 50).

Early efforts to increase efficiency and responsiveness often involved the redistribution of 'downtown' personnel to sub-district 'field' offices around the city (see Murphy, 1993a). Later, as site-based management and the key role of the principal gained attention, a few city districts (most notably Louisville and Miami) began experimenting with procedures to bring principals into a direct-reporting relationship with their general superintendent (see Kerchner et al., 1990). The city of Cincinnati received national acclaim when under two successive super-intendents it cut central-office positions firstly by 51 per cent then by an additional 20 per cent over two years (Bradley, 1993).

The New Service Ethic   The notion that bureaucracy should be minimal is popular, particularly during a time of severe financial stress in urban America. A new emphasis upon both downsizing and a closer-to-the-schools allocation of services has thus far failed to resolve two competing (and potentially contra-dictory) values. One value finds direction in a school demand-based approach to service delivery, the other value seeks a rediscovery of 'system' and 'coherence' in urban education – but now from the perspective of the organizational bottom rather than the top.

The *first* of the service values suggests that a central office should provide services to the schools 'on-demand'. While far from a fully-operative structure at this time in Chicago, that city's reform provides an illustration of some evolving organizational relationships that seem to be moving in a 'demand' direction. By 1993, four years beyond its 1989 inauguration, Chicago's decentralization found itself continuing to struggle with the delineation of its supportive role in reforming the central office. There had been charges throughout the four years that the superintendent and many central-office staff were uncommitted to decentralization, that the professional organizations (particularly the teachers' union) were far from enthusiastic reformers, and that a divided Board of Education was proving to be incapable of any role-defining leadership for the city's schools.

In the spring of 1993, the Board finally considered a consultant's proposal to establish a 'School Demand-based System' of central office and subdistrict staffing for Chicago (Seaphus, 1993). Taking cues from other experimenting districts, the central notion was that beyond the top-down imperatives of federal and state mandated programs, much of the work of 'downtown' could be reorganized to deliver services and problem-solving support to the local schools 'upon demand'. A 'School Demand-based Catalogue of Services and problem-solving Support' was to be developed, for implementation in September 1993.

Not only, of course, Chicago but also a number of other cities have shown interest in providing school-sites with options in the use of services, including the choice of using downtown or contracting-out for supplies/materials and building repairs (see Murphy and Hallinger, 1993). Elsewhere (particularly in Cincinnati), the notion has been that most of the service-providers themselves should be allocated physically to 'home' bases out in the schools away from any downtown structure of offices.

Such proposals have not escaped political controversy. A teachers' strike in Detroit, in the autumn of 1992, was at least in part in opposition to a proposal to give the school-site greater autonomy in choosing teacher personnel. An unresolved battle in Chicago in 1992, well before the 'demand-based' proposal, involved the reform-minded suggestion that curriculum development and in-service training funds/activities should be 'realigned' down to the schools. It was suggested controversially as well in Chicago that much of the decision-making in compliance with state and federal rules should additionally be left to the schools – with central office co-ordinators (for state or federal programs) serving as 'advisors, not supervisors' ('Focus Group Report', 1992).

Most interestingly, while Chicago entered into a long, formal debate over the central office role, the evidence by mid-1993 was that the city's individual schools were (on their own, quietly, and without direct leadership) already busily engaged in bottom-up restructuring of the 'demand' for services. In a series of interviews with Chicago principals through 1992–3, McPherson and Crowson (forthcoming, pp. 11–12) discovered:

'The district office is virtually nonexistent. The central office? It depends upon the department.' Each of the principals in this survey would agree with this statement. The uncoupling of the Chicago Public Schools nowhere is more evident, we suspect, than in this tearing of the administrative hierarchy.

Almost uniformly these principals described drastically changed relationships with the district [regional] and central offices. Schools seem to be much more autonomous – at least most of those represented by these principals. 'It boils down to no relationship with the district office. Parents can't run there anymore. And there's even less with the central office. The central office has nothing to do with my running this school', or, 'The central office has a dotted line relationship with us at best.'

Such heretical statements would have been unheard of fifteen years ago in a system of layered district, area, and central offices – a system of regulation and obedience and permission.

Chicago's principals were found by McPherson and Crowson (forthcoming, p. 22) to be moving (without either direction or approval from 'downtown') increasingly 'outside the system for both assistance and resources – from teachers to curricular ideas, from budget supplements to facilities improvements.' Scouting the larger urban terrain for added public or private resources; eschewing the passed-around teachers on the school system's 'list', in favour of a separate public advertisement for staff on one's own; partnering (unapproved by downtown) in a curriculum development project with an area university; or independently negotiating with other non-education agencies of city government for facilities assistance – all would be 'on-demand' expressions of school-site independence in Chicago pre-reform. Conclude McPherson and Crowson (forthcoming, p. 22), 'ask a Chicago principal, "Do you get much help from the central office?" The prototypical answer now is: "We handle things on our own."'

In review, one of the potentially significant benefits of an 'on-demand' approach to the redefinition of school-system hierarchies, a benefit that could appear to fit the Chicago situation well, is the community-environment responsiveness of service-distribution. James Cibulka (1991) was one of the first to suggest that Chicago school reform would begin to produce a widening variability among the city's schools, out of the adaptations of individual schools to their immediate community environments. Those who would now seek to understand and improve urban education, notes Cibulka (1991, p. 37) will need to look for 'school-specific organizational and environmental influences acting quite independently of institutional features.'

The adaptiveness and choice/market appeal of an 'on-demand' approach fits well into the key assumption behind Chicago reform – which is that school-site autonomy and a strong community press upon the schools will eventually lead to educational improvement. On the other hand, Richard Elmore (1993) points out that there is little evidence to date that a decentralization of services in education enhances either the efficiency of resource use or the responsiveness of schools to their communities. Indeed, the evidence in the case of New York City decentralization is that the opposite effect can just as easily develop (see Elmore, 1993; Fernandez with Underwood, 1993).

Likewise, Goldring and Sullivan (1993) note that studies thus far of the privatization and marketization of services in such other social-service arenas as health care do not offer solid evidence that efficiency and effectiveness of service-delivery are the outcomes (see also Murphy, 1991). Furthermore, John Watt (1989) warns that a decidedly less beneficial side of market-centeredness is that relatively stable and relatively affluent communities (and their schools) will likely out-resource the others. The 'widening variability' foreseen by Cibulka (1991) can become a few more steps toward a greater disadvantaging of the city's children.

A *second* service value in urban education seeks to leave school-improvement much less to chance. Instead it looks to a service ethic that focuses more carefully upon systemic redevelopment. There is the recognition that drastic bureaucratic downsizing, major changes in organizational ideologies (e.g., from scale efficiency to marketplace efficiency), and a concentration upon service-on-demand rather then service-as-control, has great popular as well as academic appeal. There appears to be little doubt to close observers of both Chicago and Kentucky reform (McPherson and Crowson, 1993, forthcoming; Murphy, 1993a,b,c), that such restructuring comes close to the 'destructive actions' that Biggart (1977) maintains were necessary to a successful early 1970s reorganization of the US Post Office Department. Destroying such stabilizing forces as old bureaucratic ideologies, informal alliances and power bases, internal communication structures, and training/indoctrination mechanisms were vital elements in successfully creative postal-service change, says Biggart (1977).

To some analysts, however, an overconcentration upon services-on-demand in an urban system of schooling poses a possible loss of some educational 'coherence' that is necessary to a successful rebuilding process or indeed to meaningful school improvement (see Smith and O'Day, 1991; also Murphy and Hallinger, 1993). In an argument much at odds with a faith in the redeeming power of destruction. Fullan and Miles (1992) note that successful change must focus on the interrelationships of *all* the main components of a system simultaneously, and must focus not just on structure but also upon deeper issues of the culture of the system.

Similarly, Gamoran and Dreeben (1986) observe that important linkages spanning the hierarchical levels of school systems (linkages key to the core technology of schools), are to be found in all manner of system-wide symbolic values, socialization patterns, ideologies, time allocations, and the like which go well beyond simple matters of service-delivery and resource 'demands'. It is interesting that despite the 'radical' restructuring in Chicago, staff and administrators in the schools still pay obeisance to an array of school-system 'policies', most long-ago lost to the procedural and enforcement concerns of the central office. These range from such 'policies' as a complex and arcane set of both visitor and staff sign-in/sign-out procedures; to a no-longer monitored 'uniform discipline code' for the schools of Chicago; to matters of curriculum, teacher and staff evaluation, student report-card distribution, school library procedures, and the use of audio-visual equipment/services.

Although they can be regarded on the one hand as examples of system 'intransigence' and the reluctance of an organizational culture to 'let go', such policies still-in-force can also be important entry-points for system change. All is not lost to a sense of hierarchy, a 'system' in the decentralized city. Thus, it is no longer difficult to understand the finding of Hannaway (1993) in her study of decentralizing districts. When all types of social control are considered, her startling observation was that:

> our analysis overall has led us to conclude that teachers in successful decentralized districts work under conditions where organizational controls over their behavior are in fact high relative to what we would expect in traditionally organized schools. Indeed, the discretion of school-level actors in many decentralized systems may be far more restricted than the discretion of school-level actors in traditionally organized systems. (Hannaway, 1993, p. 139).

The key difference, however, is that control (or coherence or system) is now to come first and foremost from the decentralized bottom, not the top. And, by 'bottom-level' is meant an aggregation of policies and procedures 'around the central task area – teaching and learning' (Elmore, 1993, p. 51). Whether more or less overall control is a product of decentralization, the simple value that looms largest in analysis, says Fullan (1993, p. 161), is that 'a preoccupation with *instruction* and *inquiry* (the constant pursuit of new ideas and practices) at *both* the school and system levels characterizes successful districts'.

To date, however, there has been remarkably little inquiry into the re-organization of school-system policy and administration arising from teaching and learning (Evertson and Murphy, 1992). Some earlier naiveté has been dispelled, that simply freeing teachers and/or communities from the straitjacket of the upper bureaucracy would necessarily lead to greater student achievement (see Murphy, 1991; Hannaway, 1993). But that which proceeds effectively from the technical core to effective hierarchical 'linkages' (Newmann, 1993) or 'coordinated codevelopment' (Fullan, 1993) in a service-to and support-of school improvement in urban education, remains much the mystery,

One model outlined (but with little detail) by Smith and O'Day (1991) suggests a combined school-site and district-level thrust to support instruction within an overarching 'systemic' framework of national standards and state goals. Productive and rewarding workplaces for teachers, emphasizing professional knowledge and responsibility, are to be the key to change at the school-site. A complementary removal of standardization and constraints (e.g., rigid time requirements, uniform class sizes, textbook conformity), in service to effective professionalization at the school-site, is to be the key district role. De-emphasizing the dividedness and separability often implied by decentralization, Smith and O'Day (1991, p. 257) stress instead the importance of a 'coherent vision and direction throughout the system'.

In like manner, Murphy and Hallinger (1993, p. 257) emphasize that successful restructuring cannot be compartmentalized. 'Improvement efforts', they stress, 'must unfold so that changes become woven into the basic fabric of the organization'. Working from what little empirical evidence there is to date on central-office and school-site responses (in tandem) to restructuring, Murphy and Hallinger (1993, p. 253) pose a systemic model with four 'general guidelines': (a) backward-map the full organizational and governance structure of the district 'from the student', (b) focus on restructuring (the continuing process) rather than a restructured 'product', (c) tailor district supports to the service of 'contextualized' needs of specific schools and communities, and (d) work toward system coherence above the easily attained fallout of further fragmentation through decentralization.

Beyond such broadly generalized 'models', there is yet little sense (in depth and in detail) as to how an urban school district should be effectively 'backward-mapped' from the core technology toward a coherent system of service-to and support-of school-site improvement.

Chicago's reform legislation in 1989 provides an example of the difficulties and problems encountered in decentralization. By the summer of 1993, Chicago's downtown office had still not finalized its 'standards document'; and the city's legislative mandate to monitor reform was all but forgotten. Persons responsible for the standards project in the central office complained (during interviews in mid-1993) that prior to reform such a task would have presented no difficulty. With its power to control and to limit 'involvement' in school policymaking, the central office staff would have just 'done it'. 'Now', continues the complaint, 'all the tinkering that's going on reflects the new, crazy politics of this place. Board members intervene, the union gets into it, community groups, the reform coalition. They all want to set their standards' (McPherson and Crowson, 1993).

In sum, a weakened central office in Chicago, no longer a bureaucratic monolith, has found itself without the clout to carry out a key role which is supportive of reform. Likewise, those who press toward coherence, 'coordinated codevelopment', and the continuation of 'system' in restructuring may fail to realize that an organization turned on its head is no longer the same organization, either at the bottom or the top. Its politics and environmental permeability have changed; its authority, rewards, and communications structures have been altered; it may have little 'service' or 'support' left to give.

2 The Monitor Role

Despite downsizing, and often a fair amount of bureaucracy-'bashing', it is not at all uncommon (as in Chicago) for the central office under reform to be expected still to engage in a monitoring of school-site behaviour and performance. It has, realistically, to be recognized that all public-sector organizations, whether centralized or decentralized, are a tempting array of incentives to individuals to use the employing organization for their own private purposes (Boyd and Crowson, 1981; Leibenstein, 1987; Boyd and Hartman, 1988).

Indeed, Vaughan (1990, p. 225) warns from the example of NASA's *Challenger* space-shuttle tragedy, that an allocation downward of regulatory autonomy can vitally affect important issues of 'social control of risky technologies'. By no means is decentralized education filled with the same sort of 'risky technologies', but a number of urban-school districts (particularly New York, Houston, and San Francisco) have recently discovered anew the value of from-the-top action to step in and 'reconstitute' the administrative staffs of poorly-performing schools (see Fernandez with Underwood, 1993; Schmidt, 1993). The recognition is that even downsized and decentralized systems must find a capacity to monitor, for there is risk indeed (particularly of the public- and political-fallout variety) in grassroots' interests, structures, and behaviours left unsupervised.

However, the trick, the basic challenge, under restructured urban education, observe Hill and Bonan (1991, p. vi), is 'how to assist schools and guarantee quality in a system whose basic premise is variety, not uniformity'. The notion is that a monitoring role must somehow manage to respect fully the diversity, site-responsiveness, professionalization, and learning-driven qualities of decentralization while simultaneously providing assurance of system-wide accountability, legality, and morality.

The recognition is that some key central-office values must change. Traditionally, centralized monitoring has emphasized compliance with: (a) state and federal regulations vis-a-vis flow-through and mandated programs (e.g., special education, bilingual education); (b) the rules and regulations and contractual commitments (particularly the teachers' contract) of the Board of Education; (c) the instructional/curricular policies of the district, producing evidence (e.g., standardized achievement-test scores), along the way, of instructional compliance; and, (d) fairness and equity (e.g., in resource allocation) as much as possible across the city's many schools.

Under decentralization, quite a different set of monitoring objectives is proposed (see particularly Hill and Bonan, 1991; Bimber, 1993). *First*, it is suggested that a monitoring function should ask whether the schools are accomplishing, over time, what *they* propose to accomplish. Accountability mechanisms under decentralization, note Hill and Bonan (1991, p. 49), 'must reflect each school's particular objectives and strategies'; tieing in with each school's specific identity, its own sense of 'needs', and its own strategies for planning performance-improvement. Hill and Bonan (1991, p. 48) write: 'accountability starts at home, with a clear vision of the school's identity and the experiences that it intends to provide children, and with a determination to maintain those qualities through close internal monitoring of processes and student outcomes.' The key central-office role, it is claimed, should be that of 'unobtrusive oversight' of the school-site plans and their fulfilment, reviewing the plans, assisting schools with their plans, and evaluating the schools' individual abilities to develop in terms of their plans (Hill and Bonan, 1991, p. 62).[3]

Second, however, the realization recently (in near-contradiction to the above) has been that decentralized systems may still require a central body that can 'step-in' with strength and authority to rescue or reconstitute 'troubled' schools. Curiously, where there was great 'unobtrusiveness' in the work of urban-school systems in the past, it was often especially to be found in the arena of school-to-school evaluation. Here quiet, no-publicity transfers of administrators (with usually the transfer-in of a known 'fire-quencher' as principal) were the not-unlikely 'solution' for troubled buildings.

Interestingly, under reform the quiet, bureaucratic remedy seems to fail public acceptability; thus increasing the numbers of cities (e.g., Houston, Cleveland, Memphis, New York, San Francisco) exploring openly 'the use of wholesale personnel changes as a way of giving a fresh start to schools that prove chronically unsuccessful in educating their students' (Schmidt, 1993, p. 22). Even while urging as a first priority a flexible, school-specific approach to monitoring, Hill and Bonan (1991, p. 63) similarly call for 'an independent school analysis done by the central-office testing and accountability unit, [so that] school staffs would be prevented from trying to glide over their problems with slick or evasive presentations.'

Third, in a continued concern over issues of equity and the possible distributive consequences of unsupervised variability, it is suggested that a central-office role should be 'to insure that idiosyncratic variations in programs, people, and policies do not result in systematic differences in the quality of education for children' (Watt, 1989; Corbett *et al.*, 1991, p. 3).[4] In a paper articulating these equity concerns, Frederick Wirt (1991) quotes political scientist Herbert Kaufman's observation from 1969, that: 'decentralization will soon be followed by disparities in practice among the numerous small units, brought on by differences in human and financial resources, that will engender demands for central intervention to restore equality and balance and concerted action' (Kaufman, 1969, p. 11).

It has long been the practice of many urban bureaucracies (including education) to use 'bureaucratic decision rules' (often effectively 'buried') in such a way as to equalize services (e.g., between white and black wards of the city) (see Toulmin, 1988; MLadenka, 1989). Thus, Kenneth Wong (1989, 1992) discovered, for example, that Chicago's downtown officials, pre-reform, very carefully and quietly pursued a 'dual strategy' in funding that city's magnet-school approach to voluntary racial integration. Despite both promoting and catering to the popular political appeal of magnet-school choice, Chicago's school bureaucrats diligently practised below-the-surface strategies of budget-parity, with allocative guidelines that did not put neighborhood schools at a resource disadvantage (Wong, 1989). Wong warned in 1989, at the beginning of Chicago's reform era, that the reform movement could have 'distributive consequences' (Wong, 1989, p. 34).

Briefly, in summary it seems illogical with decentralization, and with the power-to-the-people ideals of such reforms as Chicago's (Wong and Rollow, 1990), to outline a central-office role as monitor. Nevertheless, despite the press toward a school-site professionalism and a community responsiveness in urban education, national discussions of 'standards', 'systemic reform', and 'coherence' suggest that a larger-than-the-neighborhood accountability is still an important value. The question is how; how to prevent a stifling uniformity and possible recentralization while encouraging improvement in the benefits of the system, maintaining both variety and diversity.

The 'how' question has not yet been answered satisfactorily, but suggestions to date are that: (a) the individual school-site should be given every opportunity to improve, on *its* terms, and monitored accordingly; while, somewhat incongruously, (b) sufficient strength should be retained by a central authority of some type to step in, exert leadership, and 'reconstitute' troubled schools; and, (c) the possible distributive effects of variability should be watched most carefully. One of the most intriguing and potentially most troublesome aspects of the monitoring role under reform resides in our observation that activities (b) and (c) above seem often to have been performed in the past by 'strong' bureaucracies in quiet, unobtrusive, environmentally 'closed' ways. Now, these activities are asked of much weaker and power-dispersed bureaucracies in more openly political times.

3 The Superintendent's Leadership Role

Few positions of executive leadership have become less attractive to job candidates in recent years than the large-city superintendency. The time-in-office, in most settings across the nation, has been far too short for effective school-improvement. The conflict-laden, high-pressure job of general superintendent is an extremely difficult position in the best of times; it is a most discouraging, frustrating, and inadequately respected role in times of accelerating urban decline. The 'failures' of the public schools seem to symbolize the poor economic and social health of the entire city, with the not-always-implicit message through the community that if the schools would just improve, with better leadership, then the city itself could be 'made well'. Needless to say, fewer and fewer fully qualified candidates have been rushing to embrace this rather thankless administrative responsibility (Crowson and Boyd, 1992).

Strong superintendents stood a better chance historically of gaining control over their not-very-compliant bureaucracies. By no means would the Byzantine central office give immediate and unselfish loyalty to each of its (all-too-rapid) progression of chief executive officers. Control often had to be craftily wrested, first from folks downtown, then steadily from the regional offices and the schools. Even in these modern days of lessened control-from-the-top, Fernandez' auto-biography (*Superintendent in Miami*) discusses tough battles in New York to establish 'jurisdictional prerogatives' over the subdistricts and the schools, often describing these battles in fight-to-the-finish terms (e.g., 'it was only a glancing blow, not a knockout') (Fernandez with Underwood, 1993, p. 208).

Curiously, it is just as vital in a decentralized city system as in the days of old to seek strength in the superintendency; perhaps no longer in a controlling, stay-the-course or fight-to-the-finish sense, but strength nevertheless. Indeed, Jerome Murphy (1991, p. 512) put it well, in observing:

> . . . old administrative notions of hierarchical control and top-down
> management are of limited value today. As power and knowledge
> become more dispersed, as multiple constituencies demand attention,
> as schooling becomes more decentralized and professionalized, and as
> distrust of government grows, the Terminator approach simply will not
> work.

However, the effective superintendent for today, continues Murphy (1991, p. 512), 'must be both a tough manager with solutions and a caring educator who listens; who is an active learner, an enabler, a catalyst who makes good things happen for children'.

Making 'good things happen for children' is no less the responsibility of the chief executive officer than it is the job of school-site professionals (Murphy and Hallinger, 1988). Indeed, in a national survey of 1,200 principals across school districts of varying size, Wirt and Krug (1993) discovered that the 'single striking variable' in attributions of instructional leadership is the superintendent's combination of supervision and expectations.

Although the large-city superintendent is far removed from the classroom, it would be an error, says Joseph Murphy (1993b) to pose 'a reduced role for these players'. Likewise, in a late 1980s study of six big-city superintendents who did become well known for school-improvement, Hill, Wise, and Shapiro (1989, p. 26) note that these superintendents 'were explicit and controlling about values and priorities but gave subordinates room to create their own tactical solutions to problems.'

Significantly, the Hill *et al.* (1989, p. 20) study also demonstrated that the communication of instructional-improvement expectations downward and outward through the system worked only if effectively buttressed by the creation of a 'public mandate' from the 'outside'. Similarly, Jerome Murphy (1991, p. 512) warns that today's city superintendents must more than ever begin '. . . building alliances with mayors, legislators, governors, and the business community, as well as establishing ties with social, welfare, and youth employment agencies.' They should be 'the chief public advocates for children' (Murphy, 1991, p. 512).

Such a public advocacy role also requires strength, not a political commodity easily and readily at hand to today's urban superintendent. Indeed, Ayers (1993, p. 177) notes that most of today's restructuring and decentralization of city systems has regarded the school district as the object rather than the participating agent of reform. Thus, a good deal of influence, oversight, and power increasingly has come to reside outside the system itself, and the folks acquiring this power (e.g., reform coalitions) tend to 'plot revolutions' (see also Mirel, 1993). Similarly, political leadership during times of retrenchment and downsizing is a particularly difficult undertaking, write Morgan and Palmer, Jr (1988), for the cutback process isolates, politically, rather than unites.

What, then, is the superintendent of schools to do in providing forceful leadership and making good things happen for children; amid weakened central-office resources and now-distributed-to-the-schools controls? *First*, she can work carefully to flesh out the vision and the reality of revised values in service-to-the-schools (and backward-mapped governance and monitoring) as delineated earlier in this chapter. The symbolic as well as the put-it-into-practice power of the superintendency (in thinking children-first and in redirecting the organization from control to service), is a commodity not to be discounted. Even under decentralization, educators are inclined to look all the way upward to the CEO for clues as to their own 'direction'.

Second, the superintendent can (and should) give forceful, energetic attention to the school system's relationship with its larger urban (and state and national) environment. From the pattern maintenance of old, the new role should be a much more entrepreneurial representation of public schools (Crowson and Boyd, 1992): building 'community-wide coalitions on behalf of children' (Murphy, 1993b); 'selling' the needs (and the accomplishments) of the schools to the larger political and economic community; finding common ground and active co-operation with the city's other providers of services to children and families; engaging actively in the political fray on behalf of the schools, and, clearly setting an 'agenda' for the public schools. These are among the vital activities today of a position now torn from its tendency in the past to prefer a behind-the-scenes role rather than the front page.

Third, the superintendent should provide the district's oversight-level of leadership in moving the city's schools beyond a rhetoric of restructuring toward some truly 'deep-structure' changes in the organization of instruction. While restructuring and 'systemic' change are the order of the day, practice-oriented inquiry has not proceeded very far in illuminating that which can meaningfully cope with the 'DNA' of school systems, the institutionalized structures imbedded in organizational cultures, symbols, rules, and roles. Furthermore, ongoing programmes and even new proposals for the training of superintendents tend to concentrate upon the competencies and 'skills repertoire' of the CEO (e.g., oral and written communication, conflict management, finance and budgeting skills), with relatively little corresponding attention to the harsh realities of institutional change, whatever the skill (see Carter *et al.*, 1993). Thus, with relatively little assistance from the scholarly community on just how to change deep-structures systemically, we can only agree with Murphy (1993d) that it will be vital for 'risk-takers' and 'reflective practitioners' to inhabit these roles; people who are unafraid to give-it-a-try.

In summary, one of the least well-understood paradoxes of school-district decentralization is the continuing need for strong, even forceful (Stout, 1993) administrative leadership from the top amid strong, forceful leadership from the bottom. Part of the reason why strength is required at both ends, argues Loveless (1993, p. 5) is to be found 'in the manner in which each level of the system is connected to the larger environment'. A school-site attachment and adaptation to its unique community environment is little assisted by a chief executive office unable to participate fully in a larger, supportive process of 'urban regeneration' (Judd and Parkinson, 1990). A chief executive can guide a school district only minimally (with old bureaucratic controls in abeyance) toward a new service-of-instruction relationship with the schools (or a combined variety- and quality-maintaining form of monitoring) without a good-faith exercise of moral responsibility and strong leadership at the grassroots. And, a risk-management role for the superintendent might help him or her to be newly respected and honored as risk-taker, in the interest of systemic reform.

CONCLUSION

In an earlier analysis of changes in urban schooling, Crowson and Boyd (1992) argued that city school systems are increasingly displaying evidence of new directions in environmental adaptation, in exciting but quite separate and potentially conflicting directions. A renewed emphasis upon the school-site offers the promise of a closely adaptive match between school and community, plus an emphasis upon diversity and some measure of 'market'- or client-centredness, as well as a bottom-up professionalization of urban schooling (and with such professionalization the possibility of a newly defined core-technology-driven approach to school and school district management).

On the other hand, it was our observation that a redefined environmental 'fit' at the top of the urban school system was far from settled, that with beleaguered CEOs, evidence of lost faith in the public schools, budgets in crisis, employee organizations vowing to give no more, and round after round of 'bureaucracy-bashing', the city school system was still far from effectively restructured or reformed. We questioned whether decentralization by itself would go very far to overcome the deep deficiencies of urban education (see Boyd, 1991); and we were concerned that there seemed to be little by way of an effective balancing or an establishment of linkages between school district top and bottom, in support of school reform.

It is encouraging to note that very recently a literature has started to develop (and there is increasing experimental activity among practitioners) inquiring into the leadership role of the superintendent and the central office, plus the opportunities for a new sense of 'system', under decentralization.[5] We would agree with Michael Fullan (1993) that neither centralization nor decentralization works, but that a solid measure of *strength* in leadership is required at both ends.

The literature to date on a redefined central-office role has few details and only some rather vague models to be drawn upon. There is the suggestion that a service-to-the-schools role should replace a controlling relationship, but there is not agreement as to whether 'school-site demand' or a bit more in the way of 'coherence' should be the preferred value. As much as it hints of old-style supervision, there is the suggestion that a monitoring role is still a proper central-office responsibility. But the tricky relationship between monitoring in support of each school's plans and monitoring in the larger public interest remains a yet-unresolved administrative challenge. And, there is now a sense that urban schooling under decentralization may require even stronger leadership from the school district superintendent, a leadership that somehow manages with much-weakened organizational control and with much-weakened power politically to nevertheless 'make good things happen for children'.

NOTES

The work summarized here was supported by the office of Educational Research and Improvement (OERI) of the US Department of Education through a grant to the National Center for School Leadership at the University of Illinois, Champaign-Urbana. The opinions expressed do not necessarily reflect the position of the supporting agencies, and no official endorsement should be inferred. While absolving them of any responsibility for this paper, the authors wish to acknowledge the extremely helpful comments of Joseph Murphy and R. Bruce McPherson in their review of an earlier draft.

1 By no means is there agreement on just what it means to decentralize in educational governance and administration. A transfer of authority and decision-making responsibility downward hierarchically to the school-site is often implied, but whether the transfer is to be simply administrative in focus or political, or both, is often left unclarified. Similarly, the values behind decentralization have varied widely – from a desire to 'empower' communities and/or teachers, to a bust-up-the-bureaucracy approach to added organizational efficiency and accountability, to a search for improved 'outcomes' in

schools through a closer-to-the-client reorientation of organizational lifeways (see Bimber, 1993; Hill and Bonan, 1991; Hannaway and Carnoy, 1993).

2 We are indebted to Joe Murphy at Vanderbilt for this important observation.

3 Bimber (1993) suggests the value of a 'contract' between the central office and the individual school-sites. The contract sets goals and levels of performance but gives the local unit freedom to specify its own methods and procedures for attaining the goals.

4 Likewise, Tallerico (1993, p. 243) asks: 'How can the central educational objective of *equity* be guaranteed in a decentralized educational structure?' She goes on to note: 'Historical experience (for example, racial segregation) demonstrates that harmful inequalities may be perpetrated in the absence of centralized constraints.'

5 We admire the initiative (and the courage) of central-office personnel in Chicago to begin an 'organizational analysis project' with the 1993–94 school year – a project aimed at 'changing the institutional culture in the administration from control to service', at prioritizing central administrative functions 'on school needs', and at developing a 'demand-driven system wide strategy' (see Gillispie, 1993). There is, unfortunately, almost nothing in the extant literature, at this time, that will be of much practical assistance to Chicago's experimenters in the implementation of these organizational-reorientation objectives.

REFERENCES

Ayers, W. (1993) 'Chicago: A Restless Sea of Social Forces', in C.T. Kerchner and J.E. Koppich (eds), *A Union of Professionals: Labor Relations and Educational Reform*. New York: Teachers College Press.

Ayres, L.P. (1909) *Laggards in Our Schools: A Study of Retardation and Elimination in City School Systems*. New York: Charities Publication Committee.

Barnard, C.I. (1938) *The Functions of the Executive*. Cambridge, MA: Harvard University Press.

Barney, J.B. and Ouchi, W.G. (eds) *Organizational Economics*. San Francisco: Jossey-Bass.

Biggart, N.W. (1977) 'The creative-destructive process of organizational change: the case of the Post Office', *Administrative Science Quarterly*, 22(3), 410–426.

Bimber, B. (1993) *School Decentralization: Lessons from the Study of Bureaucracy*, Santa Monica, CA: RAND Institute on Education and Training.

Boyd, W.L. (1991) 'What makes ghetto schools succeed or fail?', *Teachers College Record*, 92, 331–362.

Boyd, W.L. and Crowson, R.L. (1981) 'The changing conception and practice of public school administration', in D.C. Berliner (ed.), *Review of Research in Education*, vol. 9. Washington, D.C.: American Educational Research Association.

Boyd, W.L. and Hartman, W. (1988) 'The politics of educational productivity', in D. Monk and J. Underwood (eds), *Microlevel School Finance: Issues and Implications for Policy*. Cambridge, MA: Ballinger.

Bradley, A. (1993) 'The business of reforming Cincinnati's schools', *Education Week*, 12(34), 1, 16–17.

Brown, D.J. (1992) 'The re-centralization of school districts', *Educational Policy*, 6(3).

Callahan, R.E. (1962) *Education and the Cult of Efficiency*. Chicago: University of Chicago Press.

Carter, D.S.G., Glass, T.E. and Hord, S. (1993) *Selecting, Preparing and Developing the School District Superintendent*. Washington, D.C.: The Falmer Press.

Chapman, J.D. (ed.) (1990) *School-Based Decision-Making and Management*. London: The Falmer Press.

Cibulka, J.G. (1991) 'Local school reform in Chicago speciality high schools: a ecological view'. Paper presented at the Annual Meeting of the American Educational Research Association (AERA), Chicago.

Corbett, H.D., Wilson, B.L. and Adduci, L. (1991) 'The central office role in school improvement'. Paper presented at the Annual Meeting of the American Educational Research Association (AERA), Chicago.

Cronin, J.M. (1973) *The Control of Urban Schools*. New York: The Free Press.

Crowson, R.L. and Boyd, W.L. (1988) 'Rational choice theory and administrative hierarchy in education', Occasional Paper, unpublished, College of Education, University of Illinois at Chicago.

Crowson, R.L. and Boyd, W.L. (1992) 'Urban schools as organizations: political perspectives', in J.G. Cibulka, R.J. Reed, and K.K. Wong (eds), *The Politics of Urban Education in the United States*. Washington, D.C.: The Falmer Press.

Crowson, R. and Hannaway, J. (1988) 'Introduction and overview: the politics of reforming school administration', in J. Hannaway and R. Crowson (eds), *The Politics of Reforming School Administration*. New York: The Falmer Press.

Crowson, R.L. and Morris, V.C. (1991) 'The superintendency and school leadership', in P.W. Thurston and P.P. Zodhiates (eds), *Advances in Educational Administration*. Greenwich, CT: JAI Press.

Crozier, M. (1964) *The Bureaucratic Phenomenon*. Chicago: University of Chicago Press.

Cuban, L. (1976) *Urban School Chiefs Under Fire*. Chicago: University of Chicago Press.

Elmore, R.F. (1993) 'School decentralization: who gains? who loses?', in J. Hannaway and M. Carnoy (eds), *Decentralization and School Improvement*. San Francisco: Jossey-Bass.

Etzioni, A. (1993) *The Spirit of Community*. New York: Crown.

Evertson, C. and Murphy, J. (1992) 'Beginning with classrooms: implications for restructuring schools', in H.H. Marshall (ed.), *Supporting Student Learning: Roots of Educational Change*. Norwood, NJ: Ablex.

Feldman, M.L. and March, J.G. (1981) 'Information in organizations as signal and symbol', *Administrative Science Quarterly*, 26, 171–186.

Fernandez, J.A. with Underwood, J. (1993) *Tales out of School: Joseph Fernandez's Crusade to Rescue American Education*. Boston: Little, Brown and Co.

Ferris, J.M. (1992) 'School-based decision making: a principal-agent perspective', *Educational Evaluation and Policy Analysis*, 14(4), 333–346.

Focus Group (1992) 'Focus Group Report: Support functions in a reformed school system', *Substance*, a monthly journal for the Chicago Public Schools, 18 6–7.

Fullan, M.G. (1993) 'Coordinating school and district development in restructuring', in J. Murphy and P. Hallinger (eds), *Restructuring Schooling: Learning from Ongoing Efforts*. Newbury Park, CA: Corwin Press, Inc.

Fullan, M.G. and Miles, M.B. (1992) 'Getting reform right: what works and what doesn't', *Phi Delta Kappan*, 745–752.

Gamoran, A. and Dreeben, R. (1986) 'Coupling and control in educational organizations', *Administrative Science Quarterly*, 31(4), 612–632.

Gillispie, C. (1993) 'A proposal for an organizational analysis and restructuring of the Chicago public schools', Chicago: Chicago Public Schools.

Gittell, M. and Hollander, T.E. (1968) *Six Urban School Districts*. New York: Praeger.

Goldring, E. and Sullivan, A.V.S. (forthcoming) 'Privatization: integrating private services in public schools', in P. Cookson and B. Schneider (eds), *Creating School Policy: Trends, Dilemmas and Prospects*..

Gouldner, A.W. (1955) *Patterns of Industrial Bureaucracy*. London: Routledge and Kegan Paul.

Gutman, A. (1987) *Democratic Education*. Princeton, NJ: Princeton University Press.

Hannaway, J. (1989) *Managers Managing: The Workings of an Administrative System*. New York: Oxford University Press.

Hannaway, J. (1993) 'Decentralization in two school districts: challenging the standard paradigm', in J. Hannaway and M. Carnoy (eds), *Decentralization and School Improvement: Can we Fulfill the Promise?* San Francisco: Jossey-Bass.

Hannaway, J. and Carnoy, M. (eds) (1993) *Decentralization and School Improvement: Can We Fulfill the Promise?* San Francisco: Jossey-Bass.

Hawley, W.D. (1993) 'Facilitating the fundamental restructuring of schools: twenty years of lessons from the high school in the community. A Report to the National Center for Educational Leadership'. Nashville, TN: Peabody College, Vanderbilt University.

Hickson, D.J. and McCullough, A.F. (1980) 'Power in organizations', in G. Salaman and K. Thompson (eds), *Control and Ideology in Organizations*. Cambridge, MA: The M.I.T. Press.

Hill, P. and Bonan, J. (1991) *Decentralization and Accountability in Public Education*. Santa Monica, CA: RAND.

Hill, P., Wise, A. and Shapiro, L. (1989) *Educational Progress: Cities Mobilize to Improve Their Schools*. Santa Monica, CA: RAND.

Judd, D. and Parkinson, M. (eds) (1990) *Leadership and Urban Regeneration: Cities in North America and Europe*. Newbury Park, CA: Sage.

Kaufman, H. (1969) 'Administrative decentralization and political power', *Public Administration Review*, 29, 3–15.

Kerchner, C.T., Koppich, J., King, B. and Weeres, J. (1990) 'This could be the start of something big: labor relations reforms in the 1990s', Paper presented at the University Council for Educational Administration (UCEA), Pittsburgh.

LaNoue, G.R. and Smith, B.L.R. (1973) *The Politics of School Decentralization*. Lexington, MA: Lexington Books.

Leibenstein, H. (1987) *Inside the Firm: The Inefficiencies of Hierarchy*. Cambridge, MA: Harvard University Press.

Loveless, T. (1993) 'Organizational coupling and the implementation of tracking reform', *Administrator's Notebook*, 35(8), 1–6.

March, J.G. (1978) 'American public school administration: a short analysis', *School Review*, 86(2), 217–250.

McPherson, R.B. and Crowson, R.L. (forthcoming) 'The principal as mini-superintendent under Chicago reform', in J. Murphy and K.S. Louis (eds), *Reshaping the Principalship: Insights from Transformational Reform Efforts*. Newbury Park, CA: Corwin.

McPherson, R.B. and Crowson, R.L. (1993) *Interview Notes, Research into the Adaptations of Central Office Personnel under Chicago School Reform*. Chicago: College of Education, University of Illinois, Chicago.

Mirel, J. (1993) 'School reform, Chicago style: educational innovation in a changing urban context, 1976–1991', *Urban Education*, 28(2), 116–149.

MLadenka, K.R. (1989) 'The distribution of an urban public service: the changing role of race and politics', *Urban Affairs Quarterly*, 24(4), 556–583.

Moe, T.M. (1984) 'The new economics of organization', *American Journal of Political Science*, 28, 739–777.

Morgan, D.R. and Palmer, W.J., Jr (1988) 'Coping with fiscal stress: predicting the use of financial management practices among U.S. cities', *Urban Affairs Quarterly*, 24(1), 69–86.

Morris, V.C., Crowson, R.L., Porter-Gehrie, C. and Hurwitz, E., Jr (1984) *Principals in Action: The Reality of Managing Schools*. Columbus, OH: Charles E. Merrill.

Murphy, J. (1991a) *Restructuring Schools: Capturing and Assessing the Phenomena*. New York: Teachers College Press.

Murphy, J.T. (1991b) 'Superintendents as saviors: from the Terminator to Pogo', *Phi Delta Kappan*, 27(7), 507–513.

Murphy, J.M. (1992) 'School effectiveness and school restructuring: contributions to educational improvement', *School Effectiveness and School Improvement* 3(2), 90–109.

Murphy, J.M. (1993a) 'The challenging role of the superintendency in restructuring districts in Kentucky', under review.

Murphy, J.M. (1993b) 'Restructuring schools in Kentucky: insights from superintendents', in K. Leithwood (ed.), *Perspectives on Effective School Leadership*. Albany: SUNY Press, forthcoming.

Murphy, J.M. (1993c) 'Restructuring in Kentucky: the changing role of the superintendent and the central office', manuscript under review, Nashville, TN: Peabody College, Vanderbilt University.

Murphy, J. (1993d) 'At the crossroads: improving preparation programs for school leaders'. A background paper prepared for the Danforth Foundation, Dept of Educational Leadership, Peabody College, Vanderbilt University, Nashville.

Murphy, J and Hallinger, P. (1988) 'The characteristics of instructionally effective school districts', *Journal of Educational Research*, 81(3), 175–181.

Murphy, J.M. and Hallinger, P. (1993) 'Restructured schooling: learning from ongoing efforts', in J. Murphy and P. Hallinger (eds), *Restructuring Schooling: Learning from Ongoing Efforts*. Newbury Park, CA: Corwin Press, Inc.

Newmann, F.M. (1993) 'Beyond common sense in educational restructuring: the issues of content and linkage', *Educational Researcher*, 22(2), 4–13, 22.

'The Perfect School' (1993) *U.S. News & World Report*, January 11, pp. 46–61.

Peterson, P.E. (1976) *School Politics, Chicago Style*. Chicago: University of Chicago Press.

Peterson, P.E. (1981) *City Limits*. Chicago: University of Chicago Press.

Rogers, D. (1968) *110 Livingston Street*. New York: Random House.

Sarason, S.B. (1993) *The Case for Change: Rethinking the Preparation of Educators*. San Francisco: Jossey-Bass.

Sayre, W. and Kaufman, H. (1960) *Governing New York City*. New York: Russell Sage.

Schmidt, P. (1993) 'Interest grows in new policy tool: Replacing staffs of failing schools', *Education Week*, 1, 22–23.

Seaphus, G. (1993) 'School demand-based central office and subdistrict office staffing', A report to the Chicago Public Schools, Quantum Education Institute, Chicago.

Seibel, T. (1992) '26 schools ring up $10,000 bell grants', *Chicago Sun-Times*, September 16, p. 22.

Sergiovanni, T. (1993) 'Organizations as communities: changing the metaphor changes the theory'. Invited address to Division A of the American Educational Research Association (AERA), Atlanta.

Smith, M.S. and O'Day, J. (1991) 'Systemic school reform', in S.H. Fuhrman and B. Malen (eds), *The Politics of Curriculum and Testing*, The 1990 Yearbook of the Politics of Education Association. London: The Falmer Press.

Smylie, M.A. and Crowson, R.L. (1993) 'Principal assessment under restructured governance', *Peabody Journal of Education*, 68(2), 64–84.

Spaulding, F.E. (1955) *School Superintendents in Action in Five Cities*. Ringe, NH: Richard R. Smith.

Spielman, F. and Vander Weele, M. (1993) 'Daley's school strategy', *Chicago Sun-Times*, April 27 p. 1.

Spring, J. (1990) *The American School, 1642–1990*, second edition. New York: Longman.

Stinchcombe, A.L. (1965) 'Social structure and organizations', in J.G. March (ed.), *Handbook of Organizations*. Chicago: Rand McNally.

Stout, R.T. (1993) 'Establishing the mission, vision, and goals', in P.B. Forsyth and M. Tallerico (eds), *City Schools: Leading the Way*. Newbury Park, CA: Corwin Press, Inc.

Tallerico, M. (1993) 'Governing urban schools', in P.B. Forsyth and M. Tallerico (eds), *City Schools: Leading the Way*. Newbury Park, CA: Corwin Press.

Toulmin, L.M. (1988) 'Equity as a decision rule in determining the distribution of urban public services', *Urban Affairs Quarterly*, 23(3), 389–413.

Tyack, D.B. (1974) *The One Best System*. Cambridge, MA: Harvard University Press.

Tyack, D. (1990) 'Restructuring in historical perspective: tinkering toward utopia', *Teachers' College Record*, 92(2), 170–191.

Tyack, D.B. (1993) 'School governance in the United States: historical puzzles and anomalies', in J. Hannaway and M. Carnoy (eds), *Decentralization and School Improvement*. San Francisco: Jossey-Bass.

Vaughan, D. (1990) 'Autonomy, interdependence, and social control: NASA and the space shuttle *Challenger*', *Administrative Science Quarterly*, 35(2), 225–257.

Watt, J. (1989) 'Devolution of power: the ideological meaning', *Journal of Educational Administration*, 27(1), 19–28.

Weber, M. (1947 tr) *The Theory of Social and Economic Organizations*, A.H. Henderson and T. Parsons (eds), New York: The Free Press (first published in 1924).

Wirt, F.W. (1991) 'Forgetting history: 19th century decentralization of education and policy'. Paper presented at the Annual Meeting of the American Educational Research Association (AERA), Chicago.

Wirt, F. and Krug, S. (1993) 'A constructivist theory of leadership: a national sample test', Paper prepared for delivery at the Annual Meeting of the American Political Science Association, Washington, D.C.

Wisby, G. (1993) 'Principal's at home in school', *Chicago Sun-Times*, April 28, p. 5.

Wong, K.K. (1989) 'Choice in public schools: their institutional functions and distributive consequences'. Paper presented at the Annual Meeting of the American Political Science Association, Chicago.

Wong, K.K. (1990) *City Choices: Education and Housing*. Albany: State University of New York Press.

Wong, K.K. (1992a) 'The politics of urban education as a field of study: an interpretive analysis', in J.G. Cibulka, R.J. Reed, and K.K. Wong (eds), *The Politics of Urban Education in the United States*. Washington, D.C.: The Falmer Press.

Wong, K.K. (1992b) 'Choice in public schools: their institutional functions and distributive consequences', in K.K. Wong (ed.), *Research in Public Policy: Politics of Policy Innovation in Chicago*, vol. 4. Greenwich, CT: JAI Press.

Wong, K.K. and Rollow, S.G. (1990) 'A case study of the recent Chicago school reform: Part II: the mobilization phase', *Administrator's Notebook*, 34(5), 1–6.

Chapter 10

Education for Urban America[1]

Paul Hill

The decline of big American cities can be measured by the collapse of their public schools. Before the immigration wave of the late 1980s, the public-school systems of the most important US metropolises, including New York, Chicago, Los Angeles, Boston, and Houston, had suffered enrolment declines averaging 30 per cent, and their student populations had become increasingly poor and welfare-dependent. Working- and middle-class students of all racial and ethnic groups have deserted the big-city public schools for suburban and private schools.

Until the 1950s, many big-city school systems were among the best in the country. The New York, Chicago, and Boston public-school systems, among others, were America's greatest sources of successful and outstanding business leaders, public officials, and scholars. Small-town and rural schools were generally considered inferior in teacher quality, classrooms and other instructional resources, and community support. Since that time, however, urban schools have declined dramatically; half the students in big-city school systems drop out before high-school graduation, four times the national average rate. The majority of students in big-city public schools drop behind the national average in reading after the fourth grade and never catch up. Only one-third of the graduates of some big-city public high schools can score well enough on the military qualifying tests to enlist in the armed forces.

Since the days of their earlier success the big-city schools have changed in many ways. Buildings constructed near the end of the 19th century are still in use, and many are suffering from decades of neglect. Spending in city schools, once the highest in the country, is now lower than in surrounding suburban areas (US Department of Education, 1991a and 1991b). Local-system governing boards, once staid collections of educated citizens, are now arenas for conflict among the politically ambitious. Most schools are burdened by layer after layer of regulations emanating from board politics, federal and state funding programmes, and court orders. Teachers are unionized, and their contracts, after decades of bargaining in which city governing boards made concessions on work rules rather than grant wage demands, constrain any attempt to adapt school programmes to new needs.

The combined effect of all these trends is to make big-city public school systems weak and inflexible – exactly the wrong characteristics for organizations that must master an exceptionally turbulent situation. City student populations are changing faster than at any time since the turn of the century, and city school budgets are declining even as their student populations increase. Since the 1960s, the student populations of most big cities have changed from majority white to majority Hispanic or black. After a period of enrolment decline caused by 'white flight', many city-school populations have grown dramatically because of immigration. Since the late 1980s, New York, Los Angeles, Chicago, and Miami have collectively enrolled nearly 100,000 new students each year who are either foreign-born or children of immigrants. City school budgets are falling as dramatically as their populations are rising. New York, Chicago and Los Angeles have had to make crippling mid-year cuts in their school budgets three times in the last five years. During the 1992–3 school year, the Los Angeles schools system cut $240 million from a general budget fund of $29 billion, and experienced several smaller cuts in state programmes and capital funds (McDonnell and Hill, 1993). Chicago must continue cutting every year and will still face a deficit of nearly $500 million in the 1997–8 school year (Booz and Hamilton, 1992).

It is hard to imagine how any organization could provide consistently good services in such a turbulent environment. Schools must have consistent and predictable funding. But funding is not enough. If existing programmes are stabilized schools will still not be effective for immigrants, for whom existing programmes and materials are not appropriate, or for native-born minority students, whom the schools were failing long before the present fiscal crisis began (McDonnell and Hill, 1993).

Big-city schools are also embedded in communities that lack sound economic bases and are burdened by crime, unemployment, teenage parenthood, child abandonment, drug use and disease. These problems, too, must be solved if children born in the inner city are to have the educational and career opportunities available to other Americans. The growth and persistence of these problems demonstrate a lack of public and private capacity to give inner-city children a fair chance in life.

In several RAND[2] studies conducted in the past few years, we have interviewed many educators who claim that the schools are helpless in the face of these problems. Nothing can be done, they claim, until the schools get more money and children get better pre-natal health care, better home environments, and more conventional adult role-models. Other educators draw a quite different conclusion: that the schools must become comprehensive social service agencies, delivering health, family planning, counselling and income-support services. These respondents may disagree about whether schools should wait for other services or aggressively seek to provide them, but they agree that the real problems are not in the schools but elsewhere and that schools would work if only children were properly cared for by their parents and the broader community.

This chapter makes the contrary argument: that public schools contribute to the problems of today's urban youth and that schools must do a better job of educating students. It admits that schools are burdened by the urban environment but contends that we cannot wait to change schools until other problems are solved. It grants that someone must address problems, such as poor student health and family instability, but argues that educators have enough to worry about in their own backyards. Better schools will not solve all the problems of American cities, but they are definitely part of the solution. The remainder of this chapter argues four points:

1   Bad public schools are making their own distinct contributions to the problems of cities.

2   There is a substantial consensus among educators and parents about how schools can be made to work for disadvantaged and minority students in the big cities.

3   Better inner-city schools are unlikely given today's methods of financing and governance.

4   Better schools are possible in the inner city but only if we make a major change in what is meant by a public school.

SCHOOLS MAKE THEIR OWN CONTRIBUTION TO URBAN ILLS

The Rodney King verdict was the spark that ignited the tinder of poor urban neighbourhoods in Los Angeles. Those arrested in the ensuing violence were largely young adult males, unemployed and embittered. These conditions were established during the years of children's supposed compulsory attendance in school. Starting in the seventh grade, low-income urban students develop poor school attendance habits; most rapidly fall behind in their classes and receive many failing marks. Those students who do attend school regularly achieve standards far lower than those expected by employers and post-secondary training institutions.

RAND studies of inner-city schools in Los Angeles and elsewhere have repeatedly encountered high-school juniors and seniors who have never read local newspapers, have no knowledge about the local economic base or the names of major local employers, and do not know the location or significance of local landmarks (McDonnell and Hill, 1993 and Hill et al., 1990). These children have grown up isolated from the broader community in ghettos that provide few avenues of access to mainstream economic, cultural, and political life. Like the poor minority children whom Robert Coles studied in Northern Ireland and South Africa, the children of America's inner cities see government and its political processes as closed and indifferent, likely to do things to them, not for them (Coles, 1986). They may serve as spectators through radio, television and movies, but they do not prepare themselves and do not expect to take part in life in environments unlike their own. Aside from the media, such children's contact with the broader society is mainly through the police, whom they regard as a hostile and punitive force, not a source of help or protection. Even those who enter the legitimate economy through jobs in fast-food establishments or small retail stores usually stay in their own neighbourhoods and deal mainly with people of similar background.

The school programmes that most inner-city minority students encounter do little to remedy their isolation from the broader community. As several RAND studies by Jeannie Oakes have shown, public high schools, especially in urban areas, 'track' students on the basis of the motivation and performance levels they display on entering the ninth grade (Oakes, 1985 and 1990). Students with poor attendance records or deficient mastery of basic skills (as is the case with a majority of students in most urban high schools) are typically assigned to remedial drill and practice on reading and arithmetic. Remedial instruction is boring; poorly motivated students seldom learn much from it or persist in it. Those students who persist in full-time remedial instruction seldom progress quickly enough to join the regular high-school curriculum. Only a few ever take the normal 'gatekeeper' courses that prepare students for college and good jobs (e.g., algebra, geometry, English literature, world history, or laboratory science).

Even when remedial instruction does teach students how to read, write and calculate, it does not teach them how those skills are used in adult life. Remedial classes teach skills in isolation from one another and leave it up to the student to see and exploit the connections. Students in such classes do not take part in writing and research projects that give others at least some experience of using skills in combination (Oakes, 1990; Hill and Bonan, 1991; Lipsitz, 1983; and Perry, 1988). Schools in general may do too little to help students learn how to integrate and use what they know, but remedial instruction does nothing to that end.

Urban public schools are also poor places to learn about how adults work in the real world. The only adults whom students observe working on a daily basis are teachers. Yet public schools are a poor model because they are not organized to be productive. They exemplify the kinds of businesses typical of the United States in the 1960s and 1970s that ran into economic difficulty in the 1980s and have now either failed or been restructured. Work is routinized and most workers (teachers) understand only their own duties, not the whole productive process. A few individuals work desperately hard and take responsibility for the results, but they are as likely to be regarded as zealots and nuisances as to be imitated and rewarded. Workers are accountable for following rules, not for contributing to overall success. Top management acts without consulting with workers to use their expertise or gain their support (Hill *et al.* 1990).

Few teachers are concerned with their school's general appearance or climate; even those who are effective in controlling their own classrooms seldom act in response to disruptions outside their classrooms or obvious student truancy or class-cutting. A norm of mutual non-interference also discourages teachers from identifying colleagues who are poorly prepared or who consistently turn out below-par students (Rosenholtz, 1989).

Many teachers think they have no warrant for action beyond their instructional duties and fear (sometimes correctly) that students or other teachers might resent interference. Many urban teachers also exercise 'leniency' in dealing with students, lowering standards for behaviour and academic attainment. Lenient treatment of students is often well intentioned, motivated by teachers' reluctance to burden students who already have difficult lives. It is often reinforced by administrators' reluctance to back teachers who become controversial because of their demands on students. But the result is an impoverished education, producing students who are not aware that their behaviour and knowledge are insufficient for a successful life in the broader community.

Many teachers and principles think of themselves as administrators of a public agency. They feel responsible to deliver a prescribed curriculum and to respect students' rights as defined by law. As one principal told a RAND researcher, 'My job is to make sure this school runs according to the policies and regulations of the school system'.

Albert Shanker of the American Federation of Teachers quotes a teacher's statement that encapsulates the problem: 'I taught them but they did not learn it'. The implication that the teacher is responsible for delivering material, but not for making sure that students master it, demonstrates teachers' bounded responsibility. Student respondents in a recent RAND survey demonstrated this attitude in another way (Hill *et al.*, 1990). Several said, 'I hate it when the teachers say, "I get paid whether you learn this or not".' Teachers may come to these attitudes through years of frustration, but students (and their parents, as well as researchers and other outsiders) often see teachers as dutiful only within the letter of their job descriptions.

The nature of teachers' work has important consequences for what students learn about adult life. Students who see teachers executing narrow routines and avoiding collaboration or responsibility for the results of their work are unlikely to imagine that their own work as adults will require risk-taking, solving of unfamiliar problems, shared responsibility, and concern for the ultimate success or failure of the enterprise in which they work. As this author has argued elsewhere, the kind of climate prevalent in urban public schools – high schools especially – teaches students that actions seldom have consequences and that 'they', not 'we', are responsible for making an organization work (Hill *et al.*, 1990).

Employers' complaints about young workers focus more on students' judgement and responsibility than on their mastery of basic skills. Employer surveys, such as those conducted by the Michigan State Employment Service, and national consultative bodies, such as Labor Secretary's Commission on Necessary Skills (SCANS) emphasize the importance of students' ability to solve problems, interpret general rules in the light of particular circumstances, collaborate, and manage interpersonal relations. These skills may require the ability to read and do arithmetic, but they also require the acceptance of responsibility, a willingness to tackle the unknown, and adaptability. These actions are seldom taught or modelled in urban schools. The result is that many low-income urban students are unprepared to operate effectively in mainstream adult roles.

WHAT IS NEEDED FROM SCHOOLS

A casual observer of school politics might think that Americans are deeply divided about what makes a good school. The debates about the need for a multicultural curriculum, instruction to maintain immigrant students' native languages, or teachers' rights to use corporal punishment represent serious differences of opinion. But by focusing attention on issues on which people disagree, these debates obscure a broad consensus about the essence of a good school. This consensus is evident from surveys of parent attitudes, from studies of teacher beliefs, and from the results of efforts to design better schools, which demonstrate agreement on a number of key elements of a good school (Johnson and Immerwahr, 1994).

- Teachers know their material and present it well.
- Each child is led to learn and accomplish as much as she can.
- Students who fall behind or encounter problems get help.
- The school works as a partner with parents, communicating clearly what their children will experience and why. Partnership means that the school respects parents' concerns and aspirations and that parents support the school's demands on students.
- Adults in the school form personal relationships with children and take responsibility for how well every child learns.
- Adults in the school set good examples of fairness, honesty, and generosity.

Two principles of effective schooling underlie this list: the first is concentrating effort on education, not delivery of social services of other non-instructional functions; the second is expecting that students, teachers, and parents will work long and hard and in as many different ways as are necessary to ensure that students learn.

Focus on Education

The first principle of effective schools is that they must educate. Many urban schools have lost their grip on that central fact. Schools must ensure that students have the opportunity to learn the bodies of knowledge that make an adult in our society. They must also help students understand the world in which they will live and work. That cannot and does not happen in schools whose leaders have become preoccupied with social services (Committee on Economic Development, 1994). Out of concern for the stresses in students' lives, many urban public schools have become centres for health care, counselling, infant day-care, and housing. Though teachers' time is seldom consumed by these activities, the attention of principals and administrators often is. Principals and senior administrators often spend major parts of their time coordinating the services of nurses and physicians, day-care workers for students' babies, psychological counsellors and security officers. Once a school becomes committed to providing such services, administrators must also work constantly to obtain grant funds and maintain the cooperation of provider agencies.

Administrators find these activities rewarding because student benefits are often quick and obvious. School administrators also have more freedom and experience less conflict in dealing with social service agencies than with the school system's central office or the teachers' union. But the result of a preoccupation with social services is that school administrators often leave the instructional program to the teachers. And though many teachers work well without supervision, the result for the school as a whole is that there is no mechanism for setting instructional priorities, establishing collaboration, and evaluating performance.

As one commentator recently said about American political parties, if one worries too much about the fringes, after a time the entire enterprise becomes fringe. Schools can easily become holding companies for diverse unco-ordinated activities that do not add up. The results, in students' educational experience and in their learning about the nature of productive adult enterprise, have been described above.

Unflagging Commitment

The second principle of effective schooling is what Robert Slavin calls 'relent-lessness' (Slavin et al., 1992). To beat the odds in dealing with disadvantaged students, schools must never let up. Teachers must keep trying, to the point of working individually with students who are not learning from regular classroom instruction. Parental support must be enlisted to ensure that students attend school every day and complete all their assignments. Students must be pressed to keep working, assured that they, their parents, and teachers can together overcome any obstacles to learning.

The example of urban Catholic schools, many of which now serve dis-advantaged minority students drawn from the same population as public school students, is instructive. Catholic high schools, in particular, are designed to put students under strong pressure to work and achieve and to ensure that all students encounter the same core of adult materials in English, science, mathe-matics, and history. They also expressly prepare students for adulthood, ensuring that they understand the local economy and political system well enough to become full participants. As the author has described elsewhere in *High Schools with Character*, the Catholic schools offer students a demanding bargain (Hill *et al.*, 1990). Students, including the many minority students who enter high school academically years behind and with poor junior-high attendance records, are told that they must work hard and co-operate with the school's efforts to help them. In return they are assured that they can succeed academically and that the school will do everything in its power to make it so. The schools are accountable to parents, who can register displeasure by taking students to other schools, but they are also aggressive in demanding that parents supervise students and reinforce the schools' demands. Catholic schools also prove their ability to deliver by introducing new students to recent graduates who, like themselves, entered high school with grave academic problems.

The focus on instruction and dedication to leading disadvantaged students through a challenging curriculum is built into urban Catholic schools. Many of them were built in the early 20th century to give immigrants a start toward full participation in American life, and they are still staffed and managed expressly for that purpose. But these capabilities are not limited to private schools. Many public schools, including one or a few in almost every inner-city area, avoid the traps of bureaucracy and preoccupation with remedial instruction. Some are renegade schools run by principals who simply defy school boards and unions. Some were also built by school boards and superintendents to attract working white and black families who threatened to leave the public school system. These schools are driven by their missions and by the dedication of their staffs, not by rules. Like the inner-city Catholic high schools, they now serve large numbers of students who are several years behind in basic skills. They teach a demanding curriculum, assuming that students faced with real mental challenges and interesting materials can learn basic skills rapidly. Though some students need an intensive first year, including weekend and summer classes from the end of the eighth grade until the beginning of the tenth, virtually all can learn standard high-school materials by the beginning of the tenth grade.

Schools built expressly to educate disadvantaged students are distinctive in may ways. Unlike most public schools, they do not assume that students' values, motivations, and abilities are fixed by early adolescence. They set out deliberately to motivate and change students. They do so by setting specific goals for what students should be able to do when they leave the school and by organizing the whole school around a definite theory or approach to instruction. They teach basic skills and standard academic subjects but integrate them with other experiences designed to prepare students to function as adults in jobs and professions. Students are introduced to the broader community, not isolated from it.

The promises such schools make about what students will encounter while in school and what they can do upon leaving are matched to demands about what the student must do to succeed. Teachers and administrators are not afraid to make demands on students. On the contrary, they assume that students need to work and that rigorous academic demands can put meaning and structure into students' lives. These schools demonstrate the rewards of hard work and build students' self-esteem by showing them that they can meet high standards.

Effective urban public schools are not all alike. Some are career-oriented, preparing students for good jobs in particular industries, such as health care, government service and finance. Some are college-prep-oriented, but their programmes are based on well-defined and integrated approaches, such as Ted Sizer's 'Essential Schools' approach or the International Baccalaureate (Sizer, 1992).

Like inner-city Catholic schools, effective public schools stand for something in particular. They are not work places for groups of autonomous teachers or holding companies for diverse social service providers. They are *schools* where adults and students work together to attain a definite outcome. These schools work. There is an unbroken chain of evidence from the early 1970s until the present that students attending public schools with these characteristics have better attendance records, gain credits more rapidly, take more demanding courses, have higher graduation rates, are more likely to graduate on time, get higher scores on the 'scholastic achievement' tests used for university admissions and are more likely to enter four-year colleges (Hill *et al.*, 1990; Lipsitz, 1983; Sizer, 1992 and Crain *et al.*, 1992).

In most central cities, parents clamour to get their children into such schools. Parents in some localities camp out overnight to be first in line to enrol their children in schools that offer specially focused programs. In New York City, which offers a small number of nonselective 'magnet' schools (in addition to the selective magnets like the Bronx High School of Science), some such schools have 20 and 30 times as many applicants as they have available seats. The schools parents want are in short supply because they differ from the dominant model of regulated and bureaucratic schooling.

NOW THE SYSTEM IS STACKED AGAINST BETTER PUBLIC SCHOOLS

Why did Americans get schools that are different from what everyone wants? The answer is complex and, because it lacks a single villain, unsatisfying. The situation has come about through the gradual accretion of small decisions, not by design. Since the mid-1960s, when schools first became the focus of social policy, they have been subject to wave after wave of rules and regulations, court orders, teacher-contract provisions, and other formal rules that bind and delimit what teachers and principals can do. Do schools have too few or too many minority students or does a desegregated school have too many segregated classes? The answer is a rule or court order. Are handicapped children neglected in some schools? The answer is a new legal principle and access to the courts for aggrieved parents. Do some students need extra help in school? The answer is a series of federal and state categorical programmes, each with its own set of controls designed to ensure that the services bought with federal and state funds go to the intended beneficiaries and no one else.

Taken one by one, most of these policies and programmes seem reasonable. So do the literally hundreds of other rules made by local school boards, state legislatures and state education agencies, Congress, the US Department of Education, and federal and state courts. So do the many rules governing when schools open and close, how many minutes teachers may teach, and how a principal may supervise and evaluate a teacher, all agreed to one by one by school boards who chose to make work rule concessions rather than meet teachers' union salary demands (McDonnell and Pascal, 1988). In the aggregate, however, the accretion of rules has created schools that no one would consciously have designed and that do not work.

A highly regulated school system does not work because no one is personally responsible for whether children learn. The people inside the system, teachers, principals, and administrators, are responsible for performing tasks specified by regulations and contracts and for respecting the turf of others. Most teachers and their supervisors care about children, and many complain that their schools are hurt by 'time servers' who do not work hard and will not cooperate with efforts to upgrade instruction. Poor performers are safe if they can demonstrate compliance and rectitude. Parents and community members who complain about poor results are often told that nothing can be done as long as no rules have been violated. School boards, caught in the web of their own rules, can do little about failing schools. Los Angeles and every other big city has dozens of schools that have abjectly failed students for years, producing several times more dropouts, truants, and semi-literate graduates than the local average. The board or superintendent may take marginal actions (e.g., replacing a principal or adding a new programme to supplement the school's inadequate core programme). A school is seldom changed fundamentally as long as it complies with all applicable regulations.

Public schools that focus on education and offer their students a specific approach to learning are rare because America's system of public control naturally produces a different kind of school. On important matters, where school boards are divided, policies are very carefully drawn to satisfy as many people as possible and to compensate pressure groups that lose on one issue so that they win on another. The natural result is a system of schools in which all are trapped in the same thicket of requirements.

The foregoing is enough to explain much of the critique of public schools. It certainly accounts for the fact that public schools try to be all things to all people and are unable to develop coherent philosophies of education. Something else is needed, however, to explain why schools in poor areas are usually worse than schools in wealthy ones.

Differences in local property tax valuation and the general economic plight of big cities limit the funding available for city schools. But some of the most striking differences in school quality are evident *within* city school districts. Even with their limited revenue bases, cities like Chicago and New York are able to create some of the best schools in the country, which coexist in the same local system with some of the worst. There are two keys to this striking inequality within cities. The first is politics: to hold on to middle-class students and demonstrate their commitment to quality, city school systems often create 'flagship schools'. These schools may or may not get more public funds than others, but the staff members are free to develop instructional themes and adapt curriculum to students' needs. Many of these flagship schools also get support from national foundations and reform networks, which further enhances their independence and flexibility.

The second key to inequality within cities is teacher allocation. Teachers' union contracts with big-city public school districts all give senior teachers first choice about jobs and school placements. Not surprisingly, senior teachers tend to congregate in schools located in safe and attractive neighbourhoods with support-ive parents and responsible students. Schools in less attractive neighbourhoods have trouble attracting and keeping senior teachers. They have to accept newer, less-experienced teachers and, in many cases, teachers who lack complete training or who scored poorly on state teachers' exams.

The teacher allocation process leads to staff instability in low-income area schools. Many teachers with good qualifications leave such schools as soon as they have the seniority to do so. It also leads to lower *de facto* funding for poverty area schools. Schools are billed for teacher salaries as if all teachers cost the same amount. But senior teachers cost two and a half times as much as beginning teachers in most cities. Since between 70 and 80 per cent of all school costs go for teachers' salaries, schools with all senior teachers can cost nearly twice as much as schools with all junior teachers.

Job protection for senior teachers poses another problem for cities with rapidly changing populations. As RAND's recent study of immigrant education showed, many schools serving immigrant populations are dominated by teachers who are left over from earlier times when all students were native-born (McDonnell and Hill, 1993). During times of budget crisis, school systems can neither create vacancies to hire new teachers with the appropriate language skills nor change school staffs rapidly as student needs change.

Not all inner-city schools are defeated by these factors. A few schools in every city attract and keep dedicated staff members and work aggressively to meet students' needs. But these schools work despite the system, not because of it. Like all systems, the public schools operate much as they were designed to most of the time. The result is that most inner-city public schools are bureaucratic, weak, unlikely to change on their own, and resistant to change from the outside.

In the past few years, superintendents and civic leaders in a number of cities have recognized that their schools were not working and have tried to create an instantaneous reform. They have declared 'site-based management' an opportunity for principals and teachers in existing schools to use their own judgement in changing school programmes to meet the needs of children. Site-based management plans in places like Miami, Chicago, Los Angeles, and New York gave teachers and parents greater influence over school-level decision making. But, as a recent RAND report shows, the roles of the superintendent, school board, and central-office bureaucracy did not change (Hill and Bonan, 1991). School communities, though urged to change themselves, are still tied up by the same inequitable school budgets, limitations on the use of funds, teacher-contract provisions, and central-office regulations. Some parent councils in Chicago exercised their authority to fire their principals; others elsewhere found new ways to use the few thousand dollars of flexible equipment and supplies money available to each school. But very few were able to focus on a basic review of the school's performance and devise significant improvements (Bryk, 1993). The existing system had kept its strings on them.

The big-city system of governance and finance that produces weak public schools is robust and persistent. Though many teachers and administrators criticize the system, most find their individual jobs safe and tolerable. Civil-service protections and union contracts ensure that schools deal fairly and consistently with adults, even if they do not work well for children. The system also deals very efficiently with challenges. Outstanding principals and community leaders can flout convention, but they are isolated and few; when they leave or retire, their schools usually regress toward the system-wide mean. Schools that receive special attention from outside funding sources and reform leaders are also allowed to distinguish themselves. But they, too often, play a role in protecting the system from criticism by focusing attention on its few excellent schools. Can big cities create public-school systems that are bound by rules and adult protections and yet be more able to promote school quality and adaptiveness? The answer is yes.

AN ALTERNATIVE PUBLIC SCHOOL SYSTEM

A solution to the problems of today's schools must overcome tendencies that are inherent in the structure of large urban public-school systems. An alternative school system must free the schools from micro-management by the school board and other political bodies; it must remedy the inequities of funding and teacher allocation that exist within most urban districts; it must allow development of schools with specific approaches to education so that staff members can feel responsible for what they produce and parents can hold them accountable; it must force school boards and superintendents to act when they discover that a school is consistently failing its students.

A radical solution preferred by some is school choice based on consumer initiative (Chubb and Moe, 1990). The plan would give every child in a locality a voucher worth the current per-pupil cost of public schooling. Parents could use the voucher to pay for tuition at any school, public or private. Parents would, presumably, seek out the better schools and avoid the weaker ones. Drawn by the possibility of lucrative tuition payments, entrepreneurs would offer alternatives to unpopular schools. In the long run, weak schools would be eliminated, strong ones would take their place, and all schools would feel the pressure of competition to maintain quality.

A choice plan including private schools raises the spectre of public funds being used to support Catholic and other sectarian schools. Some choice advocates have therefore proposed an all-public choice scheme, in which parents could choose any public school.[3]

The advantages of school choice are evident in the light of the foregoing discussion of public-school problems. School boards would not have to agree on what was the one best model of schooling for all students. Diverse tastes and demands could be satisfied by diverse schools. Schools would compete on quality, but like other sellers of complex services, they would also have to differentiate their product to appeal to purchasers' tastes and loyalty. Parents and students would, therefore, know what to expect from a school. Though schools could not discriminate in admissions, they could impose requirements related to student attendance and effort. As the research on magnet schools makes clear, students who choose a particular school knowing what it requires (even if they only consider it their least-bad alternative) have a greater incentive to meet its requirements than students who have no choice about where they will go (Hill et al., 1990; Crain et al., 1992).

Schools would be forced to attract students and would therefore pay close attention to student needs and parent preferences. Funding would be explicitly based on attendance, not driven by the locational preferences of senior teachers or by political negotiations. Schools would live and die on their reputations; teachers and principals would therefore have a strong incentive to collaborate, to press one another for good performance, to weed out weak staff members, and to work as hard as necessary to build their school's clientele. Like private schools, these schools would have to be concerned about their graduates, whether they could succeed in jobs and higher education and cope with adult life.

But choice plans, whether all-public or public-private, have a glaring problem. Vouchers may increase parents' capacity to demand better schools, but it is not clear where alternatives to the existing bad schools are to come from. Even in New York City, where Catholic schools educate over 100,000 students and constitute the twelfth-largest school system in the country, there is no room for the 1 million public-school students. If choice is to provide new opportunities for all students, a much larger supply of good schools must be created.

For choice to have any appreciable effect on the quality of schooling in big cities, a massive effort to create new schools or redevelop existing ones would be necessary. That is unlikely to happen purely through private investment. Some investors and community service organizations might venture to start one or two schools each, but only a few are likely to consider troubled central-city areas the best place to start. The demand for better schools is high in inner suburbs and in minority working-class areas, but prudent entrepreneurs will start in less challenging environments.

For the foreseeable future, a reform built solely on consumer choice will leave central cities with the problem they started with (i.e., how to create a large enough supply of good schools to serve all students). Choice does not eliminate the need for a strategy to improve public schools.

There are promising approaches to the supply problem. Several national organizations are creating new designs for schools and are building the capacity to help public-school systems form new schools (or redevelop existing ones) around these designs. These design organizations are sponsored by foundations such as RJR Nabisco, Macy, and Exxon, and many work out of major universities. Professor Henry Levin runs such an organization at Stanford, and others exist at Harvard, Yale and Brown. Other design organizations are privately sponsored and hope either to work under contract to local school districts or to run private schools with money from education vouchers.

These design organizations could provide the supply side of the market envisioned by choice advocates. They could develop school concepts, test and demonstrate their feasibility and appeal, and then offer them to parents in one or many localities. Like Montessori and the Catholic religious orders, they could ensure that the staff of a school were properly trained to run it and that a competent parent organization was available to monitor quality and help solve problems (Alis, 1995).

A national effort to create such design organizations is sponsored by the New American Schools Development Corporation (NASDC), a coalition of business leaders. Among the projects sponsored by NASDC is a Los Angeles-based effort to design an inner-city school that will use older students as tutors for younger ones and focus the efforts of all neighbourhood adults on education. Other designs sponsored by NASDC include a school based on old-fashioned character building and study of the classics; schools in which students learn basic skills in the course of research projects; and schools using computers in all phases of instruction. Starting in 1996, NASDC's design teams will be available to help communities around the country use its designs to build new schools or redevelop existing ones.

Some public agencies are creating their own design and assistance organizations. The school systems of Philadelphia and New York City are both creating new 'theme' schools that take over the building of failed neighbourhood schools and offer students choices among simple, focused, goal-oriented schools. State governments in Ohio, Oregon, and Wyoming are also developing capacities to help school systems identify and redevelop their weakest schools. All these organizations are creating alternatives to existing public schools. None seek to become the universal model for all the schools in a locality. They are creating a menu of alternative approaches that school systems can use as they try to improve or redevelop their worst schools.

However, with the exception of the efforts sponsored by the New York and Philadelphia schools, new designs for individual schools do not change the ways that public-school systems do business. One or two well-designed new schools in a city do not amount to a solution to the problems of urban education. Today's urban public-school systems are built to manage large numbers of schools via regulation and compliance enforcement. They are not built to create and nurture a variety of schools or to invest in the redevelopment of schools that have gone bad. Unless we find a new way to govern whole systems of urban schools, the new designs can only slightly increase the number of exemplary, but not imitated, public schools.

Can we find a way to govern public schools that permits and encourages variety and that moves quickly to supply better schools in place of ones that have failed their students or that nobody wants? Can we build a public-school system that nurtures the development of clear, coherent educational approaches in individual schools so that parents have real choices?

A rough blueprint for a public-school system that offers the benefits of choice is suggested in David Osborne and Ted Gaebler's book, *Reinventing Government* (Osborne and Gaebler, 1992). They argue that the key to improving schools and other public institutions is to separate governance from the delivery of services. Governance bodies like school boards naturally tend to create uniformity. Because they have formal authority over schools, they find it difficult to resist constituent pressure to settle every problem or complaint with a rule that prevents the offending circumstance from arising again. The result is that a problem that arises in one school leads to rules that constrain all schools – even those in which the problem had either been handled smoothly or had not arisen at all. Because many such problems concern the treatment of employees, public bodies like school boards gradually constrain the schools – and themselves – with elaborate civil-service employment rules and union contracts.

Osborne and Gaebler argue that public bodies can be saved from their own tendency to over-regulate. Their strategy for separating policy-making bodies from the day-to-day management of services is to have services delivered under contract. Public decision-making bodies can set basic goals and principles of operation (e.g., non-discrimination in student admissions and teacher hiring), but services will not be delivered by public employees. Services will, instead, be delivered by contractors, operating under limited-term and fixed-cost agreements. Public bodies could retain the right to terminate contracts for non-performance, and contractors would have no automatic rights of renewal. The present author has shown in detail how these ideas could be applied to public education (Hill, 1995).

Under the contracting scheme, school boards could manage a number of different contracts, with a child-development organization for some elementary schools and with a university school of education for others; with an organization like Ted Sizer's Coalition for Essential Schools for some high schools and with a college of arts and sciences or career-training academy for others. Nothing would prevent a group of teachers in existing schools from organizing themselves as contractors. Teachers' unions might offer to run a few schools in one locality; a successful local union might win contracts to provide schools in another school district or even another state.

Public-school systems would still need superintendents and some form of a central office, but their roles and powers should be modest. The superintendent's job would be to advise the board on contracting – how to attract good offers; when to warn a failing contractor or reassign some or all of its schools to other contractors. The school system's central office would support the superintendent in this basic monitoring function, but it would not directly supervise principals or teachers or provide in-service training. Contractor organizations would be responsible for those functions. The system-wide board could set general requirements for teacher qualifications and might even negotiate with contractors and the teachers' union about general wage scales. Contractors could be required to hire teachers from the existing city teaching staff, but they would be able to pick those who best fitted their schools' approaches to education. The teachers' union might operate as a guild, helping teachers find placements and trying to upgrade the skills of teachers who could not readily find work.

Contracting may be the framework for the solution of many problems of urban schools. It could, if properly implemented, allow school boards to focus on the core issues of what children need to learn and how to save children from schools that are failing them. It could also relieve school boards of the obligation to resolve every complaint about any aspect of school operations. Contracting with state-wide or national design organizations such as those discussed above would force school boards to make an explicit allocation of funds to each school, thus eliminating the current within-district inequities in school funding. Many of the teachers and administrators would come from the current teaching force, but they would work in organizations that had to maintain quality and would therefore reward good teachers and retrain or replace ineffective ones.

Schools would remain public: they would be funded from tax revenue and would operate under contracts that guaranteed fair admissions, non-discrimination, and the rights of the disadvantaged. The state could still establish requirements for teacher certification. Local school boards would be, in effect, public-investment managers, deciding which contractor's approach best fitted a neighbourhood's need. Parental choice would force school boards and superintendents to pay special attention to their shakiest investments. Schools that had become unpopular would lose students and force a reallocation of district funds. When troubled schools became too small to run economically, contractors would be forced either to negotiate for higher per-pupil payments or default on their contracts. In either case, the board and superintendent would face an action-forcing event. Even if the board shirked its duty during the life of a contract, the end of a contractor's term would force a new decision.

A board that could not get contractors to bid on a particular set of schools would know quickly that it needed to offer more money or more realistic terms. This might be a warrant for selectively allocating federal or state categorical-programme funds. If a school district consistently had trouble attracting contractors for its schools, the state government would have a clear signal that something must be done; a review of the district's contracting methods and specifications, special incentive funding for contractors, or reconstitution of the local school district. Failures would be evident and the remedies would be readily available. There would no longer by any justification for tolerating school failure or for leaving generations of children from inner-city neighbourhoods in the same ineffective hands.

Contracting with school-design organizations, such as those sponsored by the NASDC, can provide a supply of schools that make parental choice meaningful. It also provides a way out for urban communities whose schools have collapsed under the old system. No such dramatic change can be instantaneous, but effective steps can be taken now if community leaders and the school board focus on the worst inner-city schools and commit to redeveloping them via contracts with universities and design organizations that will provide a range of focused alternatives for students.

Contracting for schools will not solve all problems. Some contractors may be inadequate and will have to be assisted by others or fired. Some parents may not exercise their rights of choice aggressively and may unwittingly help deficient schools survive. School boards will have to overcome their tendency to 'solve' a problem by enacting a new policy (e.g. a new specification for contractors to meet) rather than by looking into the causes and providing needed resources. But contracting will entirely eliminate two sources of problems for today's public schools. First, it will eliminate the central-office bureaucracy that is built to control and regulate schools from the outside, replacing it with a much simpler organization built to assist the board in the selection and audit of contractors. Second, it will eliminate the need for the school board to resolve disputes by making rules that apply to all schools. Parents or interest groups with particular tastes in schooling can be encouraged to find a school that suits them rather than petitioning for general policy changes.

CONCLUSION

Many things must change before the immigrant and black students of inner-city Chicago, Detroit and Los Angeles have the same life prospects as the students of Beverly Hills. Schools cannot overcome all the problems of poverty, unemployment, crime, and community disintegration. They also need stable funding, something that only a more responsible state government can provide. But schools can do much more than they are doing.

The public-school system must change fundamentally. Enabling changes in state laws and state and federal funding programmes are necessary. But the greatest change must be local. School systems must allocate money to schools fairly. School boards, superintendents, and teachers' unions must all change their modes of operation to work with contractors who operate schools. School-system central offices would change most dramatically, from regulators of a monopoly enterprise to evaluators and managers of a set of contracts.

None of these changes is likely to come about solely through the initiative of superintendents, school boards, or teachers' unions; the changes they face are too uncomfortable. Broader community initiatives, led by the heads of neighbourhood and civil rights organizations, local general-purpose governments, and key businesses, are necessary. It is obvious that regulation, exhortation, and pressure on the existing school system cannot do the job. Only a concerted community effort to change the way that the community governs education can save the big-city public schools.

NOTES

1 Adapted, with permission, from: Steinberg, J.B., Lyon, D.W. and Vaiana, M.E. (eds) (1992) *Urban America*. Santa Monica, CA: RAND.
2 RAND is a nonprofit institution that seeks to improve public policy through research and analysis (1700 Main Street, P.O. Box 2138, Santa Monica, CA 90407-2138).
3 Parent choice of schools would require some degree of government administration. Disputes over the fairness of admissions policies and accuracy of schools' claims would inevitably lead to legal action and mandates for government oversight for publicly funded schools. (Elmore, 1986).

REFERENCES

Alis, M.B. (1995) *Building and Maintaining Multi-School Networks: Lessons to be learned from the Catholic Schools*. Working Papers in Public Policy Analysis and Management. University of Washington Graduate School of Public Affairs.

Booz, Allen and Hamilton, Inc. (1992) *Financial Outlook for the Chicago Public Schools*. Chicago.

Bryk, A.S. (1993) *A View From the Elementary Schools: The State of Reform in Chicago*. Chicago: The Consortium on Chicago School Research.

Chubb, John E. and Moe, Terry (1990) *Politics, Markets, and America's Schools*. Washington, D.C.: The Brookings Institution.

Coles, Robert (1986) *The Political Lives of Children*. Boston, Mass: Houghton Mifflin Co.

Committee on Economic Development (1994) *Putting Learning First: Governing and Managing the Schools for High Achievement*. New York: CED.

Crain, Robert *et al.* (1992) *The Effectiveness of New York City's Career Magnets*. Berkeley, CA: The National Center for Research on Vocational Education.

Elmore, Richard (1986) *Choice in Public Education*. New Brunswick, N.J.: Center for Policy Research in Education.

Hill, P.T. (1995) *Reinventing Public Education*. Santa Monica, CA: RAND.

Hill, Paul T. and Bonan, Josephine J. (1991) *Decentralization and Accountability in Public Education*. Santa Monica, CA: RAND.

Hill, Paul T., Foster, Gail E. and Gendier, Tamar (1990) *High Schools with Character*. Santa Monica, CA: RAND.

Johnson, J. and Immerwahr, J. (1994) *First Things First: What Americans Expect From the Public Schools*. New York: Public Agenda.

Lipsitz, Joan (1983) *Successful Schools for Young Adolescents*. New Brunswick, N.J.: Transaction Books.

McDonnell, Lorraine M. and Hill, P.T. (1993) *Newcomers in American Schools*. Santa Monica, CA: RAND.

McDonnell, Lorraine M. and Pascal, Anthony H. (1988) *Teacher Unions and Educational Reform*. Santa Monica, CA: RAND.

Oakes, Jeannie (1985) *Keeping Track*. New Haven: Yale University Press.

Oakes, Jeannie (1990) *Multiplying Inequalities: The Effects of Race, Social Class, and*

  Tracking on Opportunities to Learn Mathematics and Science. Santa Monica, CA: RAND.

Osborne, David, and Gaebler, Ted (1992) *Reinventing Government*. Menlo Park, CA: Addison-Wesley.

Perry, Imani (1988) 'A black student's reflection on public and private schools', *Harvard Educational Review*, 58(3), 332–336.

Rosenholtz, Susan J. (1989) *Teachers' Workplace: The Social Organization of Schools*. New York: Longman.

Sizer, Theodore R. (1992) *Horace's School: Redesigning the American High School*. New York: Houghton Mifflin Co.

Slavin, Robert *et al.* (1992) *Success for All: A Relentless Approach to Prevention and Early Intervention in Elementary Schools*. Arlington, Va: Education Research Service.

US Department of Education (1991a) *The Digest of Educational Statistics*. Washington, D.C.

US Department of Education (1991b) *The Condition of Education*. Washington, D.C.

Appendix 1

The Current Position in Urban Education

This appendix gives some details about the material referred to in Chapter 2.

ITEMS INCLUDED IN DOE 'INDEX OF LOCAL CONDITIONS' AT WARD LEVEL

i.   unemployment
ii. children in low-earning households
iii. overcrowded housing
iv. housing lacking basic amenities
v.   households with no car
vi. children in 'unsuitable' accommodation
vii. educational participation (at age 17).

Source: 1991 Census Ward Level Data.

For further details, see Department of the Environment, *Index of Local Conditions* (1994).

TECHNICAL DETAILS

Defining Urban Disadvantage

The overall data-set contained data on some 3,241 maintained secondary schools and some 18,753 primary schools. Included in this data is ward-level, 1991 census data for the ward in which the school is physically located and the three adjoining wards. The DoE 'Index of Local Conditions' values for each ward was then added to the data-set.

'Disadvantage' was based on the DoE Index, taking the top 10 per cent of schools on this measure, for primary and secondary separately.

Distributions of population densities for all wards in England were reviewed and a level of ten persons per hectare selected as a point which would include most wards in metropolitan areas and exclude a significant proportion of wards in shire counties. All wards in metropolitan areas were deemed 'urban' as were those in shire counties with population densities greater than ten persons per hectare.

Schools without ward-level data of DoE Index scores were excluded, as were schools in shire counties in wards with ten or less persons per hectare. Because of problems in linking the local area data to selective secondary schools, these were also excluded, as were GM schools. Finally, in view of some concern about the quality of some section-42 school budget data, schools with budgets of less than

£500 or more than £4,000 per pupil were discarded on the grounds that these might reflect erroneous data, or special cases. This left 10,092 maintained urban primary schools and 2,051 maintained urban comprehensive schools on which the main analysis (Tables 2.1–2.8) is based.

Inspection Data

Inspection data is based on inspectors' judgements on 676 secondary schools from the first year of the full OFSTED inspection programme drawn from the EIS database. This is approximately 75 per cent of all the secondary schools inspected in 1993/4. Judgements are recorded in terms of a seven-point scale, with 1 as the best and 7 the lowest point. The mid-point indicates a balance of strengths and weaknesses. Figures 2.3–2.7 are based on collapsing this scale by combining the top three and bottom three scales and excluding the mid-point.

Analysis

The main data was provided by OFSTED's research and analysis team, though the analysis was my responsibility. Thanks are due to Brian Wilson at the DoE for the 'Index of Local Conditions' data at ward level. For the inspection judgements I have relied on the analysis carried out by members of Chris Bryant's team of OFSTED – simply importing their tables into EXCEL.

Starting Year of the Initiatives

TITLE	Year initiative started									
	1981	1987	1988	1989	1990	1991	1992	1993	1994	1995
The 'At Risk' Support Project							1			
The Tilbury Initiative (Essex LEA)									1	
Mentoring (North Warwicks EBP)								1		
North Guilford Project (Guilford LEA)								1		
Action Research: Critical Success Factors (North Bucks TEC)								1		
Raising Achievement Project (Rochdale LEA)							1			
Pathways to School Improvement (Bath University)								1		
Middlesbrough Community Education Project (Cleveland LEA)							1			
Primary School Improvement Bretton Hall (Leeds University)									1	
Helping All Pupils to Achieve More (Bradford LEA)					1					
Partnership Review (Bradford TEC)									1	
Parental Involvement in the Core Curriculum (Tower Hamlets)					1					
Raising Standards Project (South Shields)								1		
Newspapers in Education (Teesside TEC)									1	
Post-16 Compact (Teesside TEC)					1					
Cleveland Compact (Teesside TEC)			1							
Home Instruction for Pre-School Youngsters (Teesside TGEC)								1		
IPP in Education (Teesside TEC)								1		
Case-Thinking Science (Teesside TEC)							1			
Countering Bullying (Kent LEA)								1		
Improving Results at KS4 (Kent LEA)								1		
Value Added (Kent LEA)								1		
Nettworks 94 (Gloucester LEA)									1	
Curriculum Development Focus (Rotherham)								1		
Raising Standards in the Inner City (Notts. LEA)							1			
School Improvement (Bexley)							1			
Raising Achievement in Inner City Schools (Lancashire LEA)								1		
Compact Extension (North London TEC)									1	
Vocational Education Development Centre (Devon and Cornwall TEC)								1		
School Effectiveness and Improvement Centre (London Univ)								1		
School Improvement Network (London University)								1		
Youth Work for Young People At Risk (Cambridge LEA)									1	
Truancy (Devon LEA)									1	
Two Towns Project (Staffs LEA)					1					
City Reading Project (Oxford LEA)									1	
Raising Achievement and Participation Project (Sheffield LEA)								1		
Quality Development Initiative (Birmingham LEA)						1				
Research Fellowships (Birmingham University)									1	
Literacy, Numeracy, Curriculum Enrichment etc. (Humberside)						1				

continued overleaf

Appendix 2 *continued*

	Year initiative started									
	1981	1987	1988	1989	1990	1991	1992	1993	1994	1995
Strategies to Enhance Performance at GCSE (Barnsley LEA)								1		
Improving The Quality of Education for All (Cambridge)						1				
Impact Mathematics (Harringay)								1		
Raising Standards Project (Dudley)							1			
School Effectiveness (Warwick University)		1								
Lewisham School Improvement Project (SIP)								1		
Urban Education – writing a book (Brunel University)							1			
Schools Make a Difference (Hammersmith and Fulham)								1		
African-Caribbean Project (Hammersmith and Fulham)							1			
Raising Standards in Inner City Schools (Gateshead)							1			
Black Teachers Mentoring Scheme (Goldsmiths London)									1	
Raising Reading Standards Project (Lewisham)							1			
Frequent Monitoring Programme (Wandsworth)						1				
Successful Schools (Worcester College of HE)							1			
School Measurement and Improvement Strategy (Newcastle Univ)									1	
Monitoring ALIS, YELLIS, PIPS	1									
Tower Hamlets Partnership (Exeter University)			1							
Developing Effective Schools in Greenwich (Greenwich TVEI)									1	
High Scope UK 'Young Children First' (Liverpool LEA)							1			
Peers Early Education Partnership (Oxford LEA)										1
Total	1	1	1	1	1	7	13	20	13	1

Appendix 3

Duration of the Initiatives in Months

TITLE	Duration of the initiative (mths)															
	7	8	10	12	15	16	18	22	24	27	30	31	36	48	60	No
The 'At Risk' Support Project																1
The Tilbury Initiative (Essex LEA)												1				
Mentoring (North Warwicks EBP)								1								
Action Research: Critical Success Factors (North Bucks TEC)	1															
Raising Achievement Project (Rochdale LEA)										1						
Pathways to School Improvement (Bath University)		1														
Middlesbrough Community Education Project (Cleveland LEA)														1		
Primary School Improvement Bretton Hall (Leeds University)											1					
Helping All Pupils to Achieve More (Bradford LEA)																1
A Level and GCSE Improvement Project (Barking & Dagenham)									1							
Partnership Reviews (Bradford TEC)																1
Parental Involvement in the Core Curriculum (Tower Hamlets)																1
Raising Standards Project (South Shields)				1												
Newspapers in Education (Teesside TEC)				1												
Post-16 Compact (Teesside TEC)										1						
Cleveland Compact (Teesside TEC)														1		
Home Instruction for Pre-School Youngsters (Teesside TEC)												1				
IPP in Education (Teesside TEC)																1
Case-Thinking Science (Teesside TEC)				1												
Countering Bullying (Kent LEA)				1												
Improving Results at KS4 (Kent LEA)				1												
Value Added (Kent LEA)							1									
Nettworks 94 (Gloucester LEA)			1													
Curriculum Development Focus (Rotherham)				1												
Raising Standards in the Inner City (Notts. LEA)												1				
School Improvement (Bexley)				1												
Raising Achievement in Inner City Schools (Lancashire LEA)				1												
Compact Extension (North London TEC)				1												
Vocational Education Development Centre (Devon and Corn. TEC)					1											
School Effectiveness and Improvement Centre (London Univ)																1
School Improvement Network (London University)																1
Youth Work for Young People At Risk (Cambridge LEA)				1												
Truancy (Devon LEA)												1				
Two Towns Project (Staffs LEA)															1	
City Reading Project (Oxford LEA)															1	
Raising Achievement and Participation Project (Sheffield LEA)						1										
Quality Development Initiative (Birmingham LEA)															1	
Research Fellowships (Birmingham University)									1							
Literacy, Numeracy, Curriculum Enrichment etc. (Humberside)																1

continued overleaf

Appendix 3 *continued*

	Duration of the initiative (mths)															
	7	8	10	12	15	16	18	22	24	27	30	31	36	48	60	No
Strategies to Enhance Performance at GCSE (Barnsley LEA)						1										
Improving The Quality of Education for All (Cambridge)																1
Impact Mathematics (Harringay)				1												
Raising Standards Project (Dudley)													1			
School Effectiveness (Warwick University)																1
Lewisham School Improvement Project (SIP)									1							
Urban Education – writing a book (Brunel University)							1									
Schools Make a Difference (Hammersmith and Fulham)									1							
African-Caribbean Project (Hammersmith and Fulham)													1			
Raising Standards in Inner City Schools (Gateshead)													1			
Black Teachers Mentoring Scheme (Goldsmiths London)									1							
Raising Reading Standards Project (Lewisham)													1			
Frequent Monitoring Programme (Wandsworth)				1												
Successful Schools (Worcester College of HE)					1											
School Measurement and Improvement Strategy (Newcastle Univ)													1			
Monitoring ALIS, YELLIS, PIPS																1
Tower Hamlets Partnership (Exeter University)																1
Developing Effective Schools in Greenwich (Greenwich TVEI)									1							
High Scope UK 'Young Children First' (Liverpool LEA)													1			
Peers Early Education Partnership (Oxford LEA)															1	
Total	1	1	1	12	2	2	2	1	6	1	1	1	10	1	5	12

Method of Selection of Schools

	Method of selection				
	Self-selected	All schools in an area	All schools in an area (disadvantage)	Schools identified by need	Members of existing interest group
TITLE					
The 'At-Risk' Support Project	1				
The Tilbury Initiative (Essex LEA)	1				
Mentoring (North Warwicks EBP)		1			
North Guilford Project (Guilford LEA)				1	
Action Research: Critical Success Factors (North Bucks TEC)				1	
Middlesbrough Community Education Project (Cleveland LEA)		1			
Primary School Improvement Bretton Hall (Leeds University)		1			
Parental Involvement in the Core Curriculum (Tower Hamlets)				1	
Newspapers in Education (Teesside TEC)		1			
Post-16 Compact (Teesside TEC)				1	
Cleveland Compact (Teesside TEC)		1			
Home Instruction for Pre-School Youngsters (Teesside TGEC)	1				
Case-Thinking Science (Teesside TEC)	1				
Countering Bullying (Kent LEA)	1				
Improving Results at KS4 (Kent LEA)	1				
Nettworks 94 (Gloucester LEA)	1				
Curriculum Development Focus (Rotherham)	1				
Raising Standards in the Inner City (Notts. LEA)		1			
School Improvement (Bexley)			1		
Raising Achievement in Inner City Schools (Lancashire LEA)					1
Compact Extension (North London TEC)			1		
School Effectiveness and Improvement Centre (London Univ)	1				
School Improvement Network (London University)	1				
Youth Work for Young People At Risk (Cambridge LEA)		1			
Truancy (Devon LEA)			1		
Two Towns Project (Staffs LEA)	1				
City Reading Project (Oxford LEA)		1			
Raising Achievement and Participation Project (Sheffield LEA)					1
Quality Development Initiative (Birmingham LEA)		1			
Research Fellowships (Birmingham University)	1				
Literacy, Numeracy, Curriculum Enrichment etc. (Humberside)		1			
Strategies to Enhance Performance at GCSE (Barnsley LEA)		1			
Improving The Quality of Education for All (Cambridge)	1				
Impact Mathematics (Harringay)	1				
Raising Standards Project (Dudley)			1		
School Effectiveness (Warwick University)	1				
Lewisham School Improvement Project (SIP)	1				

continued overleaf

Appendix 4 *continued*

	Method of selection				
	Self-selected	All schools in an area	All schools in an area (disadvantage)	Schools identified by need	Members of existing interest group
Schools Make a Difference (Hammersmith and Fulham)	1				
African-Caribbean Project (Hammersmith and Fulham)			1		
Raising Standards in Inner City Schools (Gateshead)		1			
Black Teachers Mentoring Scheme (Goldsmiths London)		1			
Raising Reading Standards Project (Lewisham)		1			
Frequent Monitoring Programme (Wandsworth)			1		
Successful Schools (Worcester College of HE)			1		
School Measurement and Improvement Strategy (Newcastle Univ)	1				
Monitoring ALIS, YELLIS, PIPS	1				
Tower Hamlets Partnership (Exeter University)	1				
Developing Effective Schools in Greenwich (Greenwich TVEI)					1
High Scope UK 'Young Children First' (Liverpool LEA)			1		
Peers Early Education Partnership (Oxford LEA)		1			
Total	20	15	8	4	3

Appendix 5

Educational Initiatives to Raise Standards in Urban Areas

The descriptions below are those provided by the submitting agencies. The originator of each initiative is given in Table 3.1.

A LEVEL AND GCSE IMPROVEMENT PROJECT

Low achievement and under-achievement are pervasive across the authority. The object of all the initiatives is to attack and reverse the long tail of low-achievers. The performance indicators are public examinations and movement against national norms in the National Curriculum.

ACTION RESEARCH: CRITICAL SUCCESS FACTORS

The project was intended to assist schools develop more systematic procedures for monitoring student progress and success and to establish mechanisms for using the information to raise attainment.

AFRICAN-CARIBBEAN PROJECT

No comment.

BLACK TEACHERS MENTORING SCHEME

The Black Teachers Mentoring Scheme aims (a) to address under-representation of black students entering higher education; (b) to address under-representation of black teachers in the profession and to improve retention rates of black teachers; (c) to create a support network of mentors/mentorees to facilitate (a) and (b), and (d) to produce and disseminate reports, as appropriate. The scheme will be involved in the mentoring process, serving (a) black teachers; (b) black students in training for teaching; (c) black students on Access to Education/A levels; (d) black students in year 11 of secondary schools.

CASE-THINKING SCIENCE

No comment.

CITY READING PROJECT

To raise attainment in reading across age-groups three to fourteen, particularly to increase teaching of higher-order reading skills in years 4–9.

CLEVELAND COMPACT

A partnership between schools and local industry/community which aims to improve the opportunities available to school leavers and to give them the skills and abilities to take advantage of the improved opportunities.

COMPACT EXTENSION

The mission of the Enfield/Barnet Compact Extension is to improve student achievement by enhancing the progress of identified young people at key stages of transition on to the most appropriate provision. This involves empowering young people by the provision of unbiased and sound information on all options open to them, clear progression routes and defined learning opportunities that maximize their qualifications, abilities and skills.

COUNTERING BULLYING

(i) Survey across KS2 and KS3 on what pupils (broken down by gender/age) understood by bullying, plus six case-studies of good practice. (ii) Following seminars to disseminate effective strategies for headteachers and/or designates.

CURRICULUM DEVELOPMENT FOCUS

To support new initiatives in schools aimed at raising achievement.

DEVELOPING EFFECTIVE SCHOOLS IN GREENWICH

Four-phase strategy: (1) setting scene with three participant schools; (2) diagnostic survey and feedback; (3) preparing school-improvement action plan; (4) implementing plan and evaluating. Consultants doing stages 1–3 (including Investors in People). Various support agencies involved at stage 4.

FREQUENT MONITORING PROGRAMME

The school is assisted in setting short-term targets related to longer-term objectives. Progress is monitored on a regular and frequent basis, and sources of advice, support, training etc. are identified for the school.

HELPING ALL PUPILS TO ACHIEVE MORE

HAPTAM – to get schools to identify specific developments to raise pupil achievement. These targets were then monitored by inspectorate and composite reports produced for mentors and schools. More recently, specific targeted support to specific schools and the dissemination of the work from Reading Recovery.

HIGH SCOPE UK 'YOUNG CHILDREN FIRST'

To give pupils/families confidence and self-esteem so that they will understand cause and effect and make positive choices related to learning and behaviour by ensuring early success in the education process.

HOME INSTRUCTION FOR PRE-SCHOOL YOUNGSTERS

To pilot a pre-school programme of learning development which will develop basic skills in young children and enable parents with limited schooling to provide educational enrichment to their families.

IMPACT MATHEMATICS

It is a homework scheme for mathematics in the primary school – for children aged seven to eleven.

IMPROVING RESULTS AT KS4

Following interest at a secondary deputies conference, twelve schools self-selected; in-depth survey of strategies in place/recommendations to area of strategies (context-specific) which might help them – report to all schools; follow-up work planned.

IMPROVING THE QUALITY OF EDUCATION FOR ALL

See Appendix 7.

IPP IN EDUCATION

The project is intended to support schools and colleges by funding and advice as they prepare action plans for formal commitment to IPP.

LEWISHAM SCHOOL IMPROVEMENT PROJECT

Aims: to enhance pupil progress, achievement and development. To develop the internal capacity of schools for managing change and evaluating its impact at whole-school level, classroom level and pupil level. To develop the capacity of the LEA to provide data to schools that will strengthen their ability to plan and evaluate change. To integrate the above with the LEA's ongoing INSET and support services to form a coherent approach to professional development.

LITERACY, NUMERACY, CURRICULUM ENRICHMENT ETC.

Bring about fundamental change in professional understanding and skills and pupil performance in the areas of literacy and numeracy. This is achieved through processes of audit, training (curriculum and management) and evaluation.

MENTORING

Recruitment of employer-based mentors to work with young people who are, in the opinion of their teachers, likely to underachieve. Mentors to spend at least one hour per two weeks with the young person.

MIDDLESBROUGH COMMUNITY EDUCATION PROJECT

The coalition seeks to raise standards, expectations, and improve attitudes, by drawing the community (including parents) more fully into partnerships with the education process. This long-term aim is realized by offering deliberate training and opportunities to staff and parents, and by affording children enriched experiences and resources which develop motivation for learning.

MONITORING ALIS, YELLIS, PIPS

The projects monitor 'attitudes', 'aspiration', 'achievement', and 'progress' (value added) and feed back that information to teachers and schools.

NETTWORKS 94

A joint LEA/TEC initiative to further NETTS. A project team will garner base-line information before producing a research, development and support programme which will be disseminated in March 1995.

NEWSPAPERS IN EDUCATION

To use the newspaper as a 'living textbook' and curriculum support for teachers. To raise an interest in and value of reading. To promote community values through increased awareness of local issues.

NORTH GUILDFORD PROJECT

An inter-agency project focused on schools and their attainments within the community. The overall aim is to raise standards of achievements. For this to happen, support needs to be given to families in a variety of ways.

PARENTAL INVOLVEMENT IN THE CORE CURRICULUM

The PICC project is best characterized as a learning and researching group of teachers and lecturers with the common aim of developing home–school liaison for the benefit of children's learning. The project harnesses human and financial resources in order to set up classroom-based initiatives that involve parents in the life of the school. A major gift in kind from the University of Greenwich is the release of lecturers on 'recent and relevant school experience'.

The two schools selected currently use parents as classroom assistants. The scheme is intended to provide the parents with systematic training, in reading in the first instance.

PARTNERSHIP REVIEWS

To provide a short consultancy service to local schools and colleges which will (a) audit existing provision of industry links, (b) recommend strategies to develop involvement in such activities.

PATHWAYS TO SCHOOL IMPROVEMENT

The 'Pathways to School Improvement' project is an initiative aimed at identifying the key factors which result in raised levels of pupil achievement in secondary schools. It is a qualitative study conducted in conjunction with inner-city schools which are committed to introducing measures which will result in improved performance and output.

PEERS EARLY EDUCATION PARTNERSHIP

To achieve significant improvement in educational attainment for children aged 7 in Blackbird Leys and neighbouring areas of Oxford, primarily through parental involvement and pre-school.

POST-16 COMPACT

To continue to develop Compact principles and objectives in the post-16 sector. To develop stronger links between pre-16 and higher education and post-16 education and training with the higher education sector.

PRIMARY SCHOOL IMPROVEMENT BRETTON HALL

Bretton Hall Primary School Improvement (PSI) Project is researching school-improvement strategies in primary schools. These are based on a model which includes three process factors – leadership, democracy, and development planning – which create the conditions for programmes of action to improve the school organization in four key areas – school climate, curriculum development, staff development and parental involvement.

QUALITY DEVELOPMENT INITIATIVE

The QDI is a strategy for school improvement based on a negotiated common framework of purposes, principles and working practices. It involves intensive staff training, structured networking and dissemination, external support, rigorous teacher-led monitoring and evaluation and validation via the Investors in People quality award.

RAISING ACHIEVEMENT AND PARTICIPATION PROJECT

Rapp is a joint Sheffield–TEC initiative. Two major strands form the basis of the project. A series of core themes address achievement and participation across the whole city.

Work is concentrated on a range of innovation projects in schools, groups of schools and clusters, particularly where there is greatest need in terms of achievement and participation, backed by support schemes to measure value addedness, promote post-16 education and training, survey attitudes and track and analyse post-16 destinations. Other projects have been started on basic literacy, community involvement, bilingual support and VQ assessor training.

RAISING ACHIEVEMENT IN INNER CITY SCHOOLS

To raise levels of achievement in literacy and numeracy through further development of home/community/school links. Through collaborative teamwork to identify barriers to raising levels of achievement. To disseminate successful strategies and processes for overcoming or removing those barriers.

RAISING ACHIEVEMENT PROJECT

Issues relating to under-achievement were discussed with headteachers and a small number of main contributory factors identified. Small groups of heads and teachers then identified strategies for overcoming each factor. These groups were facilitated by LEA and HE involvement. The strategies were then trialled in schools and evaluated.

RAISING READING STANDARDS PROJECT

The Lewisham Raising Reading Standards project is based in 24 schools from nursery to secondary (3 to 13 years) and located in the north of Lewisham. The overall aims of the project are to: (i) raise standards of reading and facilitate access to the National Curriculum; (ii) stimulate parental involvement in their children's education and promote effective home–school partnerships; (iii) enhance teachers' skills in working to bring about effective change.

RAISING STANDARDS IN INNER CITY SCHOOLS

To raise the standards of pupils' work across the curriculum, with particular emphasis being given to literacy. To promote the enjoyment of and increase motivation towards reading, leading to an improvement in standards of achievement. To involve parents in shared reading activities with their children. To provide practical help for teachers.

RAISING STANDARDS IN THE INNER CITY

The 'achievement contract' was an LEA/DFE funded research and development project, to raise the achievement of KS2 inner-city pupils. Using the strategies of improved attendance and punctuality, parents as partners in education, behaviours management, and total quality management.

RAISING STANDARDS PROJECT

Three main areas of emphasis: improving reading, developing learning strategies, increasing parental involvement.

RESEARCH FELLOWSHIPS

Up to 10 research fellowships (for study at M. Phil. level) are being offered (fees only: 2 years part time/1 year full time) to applicants who have experience of working with the African Caribbean community into various aspects of Afro Caribbean Education: schools – both LEA-maintained schools and supplementary schools; non-formal education; and home–school relationships.

SCHOOL EFFECTIVENESS

Publication programmes linked to short courses on school effectiveness by instructors and practitioners

SCHOOL EFFECTIVENESS AND IMPROVEMENT CENTRE

ISEIC is engaged in four key activities: development work with schools engaged in effectiveness and improvement initiatives; continuing research to expand the knowledge base about school effectiveness and the challenge of school improvement; teaching, at pre-service, in-service, diploma, master's and research-degree levels – and dissemination through conferences, workshops, publications and summaries of research studies.

SCHOOL IMPROVEMENT

To focus on pupil attainment specifically of GCSE and to assist this school to improve its image within this community.

SCHOOL IMPROVEMENTS NETWORK

The Institute of Education's School Improvement Network has been established to enable educators involved in or planning improvement initiatives to share ideas, discuss relevant issues and resolve common difficulties. Members receive a termly newsletter, termly research bulletin and annual contact list of all network members. Termly meetings are held, two in London and one elsewhere. At meetings, participants discuss issues posed by keynote speakers and hear from people engaged in improvement efforts.

SCHOOL MEASUREMENT AND IMPROVEMENT STRATEGY

The purpose is to establish a virtuous improvement cycle in schools based on good-quality data, detailed analysis and targeted strategies for dealing with areas of low achievement.

SCHOOLS MAKE A DIFFERENCE

The aim of SMAD is to lay the foundations for raising student levels of attainment, achievement and morale. The methodology is based on research on school effectiveness and school improvement. A major thrust of the project therefore addresses issues connected with school cultures and student and teacher behaviours. Consequently most of the outcomes will be process-based and qualitative rather than quantitative. Schools are being encouraged to develop process or ethos indicators to judge progress and success.

STRATEGIES TO ENHANCE PERFORMANCE AT GCSE

Aims: to raise the awareness of teaching staff of factors contributing to achievement at GCSE; to provide an overall evaluation of relative performance of secondary schools in 1993/1994; to provide comparative data across schools for the subjects – Maths, English, Science and Modern Languages; to provide data to enable schools internally to develop school/department action plans in response to the value-added analysis; to provide a coherent approach to the monitoring of achievement at GCSE.

SUCCESSFUL SCHOOLS

A fifteen-months collaborative action-research project between Worcester College of Higher Education and Sandwell, Solihull, Walsall and Wolverhampton LEAs, and involving 37 'primary' schools in urban areas. The project culminated in a national primary careers publication and a number of dissemination meetings and conferences. A major outcome was a list of important indicators of a school becoming successful. The voices of children, adults (teachers, inspectors) can be heard.

THE 'AT RISK' SUPPORT PROJECT

Enhanced support for students 'at risk' of under-achievement. The aim of the initiative is to raise the esteem and achievement of the young people of the town and to support the community in doing this, by joint activities and by funding: research into teaching and learning; management-development activities for senior staff, additional teaching and non-teaching staff to support pupils' learning in school; an increase in adult literacy opportunities; an improvement by research and action in provision for out-of-school youth activities; improvements to premises and the environment.

THE TILBURY INITIATIVE

The aim of the initiative is to raise the esteem and the achievement of the young people of the town and to support the community in doing this by joint funding; research activities into teaching and learning; management development activities for senior staff; additional teaching and non-teaching staff to support pupils' learning in schools; an increase in adult literacy opportunities; an improvement by research and action in provision for out of school youth activities; improvement to premises and the environment.

TOWER HAMLETS PARTNERSHIP

In 1988/89 Professor Wragg approached Ann Sofer and set up a programme with five elements: (1) Exeter runs a summer school for Tower Hamlets' pupils; (2) Exeter students do teaching practice in Tower Hamlets; (3) Exeter does In-

Service in Tower Hamlets; (4) Exeter does research in Tower Hamlets; (5) Exeter helps recruit teachers.

TRUANCY

Need to reduce unauthorized absences at primary and secondary level.

TWO TOWNS PROJECT

To raise aspiration, attendance and attainment levels in three high schools in Burslem and Tunstall – partners Universities, LEA, Careers Service, Colleges, TEC.

To enhance pupil involvement in education, leading to greater participation post-16 and post-18; to increase parental involvement; to raise educational standards; to increase expectations of parents, pupils and staff.

URBAN EDUCATION – WRITING A BOOK

Editing a book on urban education.

VALUE ADDED

1. Part one completed – two surveys of cost effectiveness in (i) sixth-form provision and (ii) special-school sixth form provision.
2. Work within TVEI on value added KS4/post-16 (consultant David Jesson).
3. Ongoing work by information systems on presenting exam results for different types of schools in Kent (e.g., selective, non-selective, wide-ability).
4. Work on KS1 analysis by gender age, ESL; nursery; free school meals; audit to provide broad county baseline data for KS1/2 schools.

VOCATIONAL EDUCATION DEVELOPMENT CENTRE

To establish an advice service which will give information to schools/colleges on new models for curriculum delivery and assist schools to develop formal partnerships with training providers and employers.

YOUTH WORK FOR YOUNG PEOPLE AT RISK

Providing support, skill development and youth work curriculum activity with pupils who are excluded from, or who are at risk being excluded from schools. Building on current work and good practice.

Appendix 6

GEST FUNDED PROJECTS

Three-Year Projects

LEA	Type	LEA	Type
Barnsley	RR	Leeds	
Birmingham	RR	Lewisham	
Bradford	RR +3	Manchester	
Brent	RR +1	Newcastle	
Cleveland		Nottinghamshire	RR +3
Doncaster	RR	North Tyneside	
Dudley	RR +3	Rotherham	RR
Gateshead		Sheffield	RR
Greenwich	RR +3	Southwark	RR +3
Hackney	RR +1	St Helens	RR
Hammersmith and Fulham	RR +1	Tower Hamlets	RR +3
Islington	RR +3	Wandsworth	RR +1
Lambeth	RR +1	Wirral	RR
		Wolverhampton	RR

RR = Reading Recovery
+ 1 = 1 additional year's funding
+ 3 = 3 additional years' funding

ONE-YEAR PROJECTS APPROVED 1993/4

Non-Reading Recovery

Bolton	Home/school links
Cheshire	Reading
Derbyshire	Literacy
Haringey	IMPACT maths
Humberside	Literacy and numeracy
Kirklees	Technical management
Knowsley	Fast track numeracy
Lancs	Parental involvement
Newham	Raising standards
South Tyneside	Home/school links
Walsall	Raising standards

Appendix 7

HIGHER EDUCATION SCHOOL-IMPROVEMENT NETWORKS

Our study revealed that a significant number of universities across the country are playing a major role in urban school improvement. In some cases this is a question of the university participating in an initiative alongside a TEC, and LEA or an FE institution, as, for example, in the case of Staffordshire University in the Two Towns project.

In a small number of cases the role played by the university is a great deal more ambitious. These universities have set out to link research, consultancy and sometimes their initial teacher education in order to assist schools and LEAs both regionally and sometimes nationally in bringing about improvement. The University of Bath, the University of Warwick, the University of Newcastle, the University of Cambridge and the Institute of Education in London all responded to the survey describing a role along these lines. Keele's University Centre for Successful Schools has a similar role.

The three most ambitious, on the basis of the evidence we have gathered, seem to be Newcastle, Cambridge and the Institute of Education in London.

At Newcastle, the University has developed a sophisticated model for assisting schools with the analysis of their examination results and the attitudes of the pupils. Much of the work has been developed for the 16–18 age group (A-Level Information System, ALIS), but more recently a comparable approach has been developed for the fourteen-to-sixteen age range (Year 11 Information system, YELLIS). A primary-school equivalent is at a pilot stage. The underlying philosophy of the Newcastle approach is that the provision and analysis of data will of itself contribute to improving schools. So far over 1,000 schools have chosen to participate, which suggest that ALIS and YELLIS have a significant contribution to make. The programme is not targeted particularly at urban schools, though clearly they have found participation beneficial.

At the University of Cambridge Institute of Education a school-improvement and development project known as 'Improving the Quality of Education for All' (IQEA) has been operating for three years or so and is ongoing. The group has been working with some thirty schools and representatives of the LEA or local support agency in East Anglia, North London and Yorkshire. The overall aim of the project is 'to strengthen the school's ability to provide quality education for all its pupils by building on existing good practice'. Schools contract into the programme of support and in so doing accept a set of values for school improvement which have been developed at Cambridge and have national recognition. The IQEA group co-ordinates the support arrangements, contributes to training, makes regular school visits, provides materials and monitors the school's project. It is an essential feature of the project that schools are helped to set their own priorities within the Cambridge framework, with the condition that the improvement impacts on and is owned at all 'levels' of the school organization. It is believed that an approach which works 'with' and not 'on' schools and which builds upon the particular circumstances of the school is more likely to bring about and sustain real change.

Perhaps the most ambitious scheme of all has been recently launched by the London Institute of Education. Its new International School Effectiveness and Improvement Centre (ISEIC) is intended to 'act as a national support system for improving schools'. It aims to do so through a range of activities. Its development work will involve action research with individual schools, groups of schools and LEAs. A network of associates across the country will be available to provide consultancy. A nationwide School Improvement Network has already been established to encourage the sharing of ideas.

ISEIC will also co-ordinate the Institute's extensive research programme in the areas of school effectiveness and improvement. Given the research team that it has assembled and the contracts that have already been won, ISEIC is likely to have a leading role in this field both nationally and internationally for the foreseeable future. It also has plans to disseminate knowledge of effective practice and research findings for a practitioner audience.

Appendix 8

THE QUESTIONNAIRE: SCHOOL IMPROVEMENT INITIATIVES

Please respond as fully as possible to the following questions. It is hoped that they are sufficiently broadly based to enable you to provide adequate information about your school improvement initiative without taking too much of your time. If you feel that important aspects of the initiative have not been covered, please use the space available at the end of the questionnaire to provide the additional information. We would also be grateful if you would forward to us a copy of any existing documents relating to your scheme.

1. How is the initiative referred to? _____

2. When did/will the initiative start? (*Please indicate the date as nearly as possible and/or any specific event or action which prompted the initiative – where relevant.*)

    month _____   Year _____

    event/action _____

3. Who is the originator of the initiative? (*LEA, University etc.*)

LEA	___	Youth Service	___
Further education	___	Industry/Commerce/EBPs	___
Higher education	___	Local community organizations	___
Parents' organizations	___	Police	___
Careers Service	___	Educational Welfare	___
TEC	___	Educational Psychology	___
Charitable Trust	___	Social Services	___

    Other (*please state*) _____

4. Proposed duration of the initiative (*in months*) _____ months.

5. In which areas is it intended to bring about improvement? (*please tick all relevant boxes*)

pupil/teacher expectation	___	staying on rates post-16	___
pupil attainment	___	curriculum change	___
pupil behaviour	___	truancy	___
parental involvement	___	bullying	___
pupil/ teacher morale	___	discipline	___
pupil self-esteem	___	racial awareness/tolerance	___

    other (*please state*) _____

6. Please describe briefly (*no more than 75 words*) the main characteristics of the initiative (*This information may be used to summarize your project in a report appendix*)

_____

_____

_____

_____

7. How many schools are participating in the initiative? _____

8. Are/were the schools selected for the initiative or are/were they self selected

   selected _____ self selected _____

   (*if selected, please state below the selection criteria*)

   _____

   _____

9. What kind of school(s) is/are involved? (*please select one alternative in each column*)

   A. nursery   ___   B. LEA maintained   ___
       primary only   ___   voluntary   ___
       middle   ___   grant maintained   ___
       secondary only   ___   independent   ___
       primary and secondary ___
       other _____   other _____

10. Does/will the initiative have a specific target group of children?
    Yes _____ No _____ (*if 'yes', please describe the target group below*)

    _____

    _____

11. Please indicate the different agencies, other than schools, participating in the initiative: (*please tick all those involved*)

    LEA   ___   Youth Service   ___
    Further education   ___   Industry/Commerce/EBPs   ___
    Higher education   ___   Local community organizations ___
    Parents' organizations ___   Police   ___
    Careers Service   ___   Educational Welfare   ___
    TEC   ___   Educational Psychology   ___
    Charitable Trust   ___   Social Services   ___
    Other (*please state*) _____

12. What other agencies does the initiative seek to involve?

    LEA   ___   Youth Service   ___
    Further education   ___   Industry/Commerce/EBPs   ___
    Higher education   ___   Local community organizations ___

Parents' organizations	___	Police	___
Careers Service	___	Educational Welfare	___
TEC	___	Educational Psychology	___
Charitable Trust	___	Social Services	___

Other (*please state*) _____

13. Does/will the initiative receive funding in addition to the standard school budget?

       yes _____   no _____

(if additional funding is received please answer questions 14 to 18 – otherwise more on to question 19)

14. Who provides the additional funding (*please tick all those who contribute*)

LEA	___	*name of LEA* _____
School	___	
Charitable Trust	___	*name of trust* _____
University (HEI)	___	
Industry	___	*name of industry* _____

    Other (*please state*) _____

15. What type of funding is/was received?

one-off grant	___	assistance in kind ___
revenue (i.e., ongoing funding) ___		other (please state) _____

16. What is/was the per annum level of project specific funding (i.e., over and above the standard school funding)?

one-off grant £ ____   assistance in kind £ ____ (*estimated value*)
revenue £ ____ per annum   other   £ ____

17. How many 'Full Time Equivalent Teachers' are/were appointed to the initiative?

      number of Full Time Equivalent Teachers ___

18. Are/were the FTE teachers based in individual schools or shared between schools?

number of FTEs per school ___   number of shared FTEs ___

19. Are/were permanent or temporary allowances used by schools to enhance the salaries of teachers participating in the initiative?

permanent   yes ___   no ___   temporary   yes ___   no ___

20. How much money (*if any*) is/was spent on salary enhancement for staff involved in the initiative?

    permanent

    In total £___   On each school £___   On each teacher (*on average*) £___

    temporary

    In total £___   On each school £___   On each teacher (*on average*) £___

21. Please indicate who contributes/contributed to any kind of steering group to the initiative.

LEA	___	Youth Service	___
Further education	___	Industry/Commerce/EBPs	___
Higher education	___	Local community organizations	___
Parents' organizations	___	Police	___
Careers Service	___	Educational Welfare	___
TEC	___	Educational Psychology	___
Charitable Trust	___	Social Services	___

    Other (*please state*) _____

22. Please give a brief description of the management structure of the initiative (i.e., number of management/steering groups, status of representatives, size of group(s) etc.).

    _____
    _____
    _____
    _____

23. Please state briefly how the success of the initiative is/was assessed.

    _____
    _____
    _____

24. Are/were any of the following performance indicators used to measure the success of the initiative? Where possible please specify the improvement goal in the space provided (*e.g., improve stay-on rates by 10 per cent per annum*)

    attendance _____
    punctuality _____
    pupil behaviour _____
    equal opportunities (*race*) _____
    equal opportunities (*gender*) _____
    parental involvement _____

test results (*including*
external examinations where relevant)   _____

post-16 stay on rates   _____

other   _____

other   _____

25. Will other indicators be used?   yes ___   no ___

If 'yes' please specify   _____

_____

26. Will the project be evaluated by external agency?   yes ___   no ___
(Please indicate what methods will be used to evaluate the project)

_____

_____

27. What evidence of success for the project exists so far?

_____

_____

_____

_____

28. Please give a brief description of any plans designed to ensure that the school improvement impetus continues after the agreed term of the initiative is ended.

_____

_____

_____

_____

Thank you for answering these questions. Please feel free to make further comment in the space below or on additional sheets should you feel there are important aspects of your scheme which have not been covered. Continue on the cover page opposite if necessary.

Name Index

A Level and GCSE Improvement Project 195
A Level Information System (ALIS) *see* Monitoring Alis, Yellis, Pips Project
Action Research: Critical Success Factors 195
Adduci, L. 159
Adult Literacy and Basic Skills Unit (ALBSU) 8
Allsop, T. 102
Andersson, B. E. 44
Association of Metropolitan Authorities (AMA) 20
'At Risk' Support Project 202
Audit Commission 102
Ayers, W. 161
Ayres, L. P. 147

Baker, P. 102
Barber, M. 20, 118, 121, 125
Barber Matrix 118–19, 125
Barnard, C. 150
Barth, R. 22
Biggart, N. W. 155
Bimber, B. 159
Birmingham Local Education Authority/ City of Birmingham 16, 18, 23, 83, 122–4, 127–8
Black Teachers Mentoring Scheme 195
Bonan, J. 158–9, 172, 179
Booz, A. 170
Boyd, W. L. 150, 157, 160–3
Bradley, A. 146, 152
Bretton Hall Primary School Improvement (PSI) Project 199
Brighouse, T. 16, 129–31
British Petroleum 138
Brown, D. J. 145–6
Bruner, J. 44
Bryant, C. 188
Bryk, A. S. 179
Burridge, E. 107

Callahan, R. E. 147
Cambridge University 102, 104, 108, 145
Canada 102, 104, 108, 145
Carter, D. S. G. 162
Centre for Successful Schools 10, 19, 56, 85, 92, 138–9, 205
Chapman, J. D. 145
Chartered Institute of Public Finance & Accountancy (CIPFA) 145–7, 153–5, 157, 159, 170, 178
Child Health and Education Studies (CHES) 44
Chubb, J. E. 180
Cibulka, J. 153, 155
City Challenge Scheme 94, 120
City Pride Programme 120
City Reading Project 195
Cleveland Compact 182
Coalition for Essential Schools 182
Coleman, P. 102
Coles, R. 171
Comer, J. 102
Commission for Racial Equality (CRE) 90
Committee on Economic Development 174
Community Service Volunteers 139
Compact Extension 196
Corbett, H. D. 159
Costa, A. L. 107
Countering Bullying Survey 196

Crain, R. 180
Cronin, J. M. 147
Crowson, R. L. 147–8, 150, 153–4, 155, 157, 160–2
Crozier, M. 149
Curriculum Development Focus 196

Dalin, P. 102
Darlington, R. 43–4
De'ath, E. 44
Department for Education 44
Department of Social Security 32, 34
Department of the Environment 28, 187
Developing Effective Schools in Greenwich Project 196
Dreeben, R. 151–2, 155

Elmore, R. F. 146, 154, 156
Enfield/Barnet Compact Extension 196
Essex Local Education Authority 18–19, 77, 85–9
Etzioni, A. 150
European Regional Development Programmes 120
European Social Fund 120
Evertson, C. 156

Feldman, M. L. 149
Fernandez, J. A. 145, 154, 157, 160
Ferris, J. M. 150
Fink, D. 102, 107–8, 112
Fitz-Gibbon, Carol 66

Goodman, A. 32
Gouldner, A. W. 150
Grants for Education Support and Training (GEST) 15, 58, 63, 77, 86, 94–5, 97, 204
Gray, J. 130
Green, A. 33
Greenwich Local Education Authority 196
Gutman, A. 150

Hainsworth, G. 137
Hake, C. 102
Hallinger, P. 153, 155–7, 160
Halton Board of Education 108
Halton Effective Schools Teacher Survey 112
Hamilton Inc. 170
Hammersmith and Fulham Local Education Authority 19, 85, 89–94
Hannaway, J. 147–8, 156
Hannon, P. 44
Hargreaves, D. H. 112, 115
Hartman, W. 157
Hawley, W. D. 150
Head Start Programme 43, 141
Heath, A. 34
Helping All Pupils To Achieve More Project 73, 196
Hertfordshire Reading Tests 88
Hewison, J. 44
High/Scope Programme 43–4
High Scope UK 'Young Children First' 196–7
Hill, P. 158–9, 161, 170–3, 175–6, 178–80, 182
Hillman, J. 105, 107
Hollander, T. E. 147
Holly, P. 130
Home Instruction for Pre-School Youngsters 197

Hopkins, D. 102, 107, 115, 130
Hord, S. 162
House of Commons Education Committee 26
House of Commons Select Committee on Education 83
Howes, C. 4
Hunter, P. 129–31

Impact Mathematics Scheme 197
Improving Results at Key Stage 4 197
Improving the Quality of Education for All Project 58, 205–6
Index of Local Conditions 187
Inner-City Partnership 120
Innerwahr, J. 174
Institute for Fiscal Studies 32
International School Effectiveness and Improvement Centre 58, 103–6, 108, 115, 200, 205
Investors in People Award 88, 111, 199, 197, 199

Jesson, D. 203
John Hopkins University, Centre for Research on Effective Schooling and Disadvantaged Studies 42–3
Johnson, J. 174
Jowett, S. 44
Joyce, B. R. 110
Judd, D. 162

Kallick, B. 107
Kaufman, H. 147, 159
Keele University 8, 12, 14, 20, 129, 131, 135, 137 *see also* Centre for Successful Schools
Kent Local Education Authority 58
Kerchner, C. T. 152
Kozol, J. 35
Krug, S. 160

Labor Secretary Commission on Necessary Skills (Scans) 173
Labour Party 17
LaNoue, G. R. 147
Larocque, L. 102
Lazar, L. 43–4
Learning Consortium 102, 108
Lee, T. 35
Leibenstein, H. 149, 157
Levin, H. 181
Lewisham Local Education Authority 18–19, 107–13, 197, 200
Lewisham Raising Reading Standards Project 200
Lewisham School Improvement Project 107–13, 197
Lipsitz, J. 172, 176
Literacy, Numeracy, Curriculum Enrichment, etc. Programme 197
London Institute of Education 10, 19, 58, 60, 91, 107, 205, 206 *see also* International School Effectiveness and Improvement Centre
Los Angeles Board of Education 170–1, 177
Louis, K. S. 102
Loveless, T. 162

Macbeath, J. 103, 105
McCullough, A. F. 150
McDonnell, L. M. 170–1, 177, 178

McGraw, B. 101
McGeeeney, P. 44
MacGilchrist, B. 105, 112
McGuire, J. 44
McPherson, R. B. 153–5, 157
March, J. G. 150
Michigan State Employment Service 173
Middlesbrough Community Education
    Project 77, 198
Milbank, J. E. 44
Miles, M. B. 102, 151, 155
Mirel, J. 161
Mladenka, K. R. 159
Moe, T. M. 149, 180
Monitoring Alis, Yellis, Pips Project 47
Morgan, D. R. 161
Morris, V. C. 148
Mortimore, P. 13, 47–8, 83, 96, 101,
    104–5, 114, 122, 130
Murphy, J. M. 145–6, 150–3, 155–7,
    160–2

National Commission on Education 9–10
National Education and Training Targets
    (NETTs) 7, 9, 14, 18
National Foundation for Education
    Research for England and Wales
    (NFER) 8
Nettworks 94 Initiative 198
New American Schools Development
    Corporation 181, 184
New York City 180–2
Newcastle University 205
Newmann, F. M. 146, 149, 151, 156
Newspapers in Education Project 66, 198
Noble, A. 33–4
North Guildford Project 198
Nottingham University 91
Nottinghamshire Local Education
    Authority 18, 22–3, 85, 94–8

Oakes, J. 172
Oakland, John 6
O'Day, J. 146, 151, 155–6
Office for Standards in Education 8, 15,
    17, 20, 27–8, 52, 56–7, 77, 79, 86–7,
    123, 188
Ontario Institute for Studies in Education
    102
Osborn, A. F. 44
Osborne, D. 182

Palmer, W. J. Jr. 161
Parental Involvement in the Core
    Curriculum Project 61, 198
Parkinson, M. 162
Pascal, A. H. 177
Pathways to School Improvement Project
    199
Patton, J. 121
Paul Hamlyn Foundation 131, 138
Peers Early Education Partnership 66,
    199
Perry, I. 172
Philadelphia 180–1
Porter, T. 86–7
Post-16 Compact Project 199

Prime Time Project 47
Pugh, G. 4
Pupil Attitudes to Secondary Schools
    Database 8

Quality Development Initiative 199

Raising Achievement and Participation
    Project (RAPP) 58, 77, 199–200
Raising Achievement in Inner City Schools
    Initiative 200
Raising Achievement Project 200
Raising Reading Standards Project see
    Lewisham Raising Reading Standards
Raising Standards in Inner City Schools
    Project 200
Raising Standards in the Inner City
    Project 200
Raising Standards project 200
Rand Studies 170–3, 178–9
Reading Recovery Programme 46, 48, 52,
    94, 198, 204
Reynolds, D. 103, 114, 130
Ribbins, P. 107
Richman, N. 44
Rogers, D. 147
Rosenholtz, S. 102, 114, 172
Rudduck, J. 102
Rutter, M. 48, 130

Sammons, P. 29, 105
Sandwell Local Education Authority 202
Sarason, S. B. 146
Sayre, W. 147
Schmidt, P. 157
School Curriculum and Assessment
    Authority 14, 17
School Improvement Network 10, 58,
    104–7, 113, 201
School Measurement and Improvement
    Strategy 201
School Teachers' Review Body 23
Schools Make a Difference Project 89–94,
    201–2
Schweinart, L. J. 42–3
Seibel, T. 145
Sergiovanni, T. 150
Shanker, A. 173
Shapiro, L. 161
Simon, B. 47
Single Regeneration Budget (SRB) 86,
    120
Sirotnik, K. A. 102
Sizer, T. 176, 182
Slavin, R. 42–3, 46, 51, 175
Smith, B. L. R. 147
Smith, M. S. 146, 151, 155–6
Sofer, A. 202
Spielman, F. 145
Spring, J. 147
The Staffordshire Access Scheme 138
Staffordshire Local Education Authority
    137–9, 141
Staffordshire Training and Enterprise
    Council 130, 138–9
Staffordshire University 135–6, 205
Stinchcombe, A. L. 150

Stoll, L. 102, 104–5, 107–8, 112, 114–15
Stout, R. T. 162
Strategies to Enhance Performance at
    GCSE Project 202
Student Teacher Achievement Project
    (STAR) 46–8, 52
Success for all Programme 49
Successful Schools Project 202
Sullivan, A. V. S. 155
Sylva, K. 44

Technical and Vocational Education
    Initiative (TVEI) 72, 91, 203
Technology Schools Initiative 15
Teeside Training and Enterprise 58
Thomas, S. 101, 104–5
Tilbury Initiative 77, 85–9, 202
Times Educational Supplement 124
Tizzard, B. 130
Toronto University 102
Toulmin, L. M. 159
Tower Hamlets Partnership 202–3
Training and Enterprise Councils (TECs)
    58, 60–6, 72, 78–9, 83–4, 86
Two Towns Project 58, 72–3, 130–42,
    203, 205
Tyack, D. B. 146–9

Underwood, J. 154, 157, 160
United States 31–2, 34, 41–4, 46–9, 51–2,
    104, 141, Chs 9, 10
US Department of Education 169
US News & World Report 152
Urban Aid 120

Valentine, J. 43
Van Der Weele, M. 145
Vaughan, D. 157
Vocational Education Development
    Centre 203

Walsall Local Education Authority 202
Walton, W. S. 137
Wasik, B. 46
Watson, N. 102
Watt, J. 155, 159
Webb, S. 32
Webber, R. 33
Wilson, B. L. 159
Wirt, F. 159–60
Wisby, G. 145
Wise, A. 161
Wolfendale, S. 44
Wolverhampton Local Education
    Authority 202
Wong, K. K. 147–8, 159
Worcester College of Higher Education
    202
Wragg, T. 202

Year 11 Information system (Yellis) see
    Monitoring Alis, Yellis, Pips Project
Young, M. 44
Youth Work for Young People at Risk 203

Zigler, E. 43

Subject Index

A Level Examinations 8, 17, 74
Access to education 31, 169–70
Accountability 13–14, 80, 102, 113, 158–9, 180
Administrative organization Chapter 9, 177, 179, 182
Admission criteria 14, 20–1, 138
Assessment 17, 80, 102

Bullying 68, 196

Catholic schools 175–6, 180
Centralization 16–18, 20, 145–52, 157–9, 163
Class size 46–8, 50–2, 146
Community education 136, 198
Compact schemes 72–3, 196, 199
Curriculum development/enrichment 92, 93, 130, 175–6, 199

Day nurseries 44
Decentralization 102, 145–6, 148–64
Development plans 11–12, 21, 77, 91, 105, 112, 199
Disadvantage 9, 27–9, 30–4, 42–3, 49, 51–2, 57, 85, 95, 101, 119, 155, 170–1, 184, 187
Disaffected pupils 8, 203
Discipline 11, 20, 88, 97, 135–7

Education associations 20
Education consultants 11, 84, 91, 105, 140, 198
Education, from 14 to 19 17, 86
Education vouchers 180–1
Educational finance see formula funding, local management of schools and resource allocation
Educational innovation 19–20, Chapters 3–5, 8, Appendices 2–6
Educational legislation 12
Educational policy 12–16, 31, 79
Educational priority areas 31, 41
Educational standards 7–9, 17–18, 68, 204
Evaluation 70–5, 82, 92, 111–14, 137
Examination results 7–8, 14, 37–8, 73–4, 101, 131–2, 136, 201, 203
Extracurricular activities 10, 12, 15–16, 137, 202

Formula funding 14, 31, 35–7, 96, 124

General Certificate of Secondary Education 7–8, 37–8, 73–4, 131–2, 136, 201–2
General National Vocational Qualifications 17
Grade retention 42
Grammar schools 120
Grant maintained schools 14

Head teachers 10, 11, 90, 113
Higher education institutions 58, 60, 62–6, 72, 78–9, 83–4, 135, Appendix 7
see also specific universities and institutes, e.g. London Institute of Education
Home–school relationship 45, 98, 127, 135, 200, 204
Housing 33–4

Immigrants 169–70, 178

Income Support Benefit 32
Industry–education relationship 7, 61, 63–6, 130, 172–3, 199
Information technology 126–7
Inservice teacher education 22, 91, 105, 109, 131
Inspection 13–17, 38–40, 52, 102, 105, 114, 188
Institutional co-operation 11–12, 16, 19, 58–67, 78–9, 82–4, 87, 90, 102, Chapter 6, 123, Chapter 8, Appendix 7
Intervention 16, 41, 43–6, 49

Job skills 7, 129

Leadership 9, 10, 17–19, 102, 112, 130, 149, 160–2, 199
Learning environment/networks 11, 88, 91–2
Literacy 45, 88, 124, 136, 197, 199, 204
Local education authorities 18–21, 35–7, 58–9, 60–6, 72, 77–80, 83–4, 102
see also specific LEAs, e.g. Essex Local Education Authority
Local management of schools 13–14, 19, 31, 35, 51, 96, 102, 108, 124

Magnet Schools 176–7, 180
Management teams/structures 64, 78–9, 88, 90, 93–5, 131, 140
Mentors 68, 195, 197–8
Multiculturalism/Multicultural education 120, 173

National curriculum 16–17, 44, 96, 102, 123–4, 200
Numeracy 124, 197, 200, 204
Nursery education 44, 49
see also preschool education

Organizational change Chapter 9, 182–5

Parent attitudes/expectations 20, 41, 120, 135, 173
Parent choice 20–1, 120, 176–7, 180–3
Parent participation 44, 61, 101–2, 119–20, 127, 130–1, 136, 175, 179, 198, 199–201, 204
Performance indicators/data 13–14, 16–17, 19, 22, 29–31, 74, 101–2, 139
Playground activities 97–8
Playgroups 44
Poverty see disadvantage
Preschool education 16, 41–5, 49–50, 122–3, 141, 197
Primary schools/education 47–8, 51, 80, 83, 122, 124
Professional development 11, 15, 22, 88, 95, 140, 202
Pupil attitudes/expectations 8–9, 41, 110, 130, 136, 138, 140, 171, 173, 197
Pupil behaviour 68, 88, 91, 93, 97–8, 115, 132, 135–6
Pupil-teacher ratios 35–7, 121
Pupil-teacher relationship 46, 92, 102, 126, 130
Pupil unit costs 35–7, 50

Questioning 126

Reading standards 8, 52, 169, 200
Reception classes 44

Records of achievement 132
Remedial education 172
Research and development 18
Residential programmes 135, 138
Resource allocation 15, 31, 34–7, 50–1, 63–4, 76–7, 81–2, 84, 90, 93–4, 96, 123, 124, 130, 138–40, 170, 184, 188

School culture/environment 11, 22, 91–3, 115, 130, 132, 135–6, 199, 203
School day 137, 145, 146
School effectiveness 9–12, 48, 50–1, 101–2, 108–9, 129–30, 140, 174–6, 201
School evaluation 11, 15, 17, 22, 104, 130
School improvement 6–7, 10–16, 18, 21–3, 31–5, 42–3, 48, 50, 57–75, 78, 82, 84, 90, 102–15, 122, 123, 127, Chapter 8, 155, 156, 182, 199
School policy 11, 88
School worship 21
Secondary schools 38–40, 48, 80, 89–94, 130, 189, 196–7
Self-esteem 118–19, 125, 126–7, 135, 196–7
Self-study packages 134
Social class 44, 48, 108, 119, 178
Social priority schools 31
Special educational needs 111
Standards in education see educational standards
Standardized tests 97
Staying on rates 8, 68, 129, 131–2, 139
Superintendents 160–2
Support services/staff 19, 22–3, 88, 102, 121, 123, 174

Target grouping 96–7
Target setting 7–9, 14, 18, 21–2, 80, 83, 88, 123–4, 131–2, 140, 196
Teacher appraisal 22
teacher attitudes/expectations 9, 13, 46, 90–1, 101, 118–19, 125–6, 130, 172–3, 176
Teacher education 84, 105, 139, 205
Teacher effectiveness 10, 125–7
Teacher employment 178–9
Teacher profession 121, 124
Teacher retirement 124
Teacher salaries 124
Technology education 136
Transition policy 88
Truancy 8, 68, 102, 131–2, 171–2, 203
Tutors/tutoring 134, 136, 138–9

Underachievement 7–9, 31, 40–2, 68, 86, 89, 96, 129, 171–2, 200, 202
Unemployment 34, 41, 85, 95, 101, 108, 120, 122, 129, 171
Universities see higher education institutions and specific universities, e.g. Cambridge University and London Institute of Education

Value-added methods 8, 14–15, 17, 74–5, 82, 98, 104–5, 198, 203
Values 119, 125
Vocational guidance 134, 139–40
Volunteers 133

Working-class pupils 9
Writing ability 110